2008
Moon Sign
Book

Editor/Designer: Sharon Leah
Cover Design & Art: Gavin Dayton Duffy
ISBN: 978-0-7387-0551-4

You can order Llewellyn annuals and books from *New Worlds*, Llewellyn's
magazine catalog. To request a free copy of the catalog, call toll-free
1-877-NEW-WRLD, or visit our Web site at http://www.llewellyn.com.

Llewellyn is a registered trademark of Llewellyn Worldwide, Ltd.
2134 Wooddale Drive, Woodbury, MN 55125-2989 USA
Printed in the USA

Table of Contents

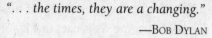

To Readers

A lot has changed in this country and around the world since 1905, when pizza was introduced in New York City by Gennaro Lombardi, and the Pennsylvania Railroad's "fastest train in the world" made the trip between New York and Chicago in eighteen hours. The *Moon Sign Book* was published for the first time in Portland, Oregon, that same year.

Today, a space shuttle can fly around Earth in ninety minutes at an altitude of about 190 miles, pizza is as close as the nearest store, and the *Moon Sign Book*, now in its 103rd year, is published in Woodbury, Minnesota.

Back in 1905, the *Moon Sign Book* was 4" X 5.75" in size, it contained about 150 pages, and sold for $1. Readers wanted to know the best times to plant their gardens and harvest their crops, when to travel, roof a building, and sell their livestock, among other things. Today, more people live in urban areas than ever before, but we still love to garden and plan our lives in sync with natural cycles. So, the daily information you expect—the Moon's sign, phase, void-of-course times, and planetary aspects, the tables of favorable and unfavorable days, and activity timing aids—are still in this almanac. For the gardeners among you, we've created a new gardening guide and forecast section that begins on page 7. There you'll find the best dates to plant, fertilize, weed, and harvest your crops in weekly tables for easy use. Be sure and check Kris Brandt Riske's weather forecasts for eight zones when you need information about short- and long-range weather trends, and Dorothy Kovach's insights on the economic trends we can expect in 2008 may put you on track toward a better financial future.

And back, due to popular demand, is the Astro Almanac! This at-a-glance timing guide, which begins on page 94, shows the best times to begin activities, from the simple things, like getting a haircut, to the complex, like buying or selling a home.

If you want to choose your own times to begin projects, plan meetings, etc., you'll find a convenient how-to guide beginning on page 106.

Why Our Almanac Is Different

Readers have asked why the *Moon Sign Book* says that the Moon is in Taurus and some almanacs indicate that the Moon is in the previous sign of Aries on the same date. It's because there are two different zodiac systems in use today: the tropical and the sidereal. The *Moon Sign Book* is based on the tropical zodiac.

The tropical zodiac takes 0 degrees of Aries to be the Spring Equinox in the Northern Hemisphere. This is the time and date when the Sun is directly overhead at noon along the equator, usually about March 20–21. The rest of the signs are positioned at 30 degree intervals from this point.

The sidereal zodiac, which is based on the location of fixed stars, uses the positions of the fixed stars to determine the starting point of 0 degrees of Aries. In the sidereal system, 0 degrees of Aries always begins at the same point. This does create a problem though, because the positions of the fixed stars, as seen from Earth, have changed since the constellations were named. The term "precession of the equinoxes" is used to describe the change.

Precession of the equinoxes describes an astronomical phenomenon brought about by the Earth's wobble as it rotates and orbits the Sun. The Earth's axis is inclined toward the Sun at an angle of about 23½ degrees, which creates our seasonal weather changes. Although the change is slight, because one complete circle of the Earth's axis takes 25,800 years to complete, we can actually see that the positions of the fixed stars seem to shift. The result is that each year, in the tropical system, the Spring Equinox occurs at a slightly different time.

Does Precession Matter?

There is an accumulative difference of about 23 degrees between the Spring Equinox (0 degrees Aries in the tropical zodiac and 0 degrees Aries in the sidereal zodiac) so that 0 degrees Aries at Spring Equinox in the tropical zodiac actually occurs at about 7 degrees Pisces in the sidereal zodiac system. You can readily see that those who use the other almanacs may be planting seeds (in the garden and in their individual lives) based on the belief that it is occurring in a fruitful sign, such as Taurus, when in fact it would be occurring in Gemini, one of the most barren signs of the zodiac. So, if you wish to plant and plan activities by the Moon, it is helpful to follow the *Moon Sign Book*. Before we go on, there are important things to understand about the Moon, her cycles, and their correlation with everyday living. For more information about gardening by the Moon, see page 60.

Weekly Almanac

Your Guide to Lunar Gardening, Weather, and the Economy for 2008

I think having land and not ruining it is the most beautiful art anyone could want to own.
— ANDY WARHOL

♑ January

Week of January 1–5

Be the change you want to see in the world.
—MAHATMA GANDHI

Jan 1, 8:32 pm- Jan 4, 9:13 am	4th	Scorpio	Plant biennials, perennials, bulbs and roots. Prune. Irrigate. Fertilize (organic).
Jan 4, 9:13 am- Jan 6, 8:43 pm	4th	Sagittarius	Cultivate. Destroy weeds and pests. Harvest fruits and root crops for food. Trim to retard growth.

Every New Year's Day, many of us resolve to change something about ourselves. Then we sort of (but not completely) forget about whatever we resolved to do—until next year. Take heart if you experience this convenient "new year" memory loss. We get a new opportunity to start over every day, and with every New Moon throughout the year. Because we do something one way today doesn't mean we have to do it the same way the next time around. Find joy wherever you can, and experience many new beginnings in the year ahead.

JANUARY

S	M	T	W	T	F	S
		1	2	3	4	5
6	7	8	9	10	11	12
13	14	15	16	17	18	19
20	21	22	23	24	25	26
27	28	29	30	31		

Jan 6, 8:43 pm- Jan 8, 6:37 am	4th	Capricorn	Plant potatoes and tubers. Trim to retard growth.
Jan 8, 6:37 am- Jan 9, 6:13 am	1st	Capricorn	Graft or bud plants. Trim to increase growth.
Jan 11, 1:44 pm- Jan 13, 7:23 pm	1st	Pisces	Plant grains, leafy annuals. Fertilize (chemical). Graft or bud plants. Irrigate. Trim to increase growth.

The first New Moon of the year appears early in the morning on January 8 from Capricorn. During the New Moon phase is when you can see something called "earthshine." It was Leonardo da Vinci who first explained that earthshine occurs when light reflecting off Earth illuminates the darkened part of the Moon. Scientists study earthshine to measure the rate of change in cloud cover and global weather phenomena, including global warming. *Albedo* is the measure of a surface's reflectivity, and reflectivity is affected by surface color and texture. The reflective quality of snow is higher than that of spruce trees, for example. If you want to know more about global weather, see Kris Brandt Riske's article on page 215.

●

January 8
6:37 am EST

Jan 15, 11:13 pm- Jan 17, 9:05 pm	2nd	Taurus	Plant annuals for hardiness. Trim to increase growth.

Days of the Week Nursery Rhyme

Monday's child is fair of face,
Tuesday's child is full of grace,
Wednesday's child is full of woe,
Thursday's child has far to go,
Friday's child is loving and giving,
Saturday's child works hard for a living,
But the child that is born on the Sabbath day
Is bonny and blithe, and good and gay.

_____

_____

_____

_____

_____

January 15
2:46 pm EST

JANUARY						
S	M	T	W	T	F	S
		1	2	3	4	5
6	7	8	9	10	11	12
13	14	15	16	17	18	19
20	21	22	23	24	25	26
27	28	29	30	31		

| Jan 22, 8:35 am-
Jan 24, 9:48 am | 3rd | Leo | Cultivate. Destroy weeds and pests. Harvest fruits and root crops for food. Trim to retard growth. |
| Jan 24, 9:48 am-
Jan 26, 5:35 pm | 3rd | Virgo | Cultivate, especially medicinal plants. Destroy weeds and pests. Trim to retard growth. |

We're familiar with SAD (Seasonal Affective Disorder) from our human perspective, but houseplants are vulnerable to SAD, too. In regions where light is limited and air is dry, if your houseplants leaves are droopy or pale, the plant is showing the stress it's under—it looks sad.

If you have a plant that is dropping its leaves, has yellow or tan splotches on the foliage, or has shriveled buds, you are probably overwatering it. If the leaves are droopy, or dropping off, or have brown or brittle edges, you are probably underwatering. If the plant foliage is pale, the leaves are small when they form, or the plant leans toward the light, it is not getting enough light or it may need fertilizing. If your plants fail to bloom or have black or brown blotches on the leaves, there may be too much temperature fluctuation in the room. Plan to inspect your plants on a regular basis, and also keep in mind that it is natural for plants to lose some leaves as they age.

◯

January 22
8:35 am EST

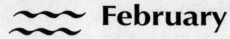

February

Week of January 27–February 2

It is even said that many ebbings and risings of the sea always come round with the moon and upon certain fixed days.

—ARISTOTLE

Jan 29, 4:35 am- Jan 29, 12:03 am	3rd	Scorpio	Plant biennials, perennials, bulbs and roots. Prune. Irrigate. Fertilize (organic).
Jan 30, 12:03 am- Jan 31, 5:08 pm	4th	Scorpio	Plant biennials, perennials, bulbs and roots. Prune. Irrigate. Fertilize (organic).
Jan 31, 5:08 pm- Feb 3, 4:52 am	4th	Sagittarius	Cultivate. Destroy weeds and pests. Harvest fruits and root crops for food. Trim to retard growth.

Birds of a feather flock together, and they're finicky about the food they eat, too. Mourning doves prefer red and white millet or cracked corn, while blue jays prefer black sunflower seeds, peanut kernels, or suet. Chickadees, on the other hand, prefer black sunflower seeds or suet, and wrens prefer just plain suet.

January 30
12:03 am EST

FEBRUARY

S	M	T	W	T	F	S
					1	2
3	4	5	6	7	8	9
10	11	12	13	14	15	16
17	18	19	20	21	22	23
24	25	26	27	28	29	

Feb 3, 4:52 am-Feb 5, 2:10 pm	4th	Capricorn	Plant potatoes and tubers. Trim to retard growth.
Feb 5, 2:10 pm-Feb 6, 10:44 pm	4th	Aquarius	Cultivate. Destroy weeds and pests. Harvest fruits and root crops for food. Trim to retard growth.
Feb 7, 8:46 pm Feb 10, 1:17 am	1st	Pisces	Plant grains, leafy annuals. Fertilize (chemical). Graft or bud plants. Irrigate. Trim to increase growth.

Good old soapy water is a safe and easy solution to rid houseplants of pests. Insects—aphids, whiteflies, spiders, etc.—that attack houseplants must be treated. It is best to start with the least toxic means possible, and that's soapy water. With small plants, you can immerse the plant foliage in soapy water, but larger plants will need to be sprayed. Repeat the process every three days to control new insect hatches. Dipping or spraying plants with soapy water will help to control aphids, spider mites, thrips, and whiteflies. To remove mealy bugs and scale, wipe the plant with a cloth or cotton swab dipped in either soapy water or rubbing alcohol.

●

February 6
10:44 pm EST

_____

_____

_____

_____

_____

Feb 12, 4:34 am– Feb 13, 10:33 pm	1st	Taurus	Plant annuals for hardiness. Trim to increase growth.
Feb 13, 10:33 pm– Feb 14, 7:19 am	2nd	Taurus	Plant annuals for hardiness. Trim to increase growth.
Feb 16, 10:12 am– Feb 18, 1:51 pm	2nd	Cancer	Plant grains, leafy annuals. Fertilize (chemical). Graft or bud plants, Irrigate. Trim to increase growth.

The Cook Islands, named after eighteenth-century explorer Captain James Cook, was the location for CBS's thirteenth *Survivor* show (fall 2006). Captain Cook was chosen by the British Admiralty to head an expedition to Tahiti in 1769 for the announced purpose of observing Venus as she passed across the face of the Sun in June of that year. He had a second "secret" mission, which was to locate the southern continent (Antarctica). Cook and his crew actually made three Pacific voyages, and it was during the second voyage, in 1772–75, that his ships came within 121 km of Antarctica but were forced to turn back because of intense cold. Cook made his last voyage in 1779. He was stabbed to death by islanders on February 14, 1779, after he stopped in Hawaii for ship repairs.

◐
February 13
10:33 pm EST

			FEBRUARY			
S	M	T	W	T	F	S
					1	2
3	4	5	6	7	8	9
10	11	12	13	14	15	16
17	18	19	20	21	22	23
24	25	26	27	28	29	

Feb 20, 10:30 pm- Feb 22, 9:14 pm	3rd	Virgo	Cultivate, especially medicinal plants. Destroy weeds and pests. Trim to retard growth.
Feb 23, 2:44 am- Feb 25 1:05 pm	3rd	Libra	Plant perennials, biennials, and bulbs.

The art of paper cutting originated in China in about the sixth century, and spread to other countries from there. In China, the intricate paper cuttings were used by women to adorn their hair, by men in sacred rites, and by peasants to cover windows and protect their homes from evil spirits. Today, paper-cutting traditions include German sherenschnitte, Polish wycinanki, Chinese hua yang, Japanese kirigami or mon-kiri, and French silhouettes (named after Etienne de Silhouette).

Children (and many adults) practice a form of paper cutting when they make paper snowflakes. On a winter day, wherever you live, get out the scissors and paper and have some fun. If you need some inspiration, visit the Web sites listed here, or others you may find online.

http://www.papersnowflakes.com, or

http://highhopes.com/snowflakes.html

◯

February 20
10:30 pm EST

March

Week of February 24–March 1

When one has faith that the spring thaw will arrive,
the winter winds seem to lose some of their punch.

—Robert L. Veninga

Feb 25, 1:05 pm– Feb 27, 10:10 pm	3rd	Scorpio	Plant biennials, perennials, bulbs and roots. Prune. Irrigate. Fertilize (organic).
Feb 28, 1:22 am– Feb 28, 9:18 pm	3rd	Sagittarius	Cultivate. Destroy weeds and pests. Harvest fruits and root crops for food. Trim to retard growth.
Mar 28, 9:18 pm– Mar 1, 1:33 pm	4th	Sagittarius	Cultivate. Destroy weeds and pests. Harvest fruits and root crops for food. Trim to retard growth.
Mar 1, 1:33 pm– Mar 3, 11:24 pm	4th	Capricorn	Plant potatoes and tubers. Trim to retard growth.

For centuries, women have complained that men procrastinate about proposing marriage. According to legend, St. Patrick decided Irish women could ask men to marry on one day every fourth year—February 29. In Scotland, in 1288, a law was passed that allowed women to propose on Leap Day, and if the man refused her proposal, he could be fined. The fine could be anything from a kiss to a new silk dress for the lady.

February 28
9:18 pm EST

FEBRUARY						
S	M	T	W	T	F	S
					1	2
3	4	5	6	7	8	9
10	11	12	13	14	15	16
17	18	19	20	21	22	23
24	25	26	27	28	29	

Mar 1, 1:33 pm- Mar 3, 11:24 pm	4th	Capricorn	Plant potatoes and tubers. Trim to retard growth.
Mar 3, 11:24 pm- Mar 6, 5:53 am	4th	Aquarius	Cultivate. Destroy weeds and pests. Harvest fruits and root crops for food. Trim to retard growth.
Mar 6, 5:53 am- Mar 7, 12:14 pm	4th	Pisces	Plant biennials, perennials, bulbs and roots. Prune. Irrigate. Fertilize (organic).
Mar 7, 12:14 pm- Mar 8, 9:23 am	1st	Pisces	Plant grains, leafy annuals. Fertilize (chemical). Graft or bud plants. Irrigate. Trim to increase growth.

You can get a jump on spring and create a stylish accessory for your home at the same time when you plant an indoor grass garden (annual ryegrass). All you need is annual ryegrass seed, a 2- or 3-inch deep planting tray with drainage holes, soil-based potting mix, slow-release fertilizer, and plastic wrap. Sow the seed in the soil-filled planting tray. Top with a fine layer of soil. Mist with warm water, and cover lightly with clear plastic wrap, allowing for some air circulation. Set the tray in a warm spot and check every couple of days. Move the tray to a sunny spot as soon as grass appears. Turn the tray every day to keep grass growing straight, mist or water lightly until grass is well established. "Mow" with scissors twice a week to encourage dense growth.

●

March 7
12:14 pm EST

MARCH

S	M	T	W	T	F	S
						1
2	3	4	5	6	7	8
9	10	11	12	13	14	15
16	17	18	19	20	21	22
23	24	25	26	27	28	29
30	31					

Mar 10, 12:13 am- Mar 12, 1:54 pm	1st	Taurus	Plant annuals for hardiness. Trim to increase growth.
Mar 14, 4:37 pm- Mar 16, 9:04 pm	2nd	Cancer	Plant grain, leafy annuals. Fertilize (chemical). Graft or bud plants. Irrigate. Trim to increase growth.

Botanists say the powerful March winds are good for trees because as their trunks and main branches flex, sap is drawn up to nourish the budding leaves. March is one of the windiest months of the year, especially in states that experience wider fluctuations in temperature. To say that windy days bring a change of season would not be an exaggeration. Wind is the result of a cooler high pressure air mass meeting a warmer low pressure mass. The closer the two pressure areas are to each other, the stronger the winds. Warm air rises as the two fronts meet, and the cooler air rushes in. The change of air temperature can be dramatic, with thermometers plunging 30 degrees or more in only an hour or two.

March 14
6:45 am EDT

Daylight Saving time begins at 2 am,
March 9

MARCH

S	M	T	W	T	F	S
						1
2	3	4	5	6	7	8
9	10	11	12	13	14	15
16	17	18	19	20	21	22
23	24	25	26	27	28	29
30	31					

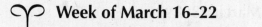

Mar 21, 11:45 am- Mar 21, 2:40 pm	2nd	Libra	Plant annuals for fragrance and beauty. Trim to increase growth.
Mar 21, 2:40 pm- Mar 23, 10:06 pm	3rd	Libra	Plant perennials, biennials, and bulbs.

Robins belong to the thrush (thrush means "wanderer") family, and they can be found throughout most of North America. Robins travel south as far as southern Florida and Guatemala, but they may also winter in more northern places. Male robins show up early, before all the snow has melted. And they begin to sing in April, when the females arrive and the birds begin pairing. The female usually lays four eggs that hatch in twelve to fourteen days. When baby robins are about fourteen days old, and before they can fly, they jump out of the nest. Their parents lead them to protective low shrubs, where they can learn to jump up on branches. Within a couple days, when the babies have gained enough strength and skill to fly and feed themselves, the parents leave them and will usually nest again.

◯
March 21
2:40 pm EDT

Mar 23, 10:06 pm- Mar 26, 10:11 am	3rd	Scorpio	Plant biennials, perennials, bulbs and roots. Prune. Irrigate. Fertilize (organic).
Mar 26, 10:11 am- Mar 28, 10:43 pm	3rd	Sagittarius	Cultivate. Destroy weeds and pests. Harvest fruits and root crops for food. Trim to retard growth.
Mar 28, 10:43 pm- Mar 29, 5:47 pm	3rd	Capricorn	Plant potatoes and tubers. Trim to retard growth.
Mar 29, 5:47 pm- Mar 31, 9:34 am	4th	Capricorn	Plant potatoes and tubers. Trim to retard growth.

Spring has arrived! It may be too early in your region to plant outdoors, but you can take advantage of this last quarter Moon phase and plant biennial seeds indoors. Some popular biennial flowers are forget-me-nots, foxglove, evening primrose, and sweet william. Biennials should be planted in rich soil, watered lightly, and kept in partial to full sun. Once a month fertilizing is recommended to keep your plants healthy and blooming. Because biennials usually require a little less care than do annuals or perennials, they're a good choice for people with limited time to devote to gardening.

March 29
5:47 pm EDT

MARCH

S	M	T	W	T	F	S
						1
2	3	4	5	6	7	8
9	10	11	12	13	14	15
16	17	18	19	20	21	22
23	24	25	26	27	28	29
30	31					

 # April

Week of March 30–April 5

People who want the most approval get the least and people who need approval the least get the most.

—WAYNE DYER

Mar 29, 5:47 pm–Mar 31, 9:34 am	4th	Capricorn	Plant potatoes and tubers. Trim to retard growth.
Mar 31, 9:34 am–Apr 2, 4:55 pm	4th	Aquarius	Cultivate. Destroy weeds and pests. Harvest fruits and root crops for food. Trim to retard growth.
Apr 2, 4:55 pm–Apr 4, 8:27 pm	4th	Pisces	Plant biennials, perennials, bulbs and roots. Prune. Irrigate. Fertilize (organic).
Apr 4, 8:27 pm–Apr 5, 10:55 pm	4th	Aries	Cultivate. Destroy weeds and pests. Harvest fruits and root crops for food. Trim to retard growth.

Now is the time to plant gladiolus, anemone, iris, and other spring bulbs. Select a well-drained site (most bulbs will rot if they are constantly wet), and check the type of light your plants will need. If you have poor soil or challenging light conditions in your yard, consider periwinkle, croscosmia, or gaillardia (blanketflower). While some plants, like gaillardia, prefer more sunlight, they will tolerate less-than-perfect growing conditions.

●
April 5
11:55 pm EDT

APRIL

S	M	T	W	T	F	S
		1	2	3	4	5
6	7	8	9	10	11	12
13	14	15	16	17	18	19
20	21	22	23	24	25	26
27	28	29	30			

Apr 6, 9:19 pm– Apr 8, 9:27 pm	1st	Taurus	Plant annuals for hardiness. Trim to increase growth.

I f weather permits in your region, early in the week is good for planting annual flowers outside. If it's still a little early and the ground hasn't warmed yet, plant your annual seeds indoors and place the flats in a warm sunny spot in your house.

Earthy, practical, and fertile Taurus is the farmer's sign. Farmers have always watched nature for signs that indicated the proper timing for different activities. They would wait to plant corn until the new leaves on oak trees were as big as a squirrel's ear, for example.

_____

_____

_____

_____

_____

◐

April 12
2:32 pm EDT

APRIL

S	M	T	W	T	F	S
		1	2	3	4	5
6	7	8	9	10	11	12
13	14	15	16	17	18	19
20	21	22	23	24	25	26
27	28	29	30			

Apr 17, 6:10 pm- Apr 20, 5:00 am	2nd	Libra	Plant annuals for fragrance and beauty. Trim to increase growth.

Spring ephemerals are a group of flowers that grow and bloom in early spring in wooded areas. Ephemeral means "lasting but a few days." Bloodroot, snow trillium, wood anemone, wild geranium, jack-in-the-pulpit, and bluebells are considered spring ephemerals. They bloom before the trees leaf out, when there's still plenty of moisture in the soil, and then they disappear without a trace by late May.

Apr 20, 5:00 am– Apr 20, 6:25 am	2nd	Scorpio	Plant grains, leafy annuals. Fertilize (chemical). Graft or bud plants. Irrigate. Trim to increase growth.
Apr 20, 6:25 am– Apr 22, 5:07 pm	3rd	Scorpio	Plant biennials, perennials, bulbs and roots. Prune. Irrigate. Fertilize (organic).
Apr 22, 5:07 pm– Apr 25, 5:47 am	3rd	Sagittarius	Cultivate. Destroy weeds and pests. Harvest fruits and root crops for food. Trim to retard growth.
Apr 25, 5:47 am– Apr 27, 5:27 pm	3rd	Capricorn	Plant potatoes and tubers. Trim to retard growth.

Celebrate Earth Day on your block or in your neighborhood. Take an active role by printing flyers (on recycled paper) and pass them out door to door with whatever information you feel is pertinent. You could invite families to walk to a local park and pick up trash along the way. Invite someone to talk to people about different trees and plantings in the park and how to avoid damaging them. Arrange to have someone available to collect the trash that your neighbors picked up.

○
April 20
6:25 am EDT

APRIL

S	M	T	W	T	F	S
		1	2	3	4	5
6	7	8	9	10	11	12
13	14	15	16	17	18	19
20	21	22	23	24	25	26
27	28	29	30			

May

Week of April 27–May 3

Don't be a blueprint. Be an original.
—ROY ACUFF

Apr 25, 5:47 am– Apr 27, 5:27 pm	3rd	Capricorn	Plant potatoes and tubers. Trim to retard growth.
Apr 27, 5:27 pm– Apr 28, 10:12 am	3rd	Aquarius	Cultivate. Destroy weeds and pests. Harvest fruits and root crops for food. Trim to retard growth.
Apr 28, 10:12 am– Apr 30, 2:11 am	4th	Aquarius	Cultivate. Destroy weeds and pests. Harvest fruits and root crops for food. Trim to retard growth.
Apr 30, 2:11 am– May 2, 6:51 am	4th	Pisces	Plant biennials, perennials, bulbs and roots. Prune. Irrigate. Fertilize (organic).
May 2, 6:51 am– May 4, 7:58 am	4th	Aries	Cultivate. Destroy weeds and pests. Harvest fruits and root crops for food. Trim to retard growth.

To find out when the projected last frost date is in your area, check with your local county extension office. It's safe to put out transplants when the last frost date is past, and you can plant seeds that have a two-week germination period two weeks prior to the last frost date.

_____

_____

_____

_____

_____

_____

April 28
10:12 am EDT

			MAY			
S	M	T	W	T	F	S
				1	2	3
4	5	6	7	8	9	10
11	12	13	14	15	16	17
18	19	20	21	22	23	24
25	26	27	28	29	30	31

May 4, 7:58 am– May 5, 8:18 am	4th	Taurus	Plant potatoes and tubers. Trim to retard growth.
May 5, 8:18 am– May 6, 7:17 am	1st	Taurus	Plant annuals for hardiness. Trim to increase growth.
May 8, 7:02 am– May 10, 9:10 am	1st	Cancer	Plant grains, leafy annuals. Fertilize (chemical). Graft or bud plants. Irrigate. Trim to increase growth.

The New Moon occurs when the Moon, in its monthly orbit, lies between the Sun and Earth. When the Moon is new, it can be seen early in the evening, but as it passes through its phases it rises later and later. We see the different Moon phases because of the way the Sun illuminates the Moon as the Moon orbits Earth. The relationship between the Sun, Earth, and the Moon is ever changing and, therefore, different angles are always being created. The appearance of the Moon (in its different phases) depends on its position in relation to the Sun.

May 5
8:18 am EDT

MAY

S	M	T	W	T	F	S
				1	2	3
4	5	6	7	8	9	10
11	12	13	14	15	16	17
18	19	20	21	22	23	24
25	26	27	28	29	30	31

May 14, 11:46 pm- May 17, 10:59 am	2nd	Libra	Plant annuals for fragrance and beauty. Trim to increase growth.
May 17, 10:59 am- May 19, 10:11 pm	2nd	Scorpio	Plant grains, leafy annuals. Fertilize (chemical). Graft or bud plants. Irrigate. Trim to increase growth

The best time to graft is when the buds on trees are just beginning to open, usually from April to early May. Healthy trees up to five years old are best suited for grafting, and there should be between one and two feet of branch between the graft and the trunk to allow for a proper crotch to form. Most varieties of a species are interchangable. Plants of the same genus but different species can be grafted, but the result is often a weak plant that may not live long. Plants from different families cannot be grafted together.

◐

May 11
11:47 pm EDT

May 17, 10:59 am- May 19, 10:11 pm	2nd	Scorpio	Plant grains, leafy annuals. Fertilize (chemical). Graft or bud plants. Irrigate. Trim to increase growth.
May 19, 10:11 pm- May 19, 11:18 pm	3rd	Scorpio	Plant biennials, perennials, bulbs and roots. Prune. Irrigate. Fertilize (organic).
May 19, 11:18 pm- May 22, 11:55 am	3rd	Sagittarius	Cultivate. Destroy weeds and pests. Harvest fruits and root crops for food. Trim to retard growth.
May 22, 11:55 am- May 24, 11:51 pm	3rd	Capricorn	Plant potatoes and tubers. Trim to retard growth.

A healthy lawn is the best cure for weeds and pests. Be aware that if you are using a combination fertilizer and herbicide, it may be taken up by the tree and shrub roots under the lawn and injure them, too. Use of residual weed killers that linger in the soil to prevent future weed growth may also kill many soil microorganisms. The result can be poorer soil, and thus poorer lawn growth and vigor. If problems occur, such as insects and diseases, check with your local garden center for answers.

○
May 19
10:11 pm EDT

MAY

S	M	T	W	T	F	S
				1	2	3
4	5	6	7	8	9	10
11	12	13	14	15	16	17
18	19	20	21	22	23	24
25	26	27	28	29	30	31

May 24, 11:51 pm– May 27, 9:38 am	3rd	Aquarius	Cultivate. Destroy weeds and pests. Harvest fruits and root crops for food. Trim to retard growth.
May 27, 9:38 am– May 27, 10:56 pm	3rd	Pisces	Plant biennials, perennials, bulbs and roots. Prune. Irrigate. Fertilize (organic).
May 27, 10:56 pm– May 29, 3:52 pm	4th	Pisces	Plant biennials, perennials, bulbs and roots. Prune. Irrigate. Fertilize (organic).
May 29, 3:52 pm– May 31, 6:18 pm	4th	Aries	Cultivate. Destroy weeds and pests. Harvest fruits and root crops for food. Trim to retard growth.

Following boat safety guidelines will ensure your safety and that of other people, and you'll have more fun.

- Always pay attention to the weather. Sudden wind shifts, lightning flashes, and choppy water all can mean a storm is brewing. Bring a portable radio to check weather reports.
- Bring along a flashlight, extra batteries, matches, a map of where you are, flares, suntan lotion, a first aid kit, and extra sunglasses. Put items that need to be protected in a watertight pouch or a container that floats.
- Tell someone where you're going, who is with you, and how long you'll be away.
- Check your boat, equipment, boat balance, engine, and fuel supply before leaving.

American Red Cross Boat Safety Guidelines

◑

May 27
10:56 pm EDT

June

Week of June 1–7

Your financial life is like a garden. If you tend a garden carefully, nourishing the flowers, pruning, and weeding, it's going to be a lot more beautiful than if you just water it half-heartedly now and then.

—SUZE ORMAN

May 31, 6:18 pm- Jun 2, 6:06 pm	4th	Taurus	Plant potatoes and tubers. Trim to retard growth.
Jun 2, 6:06 pm- Jun 3, 3:22 pm	4th	Gemini	Cultivate. Destroy weeds and pests. Harvest fruits and root crops for food. Trim to retard growth.
June 4, 5:16 pm- June 6, 6:00 pm	1st	Cancer	Plant grains, leafy annuals. Fertilize (chemical). Graft or bud plants. Irrigate. Trim to increase growth.

If you direct seeded onions, peas, lettuce, spinach, or radishes in early spring, you may have vegetables ready for harvesting now. Depending on the zone you are in, you may also be able to do a second planting for snap beans, beets, and onions at this time for harvesting later this summer or fall.

June 3
3:22 pm EDT

JUNE

S	M	T	W	T	F	S
1	2	3	4	5	6	7
8	9	10	11	12	13	14
15	16	17	18	19	20	21
22	23	24	25	26	27	28
29	30					

| Jun 11, 5:55 am-
Jun 13, 4:53 pm | 2nd | Libra | Plant annuals for fragrance and beauty. Trim to increase growth. |
| Jun 13, 4:53 pm-
Jun 16, 5:19 am | 2nd | Scorpio | Plant grains, leafy annuals. Fertilize (chemical). Graft or bud plants. Irrigate. Trim to increase growth. |

You can create a water garden even if there is no yard where you live. All you need is a plant, a small clear glass bowl or vase (even stemmed glassware works), and distilled water to create a miniature table-top water garden. Hyacinth, eelgrass, hornwort, water lettuce, marsh marigold, and sweet flag are popular choices for indoor water gardens. Consider texture and available light when you select your plant. You will need to remove all the soil from the plant roots before you place the plant on or in the water, and fertilize once a month with a colorless fertilizer. (Ask someone at your garden center to recommend a good fertilizer.) Experiment, and enjoy the results.

◐

June 10
11:03 am EDT

_____

_____

_____

_____

_____

_____

_____

Jun 18, 1:30 pm–Jun 18, 5:51 pm	3rd	Sagittarius	Cultivate. Destroy weeds and pests. Harvest fruits and root crops for food. Trim to retard growth.
Jun 18, 5:51 pm–Jun 21, 5:33 am	3rd	Capricorn	Plant potatoes and tubers. Trim to retard growth.
Jun 21, 5:33 am–Jun 23, 3:32 pm	3rd	Aquarius	Cultivate. Destroy weeds and pests. Harvest fruits and root crops for food. Trim to retard growth.

Garfield, that lazy, overweight orange tabby, made his first appearance in newspaper comic pages on June 19, 1978. True to his Gemini nature, he fears being alone and getting older. He also hates boredom and detests Mondays. One of his favorite places is the TV chair, from where he watches his favorite show, *Binky the Clown* (how Gemini is that!). Garfield's June 19 birthday is just two days before the Sun moves into Cancer, which may contribute to his fondness for food, especially lasagna, which he enjoys at Mama Leone's Italian Restaurant as often as possible. The lovable, pudgy feline turns thirty this year.

○
June 18
1:30 pm EDT

		JUNE				
S	M	T	W	T	F	S
1	2	3	4	5	6	7
8	9	10	11	12	13	14
15	16	17	18	19	20	21
22	23	24	25	26	27	28
29	30					

Jun 21, 5:33 am- Jun 23, 3:32 pm	3rd	Aquarius	Cultivate. Destroy weeds and pests. Harvest fruits and root crops for food. Trim to retard growth.
Jun 23, 3:32 pm- Jun 25, 10:49 pm	3rd	Pisces	Plant biennials, perennials, bulbs and roots. Prune. Irrigate. Fertilize (organic).
Jun 25, 10:49 pm- Jun 26, 8:10 am	3rd	Aries	Cultivate. Destroy weeds and pests. Harvest fruits and root crops for food. Trim to retard growth.
Jun 26, 8:10 am- Jun 28, 2:50 am	4th	Aries	Cultivate. Destroy weeds and pests. Harvest fruits and root crops for food. Trim to retard growth.

Research has shown that cutting grass high has many benefits for the organic lawn. Root systems develop that provide drought-resistance and hardiness, and as a result, many weeds are simply choked out. Mowing at a cutting height of at least three inches is recommended. The exception is for the last several cuts of the season, when cutting lower (down to one inch for perennial ryegrass and fine fescue, two inches for Kentucky bluegrass and tall fescue) is recommended. Mulch-cut the grass and leave clippings on the lawn. They are a great source of nitrogen and, contrary to rumors, do not contribute to thatch in an organic lawn. Keep the mower blade(s) sharp.

June 26
8:10 am EDT

♋ July

Week of June 29–July 5

In pursuit of passions, always be young. In your relationship with others, always be a grown-up. Set a standard and stay faithful to it.

—TOM BROKAW

Jun 28, 2:50 am- Jun 30, 4:03 am	4th	Taurus	Plant potatoes and tubers. Trim to retard growth.
Jun 30, 4:03 am- Jul 2, 3:53 am	4th	Gemini	Cultivate. Destroy weeds and pests. Harvest fruits and root crops for food. Trim to retard growth.
Jul 2, 3:53 am- Jul 2, 10:18 pm	4th	Cancer	Plant biennials, perennials, bulbs and roots. Prune. Irrigate. Fertilize (organic).

If you don't mind having ants in your yard but you'd rather not share your house with them, give these suggestions a try. Sprinkle scented baby powder where you see them coming in. They don't like it. You can also sprinkle a little on the shelf where you keep your honey and syrups. If you sprinkle cinnamon or black pepper on their trail, that will also deter the tiny, unwelcome guests.

July 2
10:18 pm EDT

JUNE						
S	M	T	W	T	F	S
1	2	3	4	5	6	7
8	9	10	11	12	13	14
15	16	17	18	19	20	21
22	23	24	25	26	27	28
29	30					

Jul 8, 1:31 pm– Jul 10, 12:35 pm	1st	Libra	Plant annuals for fragrance and beauty. Trim to increase growth.
Jul 10, 12:35 pm– Jul 13, 11:50 am	2nd	Scorpio	Plant grains, leafy annuals. Fertilize (chemical). Graft or bud plants. Irrigate. Trim to increase growth.

The dog days of summer are approaching, and it's important to keep in mind that pets have special needs during hot weather. Heat stroke, parasite control, and summer travel can pose problems for your pets, so take extra precautions to control mosquito and tick-related problems. Ticks are more of a problem for dogs than for cats, but cats can carry ticks in their fur, too. Fire ants can be a problem for pets, and they should be gotten rid of if they appear in your yard. Remember that sidewalks and roads can get very hot, so protect your pet's feet when you're walking with them. Let them walk in the grass if at all possible, or change your routine so you can walk your dog either earlier or later in the day, when surfaces are cooler. Heat stroke is more of a problem for dogs with short noses. And animals can get sunburned, so don't shave their fur (unless they've had skin problems). The Humane Society recommends putting sunscreen on their noses and ear tips.

July 10
12:35 am EDT

JULY

S	M	T	W	T	F	S
		1	2	3	4	5
6	7	8	9	10	11	12
13	14	15	16	17	18	19
20	21	22	23	24	25	26
27	28	29	30	31		

Jul 16, 12:20 am–Jul 18, 3:59 am	2nd	Capricorn	Graft or bud plants. Trim to increase growth.
Jul 18, 3:59 am–Jul 18, 11:40 am	3rd	Capricorn	Plant potatoes and tubers. Trim to retard growth.
Jul 18, 11:40 am–Jul 20, 9:07 pm	3rd	Aquarius	Cultivate. Destroy weeds and pests. Harvest fruits and root crops for food. Trim to retard growth.

West Nile virus first appeared in the U.S. in 1999, and it's spread by mosquitoes. Many people who contract the virus have mild symptoms that include fever, headache, body aches, skin rash, and swollen lymph glands. If WNV enters the brain, however, it can be deadly. There is no vaccine or specific treatment for WNV, but you can try to prevent contracting it by using insect repellent, eliminating mosquito breeding sites, and staying indoors between dusk and dawn. Older people are more at risk of getting the virus and should take extra precautions.

_____

_____

_____

_____

_____

○
July 18
3:59 am EDT

JULY						
S	M	T	W	T	F	S
		1	2	3	4	5
6	7	8	9	10	11	12
13	14	15	16	17	18	19
20	21	22	23	24	25	26
27	28	29	30	31		

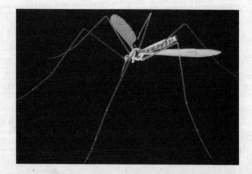

Jul 20, 9:07 pm– Jul 23, 4:22 am	3rd	Pisces	Plant biennials, perennials, bulbs and roots. Prune. Irrigate. Fertilize (organic).
Jul 23, 4:22 am– Jul 25, 9:14 am	3rd	Aries	Cultivate. Destroy weeds and pests. Harvest fruits and root crops for food. Trim to retard growth.
Jul 25, 9:14 am– Jul 25, 2:41 pm	3rd	Taurus	Plant potatoes and tubers. Trim to retard growth.
Jul 25, 2:41 pm– Jul 27, 11:55 am	4th	Taurus	Plant potatoes and tubers. Trim to retard growth.

The Red Cross has water safety tips to keep your family safe this summer. The most basic precaution is: Learn to swim! If you don't know how to swim, take some lessons at your local pool, and enroll your children in swimming classes.

- Swim with a buddy; never swim alone
- Swim in supervised areas only
- Obey all rules and posted signs
- Don't mix alcohol and swimming
- Pay attention to local weather conditions, and stop swimming at the first indication of bad weather

July 25
2:41 pm EDT

August

Week of July 27–August 2

I believe the choice to be excellent begins with aligning your thoughts and words with the intention to require more from yourself.

—OPRAH WINFREY

Jul 27, 11:55 am-Jul 29, 1:11 pm	4th	Gemini	Cultivate. Destroy weeds and pests. Harvest fruits and root crops for food. Trim to retard growth.
Jul 29, 1:11 pm-Jul 31, 2:21 pm	4th	Cancer	Plant biennials, perennials, bulbs and roots. Prune. Irrigate. Fertilize (organic).
Jul 31, 2:21 pm-Aug 1, 6:12 am	4th	Leo	Cultivate. Destroy weeds and pests. Harvest fruits and root crops for food. Trim to retard growth.

In addition to being beautiful, flowers also provide fragrance and sensual texture. When you walk through your gardens, pay a little extra attention to the "other" sensual pleasures that flowers have to offer.

August 1
6:12 am EDT

JULY

S	M	T	W	T	F	S
		1	2	3	4	5
6	7	8	9	10	11	12
13	14	15	16	17	18	19
20	21	22	23	24	25	26
27	28	29	30	31		

Aug 4, 10:28 pm– Aug 7, 7:26 am	1st	Libra	Plant annuals for fragrance and beauty. Trim to increase growth.
Aug 7, 7:26 am– Aug 8, 4:20 pm	1st	Scorpio	Plant grains, leafy annuals. Fertilize (chemical). Graft or bud plants. Irrigate. Trim to increase growth.
Aug 8, 4:20 pm– Aug 9, 7:10 pm	2nd	Scorpio	Plant grains, leafy annuals. Fertilize (chemical). Graft or bud plants. Irrigate. Trim to increase growth.

Pruning really stresses trees, and a tree that is pruned during the summer will experience even more stress because it is deprived of leaves that provide shade and allow food production. Trees are often pruned for the wrong reason. If you prune a tree because it is too large, perhaps you planted the wrong tree in your yard. You might be overwatering or overfertilizing the tree, too. Consider the tree's needs as well as your own before you bring it home and plant it.

August 8
4:20 pm EDT

| | | Au | gust | | | |
S	M	T	W	T	F	S
					1	2
3	4	5	6	7	8	9
10	11	12	13	14	15	16
17	18	19	20	21	22	23
24	25	26	27	28	29	30
31						

Aug 12, 7:42 am– Aug 14, 6:56 pm	2nd	Capricorn	Graft or bud plants. Trim to increase growth.

Herbs known to be ruled by Capricorn are:

- Wintergreen, used to remedy rheumatism in the joints
- Comfrey root, an excellent remedy for skin problems that can be applied as an ointment
- Slippery elm, a cooling and soothing digestive aid that also strengthens the bone structure

_____

_____

_____

_____

_____

○
August 16
5:16 pm EDT

AUGUST

S	M	T	W	T	F	S
					1	2
3	4	5	6	7	8	9
10	11	12	13	14	15	16
17	18	19	20	21	22	23
24	25	26	27	28	29	30
31						

Aug 17, 3:46 am- Aug 19, 10:10 am	2nd	Pisces	Plant grains, leafy annuals. Fertilize (chemical). Graft or bud plants. Irrigate. Trim to increase growth.
Aug 21, 2:38 pm- Aug 23, 5:48 pm	2nd	Taurus	Plant annuals for hardiness. Trim to increase growth.
Aug 23, 5:48 pm- Aug 25, 8:18 pm	4th	Gemini	Cultivate. Destroy weeds and pests. Harvest fruits and root crops for food. Trim to retard growth.

Even your most adored pet may not be welcome in your gardens. Dogs are indiscriminate about where they dig or flop down for a nap, and cats don't discriminate between a litter box and soft garden soil. Sprinkle ginger around your flower beds to keep cats away. They hate the smell. A whiff of cayenne pepper will send dogs into less hostile territory, and a smart dog won't return.

◑

August 23
7:49 pm EDT

Aug 25, 8:18 pm- Aug 27, 10:51 pm	4th	Cancer	Plant biennials, perennials, bulbs and roots. Prune. Irrigate. Fertilize (organic).
Aug 27, 10:51 pm- Aug 30, 2:18 am	4th	Leo	Cultivate. Destroy weeds and pests. Harvest fruits and root crops for food. Trim to retard growth.
Aug 30, 2:18 am- Aug 30, 3:58 pm	4th	Virgo	Cultivate, especially medicinal plants. Destroy weeds and pests. Trim to retard growth.

What was to become the "Great Moon Hoax" began on August 25, 1835, when the first of six articles appeared in the *New York Sun*. Although authorship was never positively determined, claims that the Moon was inhabited by winged humanoids, tail-less beaver, goats, unicorns, and other fantastic creatures resulted in a dramatic (but temporary) increase in the newspaper's circulation. The discovery was made, the articles said, by means of a telescope with a lens that weighed 14,826 pounds (after being polished) and an estimated magnifying power of 42,000 times.

August 30
3:58 pm EDT

AUGUST

S	M	T	W	T	F	S
					1	2
3	4	5	6	7	8	9
10	11	12	13	14	15	16
17	18	19	20	21	22	23
24	25	26	27	28	29	30
31						

♍ September

Week of August 31–September 6

A doctor can bury his mistakes but an architect can only advise his clients to plant vines.

—FRANK LLOYD WRIGHT

| Sep 1, 7:44 am–
Sep 3, 4:02 pm | 1st | Libra | Plant annuals for fragrance and beauty. Trim to increase growth. |
| Sep 3, 4:02 pm–
Sep 6, 3:11 am | 1st | Scorpio | Plant grains, leafy annuals. Fertilize (chemical). Graft or bud plants. Irrigate. Trim to increase growth. |

Whether you have a picnic on the deck or in the park, include some of the harvest from your garden in your meal. Lead off with chips and salsa made from tomatoes, onions, and jalapenos. Serve fresh corn on the cob, or combine fresh corn, bell peppers, and tomatoes in a salad. And don't forget the watermelon, if you have some growing in the garden, and potato salad. Or, if you plan to have a bonfire, you could wrap potatoes in aluminum foil and let them bake in the hot coals.

_____

_____

_____

_____

_____

_____

SEPTEMBER

S	M	T	W	T	F	S
		1	2	3	4	5	6
7	8	9	10	11	12	13
14	15	16	17	18	19	20
21	22	23	24	25	26	27
28	29	30				

Sep 8, 3:45 pm- Sep 11, 3:19 am	2nd	Capricorn	Graft or bud plants. Trim to increase growth.
Sep 13, 12:04 pm- Sep 15, 5:13 am	2nd	Pisces	Plant grains, leafy annuals. Fertilize (chemical). Graft or bud plants. Irrigate. Trim to increase growth.

In 2005, a 1,129-pound Atlantic Giant pumpkin took first place in the pumpkin weigh-off held in Half Moon Bay, California. First prize was $5 per pound, which put $6,145 in prize money in the winner's pocket. Lots of water, fertilizer, and hand-pollination were the key elements to this pumpkin's success. To learn more about giant pumpkins, see the "Pumpkinfest" article on page 346.

◑

September 7
10:04 am EDT

SEPTEMBER

S	M	T	W	T	F	S
	1	2	3	4	5	6
7	8	9	10	11	12	13
14	15	16	17	18	19	20
21	22	23	24	25	26	27
28	29	30				

Sep 15, 5:13 am- Sep 15, 5:39 pm	3rd	Pisces	Plant biennials, perennials, bulbs and roots. Prune. Irrigate. Fertilize (organic).
Sep 15, 5:39 pm- Sep 17, 8:56 pm	3rd	Aries	Cultivate. Destroy weeds and pests. Harvest fruits and root crops for food. Trim to retard growth.
Sep 17, 8:56 pm- Sep 19, 11:17 pm	3rd	Taurus	Plant potatoes and tubers. Trim to retard growth.
Sep 19, 11:17 pm- Sep 22, 1:48 am	3rd	Gemini	Cultivate. Destroy weeds and pests. Harvest fruits and root crops for food. Trim to retard growth.

This whole week, following the Full Moon on Monday, provides a good opportunity to clean up and divide your spring-flowering perennials. Before you divide a plant, prepare the soil in the area you want to move the new divisions to. Watering plants well the day before you divide and move them will loosen the soil and make your work easier. It's also a good idea to soak the roots for about an hour in a bucket of water before you place them in the new area. If the weather cooperates and you get an overcast day to do your garden work, that will reduce stress on the new transplanted roots. It helps to provide some temporary shade and keep the soil moist for a few weeks, too.

○
September 15
5:13 am EDT

Sep 22, 1:48 am– Sep 24, 5:13 am	4th	Cancer	Plant biennials, perennials, bulbs and roots. Prune. Irrigate. Fertilize (organic).
Sep 24, 5:13 am– Sep 26, 9:52 am	4th	Leo	Cultivate. Destroy weeds and pests. Harvest fruits and root crops for food. Trim to retard growth.
Sep 26, 9:52 am– Sep 28, 4:05 pm	4th	Virgo	Cultivate, especially medicinal plants. Destroy weeds and pests. Trim to retard growth.

When we think of medicinal plants, plants like aloe vera, nettle, and peppermint come to mind. But there are other plants with medicinal properties that we can grow in our homes or gardens that you may not have thought about. The common marigold is one of the best plants for treating local skin problems, for example. Infusions or decoctions of marigold petals can be used to treat inflammations and insect bites. Young leaves from the common mallow plant can be eaten to reduce stomach irritation, and the leaves can be rubbed on the skin to fight inflammations. Verbena is used in mouthwashes to fight bacteria and infections, and tea made with verbena leaves is used to treat insomnia and to help digestion.

September 22
1:04 am EDT

SEPTEMBER

S	M	T	W	T	F	S
	1	2	3	4	5	6
7	8	9	10	11	12	13
14	15	16	17	18	19	20
21	22	23	24	25	26	27
28	29	30				

October

Week of September 28–October 4

*Whenever men take the law into their own hands,
the loser is the law. And when the law loses, freedom languishes.*

—ROBERT F. KENNEDY

| Sep 29, 4:12 am–Oct 1, 12:26 am | 1st | Scorpio | Plant grains, leafy annuals. Fertilize (chemical). Graft or bud plants. Irrigate. Trim to increase growth. |
| Oct 1, 12:26 am–Oct 3, 11:14 am | 1st | Scorpio | Plant grains, leafy annuals. Fertilize (chemical). Graft or bud plants. Irrigate. Trim to increase growth. |

If you're not sure about which perennials to leave alone and which ones to cut back, take a few minutes and do an Internet search for advice on caring for perennials. Some plants, such as asters, astilbe, butterfly bush, and dianthus will produce stronger plants next spring if they are left standing.

—————————————————

—————————————————

—————————————————

—————————————————

—————————————————

—————————————————

●

September 29
4:12 am EDT

OCTOBER

S	M	T	W	T	F	S
			1	2	3	4
5	6	7	8	9	10	11
12	13	14	15	16	17	18
19	20	21	22	23	24	25
26	27	28	29	30	31	

Oct 5, 11:48 pm– Oct 7, 5:04 am	1st	Capricorn	Graft or bud plants. Trim to increase growth.
Oct 7, 5:04 am– Oct 8, 12:03 pm	2nd	Capricorn	Graft or bud plants. Trim to increase growth.
Oct 10, 9:31 pm– Oct 13, 3:07 am	2nd	Pisces	Plant grains, leafy annuals. Fertilize (chemical). Graft or bud plants. Irrigate. Trim to increase growth.

Healthy soil is crucial to healthy gardens, crops, and lawns. Even window boxes and patio containers need to contain healthy soil. Plants will adapt themselves to particular types of soils and climates, and in turn feed the soil they live in. The soil is also fed by the remains of animals, bugs, worms, and bacteria.

If even one species or micro-organism leaves, or is destroyed, it sets off a chain reaction through the support system that can have far-reaching implications. The disappearance of plants can cause the disappearance of animals, and so on. If you put back into the soil what you take away, the balance is maintained.

October 7
5:04 am EDT

OCTOBER

S	M	T	W	T	F	S
			1	2	3	4
5	6	7	8	9	10	11
12	13	14	15	16	17	18
19	20	21	22	23	24	25
26	27	28	29	30	31	

Oct 14, 4:02 pm- Oct 15, 5:31 am	3rd	Aries	Cultivate. Destroy weeds and pests. Harvest fruits and root crops for food. Trim to retard growth.
Oct 15, 5:31 am- Oct 17, 6:25 am	3rd	Taurus	Plant potatoes and tubers. Trim to retard growth.
Oct 17, 6:25 am- Oct 19, 7:40 am	3rd	Gemini	Cultivate. Destroy weeds and pests. Harvest fruits and root crops for food. Trim to retard growth.

Now is the time to gather grasses, flowers, attractive branches, and other items from outdoors to put into fall flower arrangements or to use for decorating your holiday wreaths. Be on the lookout for grapevines, which may be more visible now. Hydrangea can be collected in some areas. Check your flower gardens for items that can be worked into an arrangement, too. If you have extra grapevine, you can make a unique vase by simply wrapping the vine around a tall straight-sided tumbler (or any other container that you have) and securing the ends with hot glue, or a length of ribbon.

O

October 14
4:02 pm EDT

Oct 19, 7:40 am- Oct 21, 7:54 am	3rd	Cancer	Plant biennials, perennials, bulbs and roots. Prune. Irrigate. Fertilize (organic).
Oct 21, 7:54 am- Oct 21, 10:35 am	4th	Cancer	Plant biennials, perennials, bulbs and roots. Prune. Irrigate. Fertilize (organic).
Oct 21, 10:35 am- Oct 23, 3:40 pm	4th	Leo	Cultivate. Destroy weeds and pests. Harvest fruits and root crops for food. Trim to retard growth.
Oct 23, 3:40 pm- Oct 25, 10:47 pm	4th	Virgo	Cultivate, especially medicinal plants. Destroy weeds and pests. Trim to retard growth.

Be sure to provide protection—heavy mulch or a temporary cover—and sufficient water to protect your plants from serious freezing. Watering is especially important for bare-root plants and trees.

◑
October 21
7:54 am EDT

OCTOBER

S	M	T	W	T	F	S
			1	2	3	4
5	6	7	8	9	10	11
12	13	14	15	16	17	18
19	20	21	22	23	24	25
26	27	28	29	30	31	

♏ November

Week of October 26–November 1

Go out on a limb. That's where the fruit is.

—JIMMY CARTER

| Oct 28, 7:47 am-
Oct 28, 7:14 pm | 4th | Scorpio | Plant biennials, perennials, bulbs and roots. Prune. Irrigate. Fertilize (organic). |
| Oct 28, 7:14 pm-
Oct 30, 6:41 pm | 1st | Scorpio | Plant grains, leafy annuals. Fertilize (chemical). Graft or bud plants. Irrigate. Trim to increase growth. |

A gardener's hands get a lot of abuse that even wearing gloves may only minimize. Mother Nature offers help, though. To treat a cut on your hand, apply aloe vera to prevent infection. You can also bruise a handful of fresh oak leaves and apply them directly to a wound. Covering the leaves with a damp cloth (warm, if possible) will assist the leaves in fighting infection. To make a moisturizing lotion that is good for combating skin irritation, place flowers, collected from mullein and crushed up with a small amount of water (added to soften), in an earthenware bowl. Cover with almond oil and let stand for about a week. Strain and bottle.

●

October 28
7:14 pm EDT

NOVEMBER

S	M	T	W	T	F	S
						1
2	3	4	5	6	7	8
9	10	11	12	13	14	15
16	17	18	19	20	21	22
23	24	25	26	27	28	29
30						

Nov 2, 6:13 am– Nov 4, 7:01 pm	1st	Capricorn	Graft or bud plants. Trim to increase growth.
Nov 7, 5:43 am– Nov 9, 12:26 pm	2nd	Pisces	Plant grains, leafy annuals. Fertilize (chemical). Graft or bud plants. Irrigate. Trim to increase growth.

Take cuttings from plants you want to propagate when the Moon is waxing and in the sign related to the plant "type." Plants with soft, watery stems (like African violets) will do best when cuttings are taken when the Moon is in a water sign (Pisces, Cancer, or Scorpio), and plants or bushes with woody stems will do best when cuttings are taken in earth signs (Taurus and Capricorn). Wrap the cuttings in moistened paper and plant them after the Full Moon (in a sign related to the plant) to promote root growth. After the Full Moon, the plant's energy is descending and root growth will be more vigorous.

November 5
11:03 pm EST

Daylight Saving Time ends 2 pm,
November 2

NOVEMBER

S	M	T	W	T	F	S
						1
2	3	4	5	6	7	8
9	10	11	12	13	14	15
16	17	18	19	20	21	22
23	24	25	26	27	28	29
30						

Nov 11, 3:05 pm- Nov 13, 1:17 am	2nd	Taurus	Plant annuals for hardiness. Trim to increase growth.
Nov 13, 1:17 am- Nov 13, 3:11 pm	3rd	Taurus	Plant potatoes and tubers. Trim to retard growth.
Nov 13, 3:11 pm- Nov 15, 2:52 pm	3rd	Gemini	Cultivate. Destroy weeds and pests. Harvest fruits and root crops for food. Trim to retard growth.

"Peas that you would have early, sow in the Full Moon of November, if in a warm place," advised John Reid in *The Gard'ners Kalender*, first published in 1683.

To get your peas growing well, plant the seeds in raised garden beds and add compost to the soil. Compost warms the soil, and in areas that receive a lot of rain, composted soil dries faster than heavier soils. Peas make more than enough nitrogen for their own use once they are established, and the extra nitrogen stays in the soil for other plants to use. Good companion plants for peas include bush and pole beans, carrots, and cucumbers. Peas don't like to be near onions, however.

Rotating your peas to a new area in your garden next season will help prevent disease from affecting crops. Removing dead vines from your garden at the end of the season is a good disease prevention measure.

○
November 13
1:17 am EST

Nov 15, 2:52 pm– Nov 17, 4:07 pm	3rd	Cancer	Plant biennials, perennials, bulbs and roots. Prune. Irrigate. Fertilize (organic).
Nov 17, 4:07 pm– Nov 19, 4:31 pm	3rd	Leo	Cultivate. Destroy weeds and pests. Harvest fruits and root crops for food. Trim to retard growth.
Nov 19, 4:31 pm– Nov 19, 8:12 pm	4th	Leo	Cultivate. Destroy weeds and pests. Harvest fruits and root crops for food. Trim to retard growth.
Nov 19, 8:12 pm– Nov 22, 3:20 am	4th	Virgo	Cultivate, especially medicinal plants. Destroy weeds and pests. Trim to retard growth.

Organic fertilizers made from animal and plant products are slower to release because micro-organisms in the soil have to break them down before plants can use them. It is best to alternate between chemical and organic fertilizers, unless you are committed to completely natural gardening.

◐
November 19
4:31 pm EST

NOVEMBER

S	M	T	W	T	F	S
						1
2	3	4	5	6	7	8
9	10	11	12	13	14	15
16	17	18	19	20	21	22
23	24	25	26	27	28	29
30						

Nov 24, 12:54 pm- Nov 27, 12:14 am	4th	Scorpio	Plant biennials, perennials, bulbs and roots. Prune. Irrigate. Fertilize (organic).
Nov 27, 12:14 am- Nov 27, 11:54 am	4th	Sagittarius	Cultivate. Destroy weeds and pests. Harvest fruits and root crops for food. Trim to retard growth.
Nov 29, 12:48 pm- Dec 2, 1:44 am	1st	Capricorn	Graft or bud plants. Trim to increase growth.

Certified organic products have a paper trail—a series of documents—that provide proof the producer of the product is following the rules. Only companies that meet all the criteria can be certified organic, and the certificate is available to consumers upon request. But in addition to the certificate, which is issued by a certifying agency, other documents report the field history, harvest and storage records, weigh tickets, clean-truck affidavits, inventory purchase records, packaging reports, maintenance and sanitation reports, and more. All of this paperwork takes time, and time equals money, which is only one of the reasons we pay more for certified organic products.

_____

_____

_____

_____

_____

_____

December

Week of November 30–December 6

We cannot build our own future without helping others to build theirs.

—BILL CLINTON

Dec 4, 1:23 pm– Dec 5, 4:25 pm	1st	Pisces	Plant grains, leafy annuals. Fertilize (chemical). Graft or bud plants. Irrigate. Trim to increase growth.
Dec 5, 4:25 pm– Dec 6, 9:44 pm	2nd	Pisces	Plant grains, leafy annuals. Fertilize (chemical). Graft or bud plants. Irrigate. Trim to increase growth.

Crop rotation is very important if you want to grow healthy plants and minimize insect pests. Rotating crops is as important for backyard gardeners as it is for farmers. It may seem too challenging to rotate crops in a small garden, but when you consider the limited space you have to work with, it becomes even more important to protect the integrity of your soil.

December 5
4:25 pm EST

DECEMBER

S	M	T	W	T	F	S
	1	2	3	4	5	6
7	8	9	10	11	12	13
14	15	16	17	18	19	20
21	22	23	24	25	26	27
28	29	30	31			

| Dec 9, 1:52 am-
Dec 11, 2:33 am | 2nd | Taurus | Plant annuals for hardiness. Trim to increase growth. |
| Dec 13, 1:39 am-
Dec 15, 1:22 am | 3rd | Cancer | Plant biennials, perennials, bulbs and roots. Prune. Irrigate. Fertilize (organic). |

Use bee balm or coltsfoot for colds and to relieve coughing. Garlic helps your heart stay healthy and keeps colds away. Nasturtium is considered a stimulant (try it in tea), and its peppery taste makes it a good addition to salads.

Other stimulants include mint, cloves, parsley, rosemary, cinnamon, and cayenne pepper. Try to include them in your food dishes whenever possible.

O
December 12
11:37 am EST

Dec 15, 1:22 am- Dec 17, 3:35 am	3rd	Leo	Cultivate. Destroy weeds and pests. Harvest fruits and root crops for food. Trim to retard growth.
Dec 17, 3:35 am- Dec 19, 5:29 am	3rd	Virgo	Cultivate, especially medicinal plants. Destroy weeds and pests. Trim to retard growth.
Dec 19, 5:29 am- Dec 19, 9:23 am	4th	Virgo	Cultivate, especially medicinal plants. Destroy weeds and pests. Trim to retard growth.

Rose hips added to teas or fruit juices will provide extra vitamin C to your diet. Add 2 teaspoons of chopped rose hips to boiling water, cover and steep for 15 minutes, sweeten, and enjoy!

December 19
5:29 am EST

DECEMBER

S	M	T	W	T	F	S
		1	2	3	4	5	6
7	8	9	10	11	12	13
14	15	16	17	18	19	20
21	22	23	24	25	26	27
28	29	30	31			

Dec 21, 6:36 pm– Dec 24, 6:13 am	4th	Scorpio	Plant biennials, perennials, bulbs and roots. Prune. Irrigate. Fertilize (organic).
Dec 24, 6:13 am– Dec 26, 6:56 pm	4th	Sagittarius	Cultivate. Destroy weeds and pests. Harvest fruits and root crops for food. Trim to retard growth.
Dec 26, 6:56 pm– Dec 27, 7:22 am	4th	Capricorn	Plant potatoes and tubers. Trim to retard growth.
Dec 27, 7:22 am– Dec 29, 7:42 am	1st	Capricorn	Graft or bud plants. Trim to increase growth.

Common complaints at this time of year include sore throats, coughs from colds, and depression. The energy is yin (damp, cold, withdrawn), and to balance it, or alleviate the symptoms, we need to introduce yang (active, outgoing) energy through activity and what we eat or drink. Activities that get you out of the house—classes, walking, skating, or running—are yang activities.

●

December 27
7:22 am EST

Gardening by the Moon

Today, people often reject the notion of gardening according to the Moon's phase and sign. The usual nonbeliever is not a scientist but the city dweller who has never had any real contact with nature and little experience of natural rhythms.

Camille Flammarian, the French astronomer, testifies to the success of Moon planting, though:

"Cucumbers increase at Full Moon, as well as radishes, turnips, leeks, lilies, horseradish, and saffron; onions, on the contrary, are much larger and better nourished during the decline and old age of the Moon than at its increase, during its youth and fullness, which is the reason the Egyptians abstained from onions, on account of their antipathy to the Moon. Herbs gathered while the Moon increases are of great efficiency. If the vines are trimmed at night when the Moon is in the sign of Leo (the lion), Sagittarius (the scorpion), or Taurus (the bull), it will save them from field rats, moles, snails, flies, and other animals."

Dr. Clark Timmins is one of the few modern scientists to have conducted tests in Moon planting. Following is a summary of his experiments:

Beets: When sown with the Moon in Scorpio, the germination rate was 71 percent; when sown in Sagittarius, the germination rate was 58 percent.

Scotch marigold: When sown with the Moon in Cancer, the germination rate was 90 percent; when sown in Leo, the rate was 32 percent.

Carrots: When sown with the Moon in Scorpio, the germination rate was 64 percent; when sown in Sagittarius, the germination rate was 47 percent.

Tomatoes: When sown with the Moon in Cancer, the germination rate was 90 percent; but when sown with the Moon in Leo, the germination rate was 58 percent.

Two things should be emphasized. First, remember that this is only a summary of the results of the experiments; the experiments themselves were conducted in a scientific manner to eliminate any variation in soil, temperature, moisture, and so on, so that only the Moon sign is varied. Second, note that these astonishing results were obtained without regard to the phase of the Moon—the other factor we use in Moon planting, and which presumably would have increased the differential in germination rates.

Dr. Timmins also tried transplanting Cancer- and Leo-planted tomato seedlings while the Cancer Moon was waxing. The result was 100 percent survival. When transplanting was done with the waning Sagittarius Moon, there was 0 percent survival. Dr. Timmins' tests show that the Cancer-planted tomatoes had blossoms twelve days earlier than those planted under Leo; the Cancer-planted tomatoes had an average height of twenty inches at that time compared to fifteen inches for the Leo-planted; the first ripe tomatoes were gathered from the Cancer plantings eleven days ahead of the Leo plantings; and a count of the hanging fruit and its size and weight shows an advantage to the Cancer plants over the Leo plants of 45 percent.

Dr. Timmins also observed that there have been similar tests that did not indicate results favorable to the Moon planting theory. As a scientist, he asked why one set of experiments indicated a positive verification of Moon planting, and others did not. He checked these other tests and found that the experimenters had not followed the geocentric system for determining the Moon sign positions, but the heliocentric. When the times used in these other tests were converted to the geocentric system, the dates chosen often were found to be in barren, rather than fertile, signs. Without going into a technical explanation, it is sufficient to point out that geocentric and heliocentric positions often vary by as much as four days. This is a large enough differential to place the Moon in Cancer, for example, in the heliocentric system, and at the same time in Leo by the geocentric system.

Most almanacs and calendars show the Moon's signs heliocentrically—and thus incorrectly for Moon planting—while the *Moon Sign Book* is calculated correctly for planting purposes, using the geocentric system. Some readers are confused because the *Moon Sign Book* talks about first, second, third, and fourth quarters, while other almanacs refer to these same divisions as New Moon, first quarter, Full Moon, and fourth quarter. Thus the almanacs say first quarter when the *Moon Sign Book* says second quarter.

There is nothing complicated about using astrology in agriculture and horticulture in order to increase both pleasure and profit, but there is one very important rule that is often neglected—use common sense! Of course this is one rule that should be remembered in every activity we undertake, but in the case of gardening and farming by the Moon, if it is not possible to use the best dates for planting or harvesting, we must select the next best and just try to do the best we can.

This brings up the matter of the other factors to consider in your gardening work. The dates we give as best for a certain activity apply to the entire country (with slight time correction), but in your section of the country you may be buried under three feet of snow on a date we say is good to plant your flowers. So we have factors of weather, season, temperature and moisture variations, soil conditions, your own available time and opportunity, and so forth. Some astrologers like to think it is all a matter of science, but gardening is also an art. In art, you develop an instinctive identification with your work and influence it with your feelings and wishes.

The *Moon Sign Book* gives you the place of the Moon for every day of the year so that you can select the best times once you have become familiar with the rules and practices of lunar agriculture. We give you specific, easy-to-follow directions so that you can get right down to work.

We give you the best dates for planting, and also for various related activities, including cultivation, fertilizing, harvesting, irrigation, and getting rid of weeds and pests. But we cannot tell you exactly when it's good to plant. Many of these rules were learned by observation and experience; as the body of experience grew we could see various patterns emerging that allowed us to make judgments about new things. That's what you should do, too. After you have worked with lunar agriculture for a while and have gained a working knowledge, you will probably begin to try new things—and we hope you will share your experiments and findings with us. That's how the science grows.

Here's an example of what we mean: Years ago Llewellyn George suggested that we try to combine our bits of knowledge about what to expect in planting under each of the Moon signs in order to gain benefit from several lunar factors in one plant. From this came our rule for developing "thoroughbred seed." To develop thoroughbred seed, save the seed for three successive years from plants grown by the correct Moon sign and phase. You can plant in the first quarter phase and in the sign of Cancer for fruitfulness; the second year, plant seeds from the first year plants in Libra for beauty; and in the third year, plant the seeds from the second year plants in Taurus to produce hardiness. In a similar manner you can combine the fruitfulness of Cancer, the good root growth of Pisces, and the sturdiness and good vine growth of Scorpio. And don't forget the characteristics of Capricorn: hardy like Taurus, but drier and perhaps more resistant to drought and disease.

Unlike common almanacs, we consider both the Moon's phase and the Moon's sign in making our calculations for the proper timing of our work. It is perhaps a little easier to understand this if we remind you that we are all living in the center of a vast electromagnetic field that is the Earth and its environment in space. Everything that occurs within this electromagnetic field has an effect on everything else within the field. The Moon and the Sun are the most important of the factors affecting the life of the Earth, and it is their relative positions to the Earth that we project for each day of the year.

Many people claim that not only do they achieve larger crops gardening by the Moon, but that their fruits and vegetables are much tastier. A number of organic gardeners have also become lunar gardeners using the natural rhythm of life forces that we experience through the relative movements of the Sun and Moon. We provide a few basic rules and then give you day-by-day guidance for your gardening work. You will be able to choose the best dates to meet your own needs and opportunities.

Planting by the Moon's Phases

During the increasing or waxing light—from New Moon to Full Moon—plant annuals that produce their yield above the ground. An annual is a plant that completes its entire life cycle within one growing season and has to be seeded each year. During the decreasing or waning light—from Full Moon to New Moon—plant biennials, perennials, and bulb and root plants. Biennials include crops that are planted one season to winter over and produce crops the next, such as winter wheat. Perennials and bulb and root plants include all plants that grow from the same root each year.

A simpler, less-accurate rule is to plant crops that produce above the ground during the waxing Moon, and to plant crops that produce below the ground during the waning Moon. Thus the old adage, "Plant potatoes during the dark of the Moon." Llewellyn George's system divided the lunar month into quarters. The first two from New Moon to Full Moon are the first and second quarters, and the last two from Full Moon to New Moon the third and fourth quarters. Using these divisions, we can increase our accuracy in timing our efforts to coincide with natural forces.

First Quarter

Plant annuals producing their yield above the ground, which are generally of the leafy kind that produce their seed outside the fruit. Some examples are asparagus, broccoli, brussels sprouts, cabbage, cauliflower, celery, cress, endive, kohlrabi, lettuce, parsley, and spinach. Cucumbers are an exception, as they do best in the first quarter rather than the second, even though the seeds are inside the fruit. Also plant cereals and grains.

Second Quarter

Plant annuals producing their yield above the ground, which are generally of the viney kind that produce their seed inside the fruit. Some examples include beans, eggplant, melons, peas, peppers, pumpkins, squash, tomatoes, etc. These are not hard-and-fast divisions. If you can't plant during the first quarter, plant during the second, and vice versa. There are many plants that seem to do equally well planted in either quarter, such as watermelon, hay, and cereals and grains.

Third Quarter

Plant biennials, perennials, bulbs, root plants, trees, shrubs, berries, grapes, strawberries, beets, carrots, onions, parsnips, rutabagas, potatoes, radishes, peanuts, rhubarb, turnips, winter wheat, etc.

Fourth Quarter

This is the best time to cultivate, turn sod, pull weeds, and destroy pests of all kinds, especially when the Moon is in Aries, Leo, Virgo, Gemini, Aquarius, and Sagittarius.

The Moon in the Signs

Moon in Aries

Barren, dry, fiery, and masculine. Use for destroying noxious weeds.

Moon in Taurus

Productive, moist, earthy, and feminine. Use for planting many crops when hardiness is important, particularly root crops. Also used for lettuce, cabbage, and similar leafy vegetables.

Moon in Gemini

Barren and dry, airy and masculine. Use for destroying noxious growths, weeds, and pests, and for cultivation.

Moon in Cancer

Fruitful, moist, feminine. Use for planting and irrigation.

Moon in Leo

Barren, dry, fiery, masculine. Use for killing weeds or cultivation.

Moon in Virgo

Barren, moist, earthy, and feminine. Use for cultivation and destroying weeds and pests.

Moon in Libra

Semi-fruitful, moist, and airy. Use for planting crops that need good pulp growth. A very good sign for flowers and vines. Also used for seeding hay, corn fodder, and the like.

Moon in Scorpio

Very fruitful and moist, watery and feminine. Nearly as productive as Cancer; use for the same purposes. Especially good for vine growth and sturdiness.

Moon in Sagittarius

Barren and dry, fiery and masculine. Use for planting onions, seeding hay, and for cultivation.

Moon in Capricorn

Productive and dry, earthy and feminine. Use for planting potatoes and other tubers.

Moon in Aquarius

Barren, dry, airy, and masculine. Use for cultivation and destroying noxious growths and pests.

Moon in Pisces

Very fruitful, moist, watery, and feminine. Especially good for root growth.

A Guide to Planting

Using Phase & Sign Rulerships

Plant	Quarter	Sign
Annuals	1st or 2nd	Any
Apple tree	2nd or 3rd	Cancer, Pisces, Virgo
Artichoke	1st	Cancer, Pisces
Asparagus	1st	Cancer, Scorpio, Pisces
Aster	1st or 2nd	Virgo, Libra
Barley	1st or 2nd	Cancer Pisces, Libra, Capricorn, Virgo
Beans (bush & pole)	2nd	Cancer, Taurus, Pisces, Libra
Beans (kidney, white, & navy)	1st or 2nd	Cancer, Pisces
Beech tree	2nd or 3rd	Virgo, Taurus
Beets	3rd	Cancer, Capricorn, Pisces, Libra
Biennials	3rd or 4th	Any
Broccoli	1st	Cancer, Scorpio, Pisces, Libra
Brussels sprouts	1st	Cancer, Scorpio, Pisces, Libra
Buckwheat	1st or 2nd	Capricorn
Bulbs	3rd	Cancer, Scorpio, Pisces
Bulbs for seed	2nd or 3rd	Any
Cabbage	1st	Cancer, Scorpio, Pisces, Taurus, Libra
Canes (raspberry, blackberry, & gooseberry)	2nd	Cancer, Scorpio, Pisces
Cantaloupe	1st or 2nd	Cancer, Scorpio, Pisces, Taurus, Libra
Carrots	3rd	Cancer, Scorpio, Pisces, Taurus, Libra
Cauliflower	1st	Cancer, Scorpio, Pisces, Libra
Celeriac	3rd	Cancer, Scorpio, Pisces
Celery	1st	Cancer, Scorpio, Pisces
Cereals	1st or 2nd	Cancer, Scorpio, Pisces, Libra
Chard	1st or 2nd	Cancer, Scorpio, Pisces
Chicory	2nd or 3rd	Cancer, Scorpio, Pisces
Chrysanthemum	1st or 2nd	Virgo

Plant	Quarter	Sign
Clover	1st or 2nd	Cancer, Scorpio, Pisces
Corn	1st	Cancer, Scorpio, Pisces
Corn for fodder	1st or 2nd	Libra
Coryopsis	2nd or 3rd	Libra
Cosmo	2nd or 3rd	Libra
Cress	1st	Cancer, Scorpio, Pisces
Crocus	1st or 2nd	Virgo
Cucumber	1st	Cancer, Scorpio, Pisces
Daffodil	1st or 2nd	Libra, Virgo
Dahlia	1st or 2nd	Libra, Virgo
Deciduous trees	2nd or 3rd	Cancer, Scorpio, Pisces, Virgo, Libra
Eggplant	2nd	Cancer, Scorpio, Pisces, Libra
Endive	1st	Cancer, Scorpio, Pisces, Libra
Flowers	1st	Cancer, Scorpio, Pisces, Libra, Taurus, Virgo
Garlic	3rd	Libra, Taurus, Pisces
Gladiola	1st or 2nd	Libra, Virgo
Gourds	1st or 2nd	Cancer, Scorpio, Pisces, Libra
Grapes	2nd or 3rd	Cancer, Scorpio, Pisces, Virgo
Hay	1st or 2nd	Cancer, Scorpio, Pisces, Libra, Taurus
Herbs	1st or 2nd	Cancer, Scorpio, Pisces
Honeysuckle	1st or 2nd	Scorpio, Virgo
Hops	1st or 2nd	Scorpio, Libra
Horseradish	1st or 2nd	Cancer, Scorpio, Pisces
Houseplants	1st	Cancer, Scorpio, Pisces, Libra
Hyacinth	3rd	Cancer, Scorpio, Pisces
Iris	1st or 2nd	Cancer, Virgo
Kohlrabi	1st or 2nd	Cancer, Scorpio, Pisces, Libra
Leek	1st or 2nd	Cancer, Pisces
Lettuce	1st	Cancer, Scorpio, Pisces, Libra, Taurus
Lily	1st or 2nd	Cancer, Scorpio, Pisces
Maple tree	2nd or 3rd	Taurus, Virgo, Cancer, Pisces
Melon	2nd	Cancer, Scorpio, Pisces

Plant	Quarter	Sign
Morning glory	1st or 2nd	Cancer, Scorpio, Pisces, Virgo
Oak tree	2nd or 3rd	Taurus, Virgo, Cancer, Pisces
Okra	1st or 2nd	Cancer, Scorpio, Pisces, Libra
Oats	1st or 2nd	Cancer, Scorpio, Pisces, Libra
Onion seed	2nd	Cancer, Scorpio, Sagittarius
Onion set	3rd or 4th	Cancer, Pisces, Taurus, Libra
Pansies	1st or 2nd	Cancer, Scorpio, Pisces
Parsley	1st	Cancer, Scorpio, Pisces, Libra
Parsnip	3rd	Cancer, Scorpio, Taurus, Capricorn
Peach tree	2nd or 3rd	Cancer, Taurus, Virgo, Libra
Peanuts	3rd	Cancer, Scorpio, Pisces
Pear tree	2nd or 3rd	Cancer, Scorpio, Pisces, Libra
Peas	2nd	Cancer, Scorpio, Pisces, Libra
Peony	1st or 2nd	Virgo
Peppers	2nd	Cancer, Scorpio, Pisces
Perennials	3rd	Any
Petunia	1st or 2nd	Libra, Virgo
Plum tree	2nd or 3rd	Cancer, Pisces, Taurus, Virgo
Poppies	1st or 2nd	Virgo
Portulaca	1st or 2nd	Virgo
Potatoes	3rd	Cancer, Scorpio, Libra, Taurus, Capricorn
Privet	1st or 2nd	Taurus, Libra
Pumpkin	2nd	Cancer, Scorpio, Pisces, Libra
Quince	1st or 2nd	Capricorn
Radishes	3rd	Cancer, Scorpio, Pisces, Libra, Capricorn
Rhubarb	3rd	Cancer, Pisces
Rice	1st or 2nd	Scorpio
Roses	1st or 2nd	Cancer, Virgo
Rutabaga	3rd	Cancer, Scorpio, Pisces, Taurus
Saffron	1st or 2nd	Cancer, Scorpio, Pisces
Sage	3rd	Cancer, Scorpio, Pisces

Plant	Quarter	Sign
Salsify	1st	Cancer, Scorpio, Pisces
Shallot	2nd	Scorpio
Spinach	1st	Cancer, Scorpio, Pisces
Squash	2nd	Cancer, Scorpio, Pisces, Libra
Strawberries	3rd	Cancer, Scorpio, Pisces
String beans	1st or 2nd	Taurus
Sunflowers	1st or 2nd	Libra, Cancer
Sweet peas	1st or 2nd	Any
Tomatoes	2nd	Cancer, Scorpio, Pisces, Capricorn
Shade trees	3rd	Taurus, Capricorn
Ornamental trees	2nd	Libra, Taurus
Trumpet vine	1st or 2nd	Cancer, Scorpio, Pisces
Tubers for seed	3rd	Cancer, Scorpio, Pisces, Libra
Tulips	1st or 2nd	Libra, Virgo
Turnips	3rd	Cancer, Scorpio, Pisces, Taurus, Capricorn, Libra
Valerian	1st or 2nd	Virgo, Gemini
Watermelon	1st or 2nd	Cancer, Scorpio, Pisces, Libra
Wheat	1st or 2nd	Cancer, Scorpio, Pisces, Libra

Companion Planting Guide

Plant	Companions	Hindered by
Asparagus	Tomatoes, parsley, basil	None known
Beans	Tomatoes, carrots, cucumbers, garlic, cabbage, beets, corn	Onions, gladiolas
Beets	Onions, cabbage, lettuce, mint, catnip	Pole beans
Broccoli	Beans, celery, potatoes, onions	Tomatoes
Cabbage	Peppermint, sage, thyme, tomatoes	Strawberries, grapes
Carrots	Peas, lettuce, chives, radishes, leeks, onions, sage	Dill, anise
Citrus trees	Guava, live oak, rubber trees, peppers	None known
Corn	Potatoes, beans, peas, melon, squash, pumpkin, sunflowers, soybeans	Quack grass, wheat straw mulch
Cucumbers	Beans, cabbage, radishes, sunflowers, lettuce, broccoli, squash	Aromatic herbs
Eggplant	Green beans, lettuce, kale	None known
Grapes	Peas, beans, blackberries	Cabbage, radishes
Melons	Corn, peas	Potatoes, gourds
Onions, leeks	Beets, chamomile, carrots, lettuce	Peas, beans, sage
Parsnip	Peas	None known
Peas	Radishes, carrots, corn, cucumbers, beans, tomatoes, spinach, turnips	Onion, garlic
Potatoes	Beans, corn, peas, cabbage, hemp, cucumbers, eggplant, catnip	Raspberries, pumpkins, tomatoes, sunflowers
Radishes	Peas, lettuce, nasturtiums, cucumbers	Hyssop
Spinach	Strawberries	None known
Squash/Pumpkin	Nasturtiums, corn, mint, catnip	Potatoes
Tomatoes	Asparagus, parsley, chives, onions, carrots, marigolds, nasturtiums, dill	Black walnut roots, fennel, potatoes
Turnips	Peas, beans, brussels sprouts	Potatoes

Plant	Companions	Uses
Anise	Coriander	Flavor candy, pastry, cheeses, cookies
Basil	Tomatoes	Dislikes rue; repels flies and mosquitoes
Borage	Tomatoes, squash	Use in teas
Buttercup	Clover	Hinders delphinium, peonies, monkshood, columbine

Plant	Companions	Uses
Catnip		Repels flea beetles
Chamomile	Peppermint, wheat, onions, cabbage	Roman chamomile may control damping-off disease; use in herbal sprays
Chervil	Radishes	Good in soups and other dishes
Chives	Carrots	Use in spray to deter black spot on roses
Coriander	Plant anywhere	Hinders seed formation in fennel
Cosmos		Repels corn earworms
Dill	Cabbage	Hinders carrots and tomatoes
Fennel	Plant in borders away from garden	Disliked by all garden plants
Horseradish		Repels potato bugs
Horsetail		Makes fungicide spray
Hyssop		Attracts cabbage fly away from cabbage; harmful to radishes
Lavender	Plant anywhere	Use in spray to control insects on cotton, repels clothes moths
Lovage		Lures horn worms away from tomatoes
Marigolds		Pest repellent; use against Mexican bean beetles and nematodes
Mint	Cabbage, tomatoes	Repels ants, flea beetles, and cabbage worm butterflies
Morning glory	Corn	Helps melon germination
Nasturtiums	Cabbage, cucumbers	Deters aphids, squash bugs, and pumpkin beetles
Okra	Eggplant	Will attract leafhopper (use to trap insects away from other plants)
Parsley	Tomatoes, asparagus	Freeze chopped up leaves to flavor foods
Purslane		Good ground cover
Rosemary		Repels cabbage moths, bean beetles, and carrot flies
Savory		Plant with onions to give them added sweetness
Tansy		Deters Japanese beetles, striped cucumber beetles, and squash bugs
Thyme		Repels cabbage worms
Yarrow		Increases essential oils of neighbors

Moon Void-of-Course

By Kim Rogers-Gallagher

The Moon circles the Earth in about twenty-eight days, moving through each zodiac sign in two-and-a-half days. As she passes through the thirty degrees of each sign, she "visits" with the planets in numerical order, forming aspects with them. Because she moves one degree in just two to two-and-a-half hours, her influence on each planet lasts only a few hours. She eventually reaches the planet that's in the highest degree of any sign, and forms what will be her final aspect before leaving the sign. From this point until she enters the next sign, she is referred to as void-of-course.

Think of it this way: the Moon is the emotional "tone" of the day, carrying feelings with her particular to the sign she's "wearing" at the moment. After she has contacted each of the planets, she symbolically "rests" before changing her costume, so her instinct is temporarily on hold. It's during this time that many people feel "fuzzy" or "vague." Plans or decisions made now often do not pan out. Without the instinctual "knowing" the Moon provides as she touches each planet, we tend to be unrealistic or exercise poor judgment. The traditional definition of the void Moon is that "nothing will come of this." Actions initiated under a void Moon are often wasted, irrelevant, or incorrect—usually because information is hidden, missing, or has been overlooked.

Although it's not a good time to initiate plans, routine tasks seem to go along just fine. This period is ideal for reflection. On the lighter side, remember there are good uses for the void Moon. It is the period when the universe seems to be most open to loopholes. It's a great time to make plans you don't want to fulfill or schedule things you don't want to do. See the table on pages 75–80 for a schedule of the Moon's void-of-course times.

Moon Void-of-Course Dates

Last Aspect　　　　　　**Moon Enters New Sign**

		January		
1	7:33 pm	1	Scorpio	8:32 pm
3	7:30 pm	4	Sagittarius	9:13 am
6	7:27 pm	6	Capricorn	8:43 pm
8	6:37 am	9	Aquarius	6:13 am
11	12:52 pm	11	Pisces	1:44 pm
13	6:41 pm	13	Aries	7:23 pm
15	10:39 pm	15	Taurus	11:13 pm
17	9:05 pm	17	Gemini	1:30 am
20	2:46 am	20	Cancer	3:05 am
21	5:56 am	22	Leo	5:20 am
24	9:43 am	24	Virgo	9:48 am
26	6:32 am	26	Libra	5:35 pm
28	4:47 pm	29	Scorpio	4:35 pm
31	3:34 am	31	Sagittarius	5:08 pm
		February		
2	5:21 pm	3	Capricorn	4:52 am
4	1:20 pm	5	Aquarius	2:10 pm
7	10:50 am	7	Pisces	8:46 pm
9	4:05 pm	9	Aries	1:17 am
11	8:00 pm	12	Taurus	4:34 am
14	12:05 am	14	Gemini	7:19 am
16	5:17 am	16	Cancer	10:12 am
17	4:13 pm	18	Leo	1:51 pm
20	12:52 pm	20	Virgo	7:06 pm
22	9:14 pm	22	Libra	2:44 am
25	8:35 am	25	Scorpio	1:05 pm
27	9:53 am	27	Sagittarius	1:22 am

Last Aspect			Moon Enters New Sign	
		March		
1	11:54 am	1	Capricorn	1:33 pm
3	1:16 am	3	Aquarius	11:24 pm
5	4:46 pm	6	Pisces	5:53 am
7	2:04 pm	8	Aries	9:23 am
10	7:09 am	10	Taurus	12:13 am
12	1:26 pm	12	Gemini	1:54 pm
14	4:23 pm	14	Cancer	4:37 pm
16	2:58 pm	16	Leo	9:04 pm
18	2:38 pm	18	Virgo	3:25 am
20	3:28 pm	21	Libra	11:45 am
23	8:41 am	23	Scorpio	10:06 pm
25	8:36 pm	26	Sagittarius	10:11 am
28	9:21 am	28	Capricorn	10:43 pm
31	12:54 am	31	Aquarius	9:34 am
		April		
2	5:13 am	2	Pisces	4:55 pm
4	5:43 pm	4	Aries	8:27 pm
6	11:01 am	6	Taurus	9:19 pm
8	11:12 am	8	Gemini	9:27 pm
10	12:11 pm	10	Cancer	10:43 pm
12	2:32 pm	13	Leo	2:29 am
15	12:56 am	15	Virgo	9:06 am
17	1:59 am	17	Libra	6:10 pm
19	4:54 pm	20	Scorpio	5:00 am
22	4:53 am	22	Sagittarius	5:07 pm
24	5:37 pm	25	Capricorn	5:47 am
27	10:18 am	27	Aquarius	5:27 pm
30	1:25 am	30	Pisces	2:11 am

Last Aspect		Moon Enters New Sign		
		May		
2	5:34 am	2	Aries	6:51 am
4	3:16 am	4	Taurus	7:58 am
6	4:21 am	6	Gemini	7:17 am
7	9:36 pm	8	Cancer	7:02 am
9	8:06 pm	10	Leo	9:10 am
12	4:09 am	12	Virgo	2:48 pm
14	12:38 pm	14	Libra	11:46 pm
16	11:29 pm	17	Scorpio	10:59 am
19	10:11 pm	19	Sagittarius	11:18 pm
22	12:19 am	22	Capricorn	11:55 am
24	8:26 am	24	Aquarius	11:51 pm
26	10:49 pm	27	Pisces	9:38 am
29	2:23 am	29	Aries	3:52 pm
31	8:54 am	31	Taurus	6:18 pm
		June		
2	9:02 am	2	Gemini	6:06 pm
4	8:08 am	4	Cancer	5:16 pm
6	5:32 am	6	Leo	6:00 pm
8	11:40 am	8	Virgo	10:01 pm
10	3:42 pm	11	Libra	5:55 am
13	5:15 am	13	Scorpio	4:53 pm
15	5:29 pm	16	Sagittarius	5:19 am
18	5:37 pm	18	Capricorn	5:51 pm
20	3:02 pm	21	Aquarius	5:33 am
23	3:04 pm	23	Pisces	3:32 pm
25	10:16 pm	25	Aries	10:49 pm
28	2:14 am	28	Taurus	2:50 am
30	2:43 am	30	Gemini	4:03 am

Last Aspect		Moon Enters New Sign		
		July		
2	3:08 am	2	Cancer	3:53 am
3	4:13 pm	4	Leo	4:15 am
6	6:04 am	6	Virgo	7:04 am
8	12:21 pm	8	Libra	1:31 pm
10	10:14 pm	10	Scorpio	11:35 pm
12	11:05 pm	13	Sagittarius	11:50 am
15	10:44 pm	16	Capricorn	12:20 am
18	3:59 am	18	Aquarius	11:40 am
20	7:25 pm	20	Pisces	9:07 pm
23	2:39 am	23	Aries	4:22 am
25	7:30 am	25	Taurus	9:14 am
27	12:52 am	27	Gemini	11:55 am
29	11:25 am	29	Cancer	1:11 pm
31	1:31 am	31	Leo	2:21 pm
		August		
2	2:59 pm	2	Virgo	4:59 pm
4	8:16 pm	4	Libra	10:28 pm
7	5:01 am	7	Scorpio	7:26 am
9	5:02 pm	9	Sagittarius	7:10 pm
12	5:04 am	12	Capricorn	7:42 am
14	1:09 pm	14	Aquarius	6:56 pm
17	1:14 am	17	Pisces	3:46 am
19	7:41 am	19	Aries	10:10 am
21	12:53 pm	21	Taurus	2:38 pm
23	5:19 am	23	Gemini	5:48 pm
25	5:52 pm	25	Cancer	8:18 pm
27	8:13 pm	27	Leo	10:51 pm
29	11:44 pm	29	Virgo	2:18 am

		September		
1	5:01 am	1	Libra	7:44 am
3	1:09 pm	3	Scorpio	4:02 pm
5	11:45 am	6	Sagittarius	3:11 am
8	12:43 pm	8	Capricorn	3:45 pm
10	9:15 am	11	Aquarius	3:19 am
13	9:19 am	13	Pisces	12:04 pm
15	3:03 pm	15	Aries	5:39 pm
17	6:26 pm	17	Taurus	8:56 pm
19	6:51 pm	19	Gemini	11:17 pm
22	1:04 am	22	Cancer	1:48 am
23	5:16 pm	24	Leo	5:13 am
26	7:20 am	26	Virgo	9:52 am
28	1:31 pm	28	Libra	4:05 pm
30	9:47 pm	1 October	Scorpio	12:26 am
		October		
2	6:46 pm	3	Sagittarius	11:14 am
5	9:08 pm	5	Capricorn	11:48 pm
7	3:37 pm	8	Aquarius	12:03 pm
10	7:13 pm	10	Pisces	9:31 pm
13	1:02 am	13	Aries	3:07 am
15	3:36 am	15	Taurus	5:31 am
17	3:33 am	17	Gemini	6:25 am
19	5:52 am	19	Cancer	7:40 am
21	7:54 am	21	Leo	10:35 am
23	1:53 pm	23	Virgo	3:40 pm
25	9:02 pm	25	Libra	10:47 pm
28	6:05 am	28	Scorpio	7:47 am
30	1:45 am	30	Sagittarius	6:41 pm

Last Aspect			Moon Enters New Sign	
		November		
2	4:41 am	2	Capricorn	6:13 am
4	1:47 am	4	Aquarius	7:01 pm
7	4:33 am	7	Pisces	5:43 am
9	11:28 am	9	Aries	12:26 pm
11	2:17 pm	11	Taurus	3:05 pm
13	12:12 pm	13	Gemini	3:11 pm
15	2:17 pm	15	Cancer	2:52 pm
17	8:43 am	17	Leo	4:07 pm
19	7:48 pm	19	Virgo	8:12 pm
22	3:02 am	22	Libra	3:20 am
24	12:45 pm	24	Scorpio	12:54 pm
26	7:32 am	27	Sagittarius	12:14 am
28	7:53 pm	29	Capricorn	12:48 pm
		December		
1	10:44 am	2	Aquarius	1:44 am
3	9:14 pm	4	Pisces	1:23 pm
6	7:43 pm	6	Aries	9:44 pm
8	4:35 pm	8	Taurus	1:52 am
10	5:23 pm	11	Gemini	2:33 am
12	1:01 pm	13	Cancer	1:39 am
14	5:27 pm	15	Leo	1:22 am
16	7:45 pm	17	Virgo	3:35 am
19	5:29 am	19	Libra	9:23 am
21	11:57 am	21	Scorpio	6:36 pm
24	12:29 am	24	Sagittarius	6:13 am
26	6:25 pm	26	Capricorn	6:56 pm
29	4:20 am	29	Aquarius	7:42 am
31	1:34 pm	31	Pisces	7:27 pm

The Moon's Rhythm

The Moon journeys around Earth in an elliptical orbit that takes about 27.33 days, which is known as a sidereal month (period of revolution of one body about another). She can move up to 15 degrees or as few as 11 degrees in a day, with the fastest motion occurring when the Moon is at perigee (closest approach to Earth). The Moon is never retrograde, but when her motion is slow, the effect is similar to a retrograde period.

Astrologers have observed that people born on a day when the Moon is fast will process information differently from those who are born when the Moon is slow in motion. People born when the Moon is fast process information quickly and tend to react quickly, while those born during a slow Moon will be more deliberate.

The time from New Moon to New Moon is called the synodic month (involving a conjunction), and the average time span between this Sun-Moon alignment is 29.53 days. Since 29.53 won't divide into 365 evenly, we can have a month with two Full Moons (December 2009) or two New Moons (August 2008).

Moon Aspects

The aspects the Moon will make during the times you are considering are also important. A trine or sextile, and sometimes a conjunction, are considered favorable aspects. A trine or sextile between the Sun and Moon is an excellent foundation for success. Whether or not a conjunction is considered favorable depends upon the planet the Moon is making a conjunction to. If it's joining the Sun, Venus, Mercury, Jupiter, or even Saturn, the aspect is favorable. If the Moon joins Pluto or Mars, however, that would not be considered favorable. There may be exceptions, but it would depend on what you are electing to do. For example, a trine to Pluto might hasten the end of a relationship you want to be free of.

It is important to avoid times when the Moon makes an aspect to or is conjoining any retrograde planet, unless, of course, you want the thing started to end in failure.

After the Moon has completed an aspect to a planet, that planetary energy has passed. For example, if the Moon squares Saturn at 10:00 am, you can disregard Saturn's influence on your activity if it will occur after that time. You should always look ahead at aspects the Moon will make on the day in question, though, because if the Moon opposes Mars at 11:30 pm on that day, you can expect events that stretch into the evening to be affected by the Moon-Mars aspect. A testy conversation might lead to an argument, or more.

Moon Signs

Much agricultural work is ruled by earth signs—Virgo, Capricorn, and Taurus; and the air signs—Gemini, Aquarius, and Libra—rule flying and intellectual pursuits.

Each planet has one or two signs in which its characteristics are enhanced or "dignified," and the planet is said to "rule" that sign. The Sun rules Leo and the Moon rules Cancer, for example. The ruling planet for each sign is listed below. These should not be considered complete lists. We recommend that you purchase a book of planetary rulerships for more complete information.

Aries Moon

The energy of an Aries Moon is masculine, dry, barren, and fiery. Aries provides great start-up energy, but things started at this time may be the result of impulsive action that lacks research or necessary support. Aries lacks staying power.

Use this assertive, outgoing Moon sign to initiate change, but have a plan in place for someone to pick up the reins when you're impatient to move on to the next thing. Work that requires skillful, but not necessarily patient, use of tools—hammering, cutting down trees, etc.—is appropriate in Aries. Expect things to occur rapidly but to also quickly pass. If you are prone to injury or accidents, exercise caution and good judgment in Aries-related activities.

RULER: Mars
IMPULSE: Action
RULES: Head and face

Taurus Moon

A Taurus Moon's energy is feminine, semi-fruitful, and earthy. The Moon is exalted—very strong—in Taurus. Taurus is known as the farmer's sign because of its associations with farmland and precipitation that is the typical day-long "soaker" variety. Taurus energy is good to incorporate into your plans when patience, practicality, and perseverance are needed. Be aware, though, that you may also experience stubbornness in this sign.

Things started in Taurus tend to be long lasting and to increase in value. This can be very supportive energy in a marriage election. On the downside, the fixed energy of this sign resists change or the letting go of even the most difficult situations. A divorce following a marriage that occurred during a Taurus Moon may be difficult and costly to end. Things begun now tend to become habitual and hard to alter. If you want to make changes in something you start, it would be better to wait for Gemini. This is a good time to get a loan, but expect the people in charge of money to be cautious and slow to make decisions.

RULER: Venus
IMPULSE Stability
RULES: Neck, throat, and voice

Gemini Moon

A Gemini Moon's energy is masculine, dry, barren, and airy. People are more changeable than usual and may prefer to follow intellectual pursuits and play mental games rather than apply themselves to practical concerns.

This sign is not favored for agricultural matters, but it is an excellent time to prepare for activities, to run errands, and write letters. Plan to use a Gemini Moon to exchange ideas, meet people, go on vacations that include walking or biking, or be in situations that require versatility and quick thinking on your feet.

RULER: Mercury
IMPULSE: Versatility
RULES: Shoulders, hands, arms, lungs, and nervous system

Cancer Moon

A Cancer Moon's energy is feminine, fruitful, moist, and very strong. Use this sign when you want to grow things—flowers, fruits, vegetables, commodities, stocks, or collections—for example. This sensitive sign stimulates rapport between people. Considered the most fertile of the signs, it is often associated with mothering. You can use this moontime to build personal friendships that support mutual growth.

Cancer is associated with emotions and feelings. Prominent Cancer energy promotes growth, but it can also turn people pouty and prone to withdrawing into their shells.

RULER: The Moon
IMPULSE Tenacity
RULES: Chest area, breasts, and stomach

Leo Moon

A Leo Moon's energy is masculine, hot, dry, fiery, and barren. Use it whenever you need to put on a show, make a presentation, or entertain colleagues or guests. This is a proud yet playful energy that exudes self-confidence and is often associated with romance.

This is an excellent time for fund-raisers and ceremonies, or to be straight forward, frank, and honest about something. It is advisable not to put yourself in a position of needing public approval or where you might have to cope with underhandedness, as trouble in these areas can bring out the worst Leo traits. There is a tendency in this sign to become arrogant or self-centered.

RULER: The Sun

IMPULSE: I am

RULES: Heart and upper back

Virgo Moon

A Virgo Moon is feminine, dry, barren, earthy energy. It is favorable for anything that needs painstaking attention—especially those things where exactness rather than innovation is preferred.

Use this sign for activities when you must analyze information, or when you must determine the value of something. Virgo is the sign of bargain hunting. It's friendly toward agricultural matters with an emphasis on animals and harvesting vegetables. It is an excellent time to care for animals, especially training them and veterinary work.

This sign is most beneficial when decisions have already been made and now need to be carried out. The inclination here is to see details rather than the bigger picture.

There is a tendency in this sign to overdo. Precautions should be taken to avoid becoming too dull from all work and no play. Build a little relaxation and pleasure into your routine from the beginning.

RULER: Mercury

IMPULSE: Discriminating

RULES: Abdomen and intestines

Libra Moon

A Libra Moon's energy is masculine, semi-fruitful, and airy. This energy will benefit any attempt to bring beauty to a place or thing. Libra is considered good energy for starting things of an intellectual nature. Libra is the sign of partnership and unions, which make it an excellent time to form partnerships of any kind, to make agreements, and to negotiate. Even though this sign is good for initiating things, it is crucial to work with a partner who will provide incentive and encouragement, however. A Libra Moon accentuates teamwork (particularly teams of two) and artistic work (especially work that involves color). Make use of this sign when you are decorating your home or shopping for better quality clothing.

RULER: Venus

IMPULSE: Balance

RULES: Lower back, kidneys, and buttocks

Scorpio Moon

The Scorpio Moon is feminine, fruitful, cold, and moist. It is useful when intensity (that sometimes borders on obsession) is needed. Scorpio is considered a very psychic sign. Use this Moon sign when you must back up something you strongly believe in, such as union or employer relations. There is strong group loyalty here, but a Scorpio Moon is also a good time to end connections thoroughly. This is also a good time to conduct research.

The desire nature is so strong here that there is a tendency to manipulate situations to get what one wants, or to not see one's responsibility in an act.

RULER: Pluto, Mars (traditional)

IMPULSE: Transformation

RULES: Reproductive organs, genitals, groin, and pelvis

Sagittarius Moon

The Moon's energy is masculine, dry, barren, and fiery in Sagittarius, encouraging flights of imagination and confidence in the flow of life. Sagittarius is the most philosophical sign. Candor and honesty are enhanced when the Moon is here. This is an excellent time to "get things off your chest," and to deal with institutions of higher learning, publishing companies, and the law. It's also a good time for sport and adventure.

Sagittarians are the crusaders of this world. This is a good time to tackle things that need improvement, but don't try to be the diplomat while influenced by this energy. Opinions can run strong and the tendency to proselytize is increased.

RULER: Jupiter

IMPULSE: Expansion

RULES: Thighs and hips

Capricorn Moon

In Capricorn the Moon's energy is feminine, semi-fruitful, and earthy. Because Cancer and Capricorn are polar opposites, the Moon's energy is thought to be weakened here. This energy encourages the need for structure, discipline, and organization. This is a good time to set goals and plan for the future, tend to family business, and to take care of details requiring patience or a businesslike manner. Institutional activities are favored. This sign should be avoided if you're seeking favors, as those in authority can be insensitive under this influence.

RULER: Saturn

IMPULSE: Ambitious

RULES: Bones, skin, and knees

Aquarius Moon

An Aquarius Moon's energy is masculine, barren, dry, and airy. Activities that are unique, individualistic, concerned with humanitarian issues, society as a whole, and making improvements are favored under this Moon. It is this quality of making improvements that has caused this sign to be associated with inventors and new inventions.

An Aquarius Moon promotes the gathering of social groups for friendly exchanges. People tend to react and speak from an intellectual rather than emotional viewpoint when the Moon is in this sign.

RULER: Uranus and Saturn

IMPULSE: Reformer

RULES: Calves and ankles

Pisces Moon

A Pisces Moon is feminine, fruitful, cool, and moist. This is an excellent time to retreat, meditate, sleep, pray, or make that dreamed-of escape into a fantasy vacation. However, things are not always what they seem to be with the Moon in Pisces. Personal boundaries tend to be fuzzy, and you may not be seeing things clearly. People tend to be idealistic under this sign, which can prevent them from seeing reality.

There is a live and let live philosophy attached to this sign, which in the idealistic world may work well enough, but chaos is frequently the result. That's why this sign is also associated with alcohol and drug abuse, drug trafficking, and counterfeiting. On the lighter side, many musicians and artists are ruled by Pisces. It's only when they move too far away from reality that the dark side of substance abuse, suicide, or crime takes away life.

RULER: Jupiter and Neptune

IMPULSE: Empathetic

RULES: Feet

More About Zodiac Signs

Element (Triplicity)

Each of the zodiac signs is classified as belonging to an element, and these are the four basic elements:

Fire Signs

Aries, Sagittarius, and Leo are action-oriented, outgoing, energetic, and spontaneous.

Earth Signs

Taurus, Capricorn, and Virgo are stable, conservative, practical, and oriented to the physical and material realm.

Air Signs

Gemini, Aquarius, and Libra are sociable and critical, and they tend to represent intellectual responses rather than feelings.

Water Signs

Cancer, Scorpio, and Pisces are emotional, receptive, intuitive, and can be very sensitive.

Quality (Quadruplicity)

Each zodiac sign is further classified as being cardinal, mutable, or fixed. There are four signs in each quadruplicity, one sign from each element.

Cardinal Signs

Aries, Cancer, Libra, and Capricorn represent beginnings and initiate new action. They initiate each new season in the cycle of the year.

Fixed Signs

Taurus, Leo, Scorpio, and Aquarius want to maintain the status quo through stubbornness and persistence; they represent that "between" time. For example, Leo is the month when summer really feels like summer.

Mutable Signs

Pisces, Gemini, Virgo, and Sagittarius adapt to change and tolerate situations. They represent the last month of each season, when things are changing in preparation for the coming season.

Nature and Fertility

In addition to a sign's element and quality, each sign is further classified as either fruitful, semi-fruitful, or barren. This classification is the most important for readers who use the gardening information in the *Moon Sign Book* because the timing of most events depends on the fertility of the sign occupied by the Moon. The water signs of Cancer, Scorpio, and Pisces are the most fruitful. The semi-fruitful signs are the earth signs Taurus and Capricorn, and the air sign Libra. The barren signs correspond to the fire signs Aries, Leo, and Sagittarius; the air signs Gemini and Aquarius; and earth-sign Virgo.

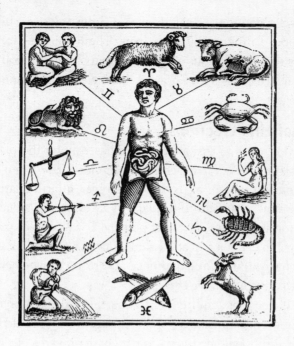

Good Timing

By Sharon Leah

Electional astrology is the art of electing times to begin any undertaking. Say, for example, you want to start a business. That business will experience ups and downs, as well as reach its potential, according to the promise held in the universe at the time the business was started—its birth time. The horoscope (birth chart) set for the date, time, and place that a business starts would indicate the outcome—its potential to succeed.

So, you might ask yourself the question: If the horoscope for a business start can show success or failure, why not begin at a time that is more favorable to the venture? Well, you can.

While no time is perfect, there are better times and better days to undertake specific activities. There are thousands of examples that prove electional astrology is not only practical, but that it can make a difference in our lives. There are rules for electing times to begin various activities—even shopping. You'll find detailed instructions about how to make elections beginning on page 106.

Personalizing Elections

The election rules in this almanac are based upon the planetary positions at the time for which the election is made. They do not depend on any type of birth chart. However, a birth chart based upon the time, date, and birthplace of an event has advantages. No election is effective for every person. For example, you may leave home to begin a trip at the same time as a friend, but each of you will have a different experience according to whether or not your birth chart favors the trip.

Not all elections require a birth chart, but the timing of very important events—business starts, marriages, etc.—would benefit from the additional accuracy a birth chart provides. To order a birth chart for yourself or a planned event, visit our Web site at www.llewellyn.com.

Some Things to Consider

You've probably experienced good timing in your life. Maybe you were at the right place at the right time to meet a friend whom you hadn't seen in years. Frequently, when something like that happens, it is the result of following an intuitive impulse—that "gut instinct." Consider for a moment that you were actually responding to planetary energies. Electional astrology is a tool that can help you to align with energies, present and future, that are available to us through planetary placements.

Significators

Decide upon the important significators (planet, sign, and house ruling the matter) for which the election is being made. The Moon is the most important significator in any election, so the

Moon should always be fortified (strong by sign, and making favorable aspects to other planets). The Moon's aspects to other planets are more important than the sign the Moon is in.

Other important considerations are the significators of the Ascendant and Midheaven—the house ruling the election matter, and the ruler of the sign on that house cusp. Finally, any planet or sign that has a general rulership over the matter in question should be taken into consideration.

Nature and Fertility

Determine the general nature of the sign that is appropriate for your election. For example, much agricultural work is ruled by the earth signs of Virgo, Capricorn, and Taurus; while the air signs—Gemini, Aquarius, and Libra—rule intellectual pursuits.

One Final Comment

Use common sense. If you must do something, like plant your garden or take an airplane trip on a day that doesn't have the best aspects, proceed anyway, but try to minimize problems. For example, leave early for the airport to avoid being left behind due to delays in the security lanes. When you have no other choice, do the best that you can under the circumstances at the time.

If you want to personalize your elections, please turn to page 106 for more information. If you want a quick and easy answer, you can refer to Llewellyn's Astro Almanac (pages 94–105).

Llewellyn's Astro Almanac

The Astro Almanac tables, beginning on the next page, can help you find the dates best suited to particular activities. The dates provided are determined from the Moon's sign, phase, and aspects to other planets. Please note that the Astro Almanac does not take personal factors, such as your Sun and Moon sign, into account. The dates are general, and they will apply for everyone. Some activities will not have suitable dates during a particular month, so no dates will be shown.

Astro Almanac Tables

Activity	January
Advertise in Print	3, 10, 14, 15, 28
Automobile (Buy)	2
Animals (Neuter or spay)	7
Animals (Sell or buy)	24, 25
Build (Start excavation)	
Business (Start new)	16, 17
Can Fruits and Vegetables	2, 3, 29, 30, 31
Concrete (Pour)	23, 24
Consultants (Begin work with)	3, 7, 11, 16, 25
Contracts (Bid on)	7
Copyrights/Patents (Apply for)	3, 7, 11, 16, 25
Cultivate	24, 25, 26
Cut Wood	25, 26
Entertain Guests	1, 24, 28
Fertilize and Compost (Chemical)	12, 13
Fertilize and Compost (Organic)	2, 3, 29, 30, 31
Habits (Break)	
Hair (Cut for fast growth)	12, 13, 20, 21
Hair (Cut for slow growth)	24, 25
Hair (Cut for thicker hair)	21, 22
Harvest (Crops to dry)	4, 5, 6, 25, 26
Job (Start new)	2, 4, 7, 16, 29
Legal (Gain damages or start proceeding)	16
Loan (Ask for)	24
Massage (Relaxing)	16, 17, 22, 23
Mushrooms (Pick)	21, 22, 23
Promotion (Ask for)	3, 14, 28
Prune to Promote Healing	7, 8, 9
Prune to Retard Growth	2, 3
Sauerkraut (Make)	21, 22, 23
Spray Pests and Weeds	23, 24
Wean Children	4, 5, 6, 7
Weight (Reduce)	23, 24

Activity	February
Advertise in Print	2, 6, 23, 29
Automobile (Buy)	3, 4, 6, 12
Animals (Neuter or spay)	3, 4
Animals (Sell or buy)	8, 9, 12
Build (Start excavation)	7
Business (Start new)	12, 13
Can Fruits and Vegetables	25, 26
Concrete (Pour)	
Consultants (Begin work with)	4, 6, 21, 23, 26
Contracts (Bid on)	3, 4
Copyrights/Patents (Apply for)	2, 4, 8, 21
Cultivate	21, 22, 29
Cut Wood	3, 4, 21, 22
Entertain Guests	20, 23, 24
Fertilize and Compost (Chemical)	7, 8
Fertilize and Compost (Organic)	26, 27
Habits (Break)	5
Hair (Cut for fast growth)	8, 9
Hair (Cut for slow growth)	21, 22
Hair (Cut for thicker hair)	29, 20, 21
Harvest (Crops to dry)	1, 2, 21, 22, 29
Job (Start new)	4, 8, 21, 23, 29
Legal (Gain damages or start proceeding)	8
Loan (Ask for)	
Massage (Relaxing)	12, 13, 18, 19, 20
Mushrooms (Pick)	19, 20, 21
Promotion (Ask for)	6, 29
Prune to Promote Healing	3, 4, 5
Prune to Retard Growth	25, 26
Sauerkraut (Make)	19, 20, 21
Spray Pests and Weeds	4, 5
Wean Children	1, 2, 3, 4, 5
Weight (Reduce)	4, 5

Activity	March
Advertise in Print	5, 10, 14, 25
Automobile (Buy)	10, 14, 25
Animals (Neuter or spay)	27, 28, 29, 30
Animals (Sell or buy)	
Build (Start excavation)	10, 11
Business (Start new)	19, 20
Can Fruits and Vegetables	6, 7, 24, 25
Concrete (Pour)	
Consultants (Begin work with)	2, 5, 10, 11, 14, 25
Contracts (Bid on)	2, 14, 28, 29, 30
Copyrights/Patents (Apply for)	7, 10, 24, 25
Cultivate	4, 5
Cut Wood	29, 30 ,31
Entertain Guests	18, 22, 23
Fertilize and Compost (Chemical)	19, 20
Fertilize and Compost (Organic)	6, 24, 25
Habits (Break)	4, 5
Hair (Cut for fast growth)	15, 16
Hair (Cut for slow growth)	
Hair (Cut for thicker hair)	20, 21, 22
Harvest (Crops to dry)	1, 4, 5, 26, 27
Job (Start new)	10, 11, 14
Legal (Gain damages or start proceeding)	17, 18
Loan (Ask for)	
Massage (Relaxing)	11, 12, 17, 18
Mushrooms (Pick)	20, 21, 22
Promotion (Ask for)	2, 5, 7, 10, 14
Prune to Promote Healing	2, 3, 29, 30
Prune to Retard Growth	25, 26
Sauerkraut (Make)	20, 21, 22
Spray Pests and Weeds	4, 5
Wean Children	1, 2, 3, 4, 5
Weight (Reduce)	4, 5, 31

Activity	April
Advertise in Print	4, 9, 26, 30
Automobile (Buy)	8, 15, 21,24, 26
Animals (Neuter or spay)	1, 2, 29, 30
Animals (Sell or buy)	15, 16
Build (Start excavation)	7, 8
Business (Start new)	7, 8, 15, 16
Can Fruits and Vegetables	3, 4, 30
Concrete (Pour)	27, 28
Consultants (Begin work with)	4, 9, 13, 14, 26
Contracts (Bid on)	8, 15, 21, 24, 26
Copyrights/Patents (Apply for)	8, 9, 25, 26
Cultivate	1, 4, 5, 28, 29
Cut Wood	25, 26
Entertain Guests	13, 14, 18, 19
Fertilize and Compost (Chemical)	15, 16
Fertilize and Compost (Organic)	3, 4, 21, 22
Habits (Break)	28, 29
Hair (Cut for fast growth)	11, 12
Hair (Cut for slow growth)	20, 21
Hair (Cut for thicker hair)	19, 20, 21
Harvest (Crops to dry)	1, 2, 23, 24, 28, 29
Job (Start new)	7, 9, 13, 14, 18
Legal (Gain damages or start proceeding)	8, 9, 13, 18
Loan (Ask for)	
Massage (Relaxing)	7, 8, 13, 14, 15
Mushrooms (Pick)	19, 20, 21
Promotion (Ask for)	9, 14, 18
Prune to Promote Healing	25, 26, 27
Prune to Retard Growth	21, 22
Sauerkraut (Make)	19, 20, 21
Spray Pests and Weeds	28, 29
Wean Children	23, 24, 25, 26, 27
Weight (Reduce)	28, 29

Activity	May
Advertise in Print	9, 18, 31
Automobile (Buy)	4, 8, 17, 22, 24, 31
Animals (Neuter or spay)	20, 21, 22, 24
Animals (Sell or buy)	1, 13, 14, 28, 29
Build (Start excavation)	5, 6
Business (Start new)	5, 6
Can Fruits and Vegetables	1, 27, 28, 29
Concrete (Pour)	22, 23
Consultants (Begin work with)	1, 5, 7, 24, 26
Contracts (Bid on)	24, 26
Copyrights/Patents (Apply for)	24, 26
Cultivate	3, 20, 21, 15, 26, 30, 31
Cut Wood	22, 23, 24
Entertain Guests	10, 11, 15
Fertilize and Compost (Chemical)	13, 14
Fertilize and Compost (Organic)	27, 28
Habits (Break)	
Hair (Cut for fast growth)	8, 9
Hair (Cut for slow growth)	20, 31
Hair (Cut for thicker hair)	
Harvest (Crops to dry)	25, 26, 30
Job (Start new)	8, 17, 18
Legal (Gain damages or start proceeding)	12, 14, 18
Loan (Ask for)	
Massage (Relaxing)	4, 5, 6, 10, 11, 12
Mushrooms (Pick)	18, 19, 20
Promotion (Ask for)	7, 8, 13, 14
Prune to Promote Healing	22, 23
Prune to Retard Growth	
Sauerkraut (Make)	18, 19, 20
Spray Pests and Weeds	25, 26
Wean Children	1, 2
Weight (Reduce)	25, 26

Activity	June
Advertise in Print	7, 12, 15
Automobile (Buy)	4, 7, 9, 13, 19, 22, 28
Animals (Neuter or spay)	21, 22
Animals (Sell or buy)	8, 9
Build (Start excavation)	7, 8
Business (Start new)	9
Can Fruits and Vegetables	24, 25
Concrete (Pour)	
Consultants (Begin work with)	7, 12, 15
Contracts (Bid on)	19, 20
Copyrights/Patents (Apply for)	30
Cultivate	21, 22, 23
Cut Wood	28, 29
Entertain Guests	6, 7, 13, 14
Fertilize and Compost (Chemical)	9, 10
Fertilize and Compost (Organic)	24, 25
Habits (Break)	29, 30
Hair (Cut for fast growth)	5, 6
Hair (Cut for slow growth)	20, 21
Hair (Cut for thicker hair)	18
Harvest (Crops to dry)	3, 27
Job (Start new)	5, 6, 13
Legal (Gain damages or start proceeding)	5
Loan (Ask for)	5, 13
Massage (Relaxing)	7, 8, 28, 29
Mushrooms (Pick)	17, 18, 19
Promotion (Ask for)	7, 12, 15
Prune to Promote Healing	19, 20, 21
Prune to Retard Growth	
Sauerkraut (Make)	17, 18, 19
Spray Pests and Weeds	5, 13, 19
Wean Children	21, 22, 23, 24
Weight (Reduce)	3, 30

Activity	July
Advertise in Print	3, 5, 11, 22
Automobile (Buy)	3, 5, 11, 12, 14, 22, 26
Animals (Neuter or spay)	21, 22
Animals (Sell or buy)	7, 21, 22
Build (Start excavation)	4, 5
Business (Start new)	6, 7, 8
Can Fruits and Vegetables	22, 29, 30
Concrete (Pour)	25, 26
Consultants (Begin work with)	7, 21, 22
Contracts (Bid on)	1, 2, 16, 17, 18
Copyrights/Patents (Apply for)	7, 21, 22
Cultivate	23, 24, 27, 28
Cut Wood	26, 27
Entertain Guests	4, 5, 10
Fertilize and Compost (Chemical)	6, 7
Fertilize and Compost (Organic)	21, 22, 30, 31
Habits (Break)	
Hair (Cut for fast growth)	2, 3
Hair (Cut for slow growth)	23, 24, 28, 29
Hair (Cut for thicker hair)	17, 18, 19
Harvest (Crops to dry)	19, 20, 24, 25, 28, 29
Job (Start new)	3, 7, 11, 14
Legal (Gain damages or start proceeding)	7, 12, 14
Loan (Ask for)	26
Massage (Relaxing)	4, 5, 25, 26
Mushrooms (Pick)	17, 18, 19
Promotion (Ask for)	1, 5, 12
Prune to Promote Healing	
Prune to Retard Growth	
Sauerkraut (Make)	17, 18, 19
Spray Pests and Weeds	18, 19, 24
Wean Children	1, 27, 28, 29
Weight (Reduce)	27, 28

Activity	August
Advertise in Print	1, 2, 6, 12, 27
Automobile (Buy)	1, 3, 6, 12, 13, 22, 27
Animals (Neuter or spay)	18
Animals (Sell or buy)	3, 4, 17, 18, 19
Build (Start excavation)	
Business (Start new)	12, 13, 14
Can Fruits and Vegetables	26, 27
Concrete (Pour)	21, 22, 23
Consultants (Begin work with)	1, 3, 6, 12, 16, 22
Contracts (Bid on)	3, 12, 13
Copyrights/Patents (Apply for)	1, 3, 6, 8, 12, 13, 22, 27
Cultivate	20, 21, 24, 25
Cut Wood	22, 23
Entertain Guests	1, 2, 5, 6, 28, 29
Fertilize and Compost (Chemical)	3, 4
Fertilize and Compost (Organic)	25, 26
Habits (Break)	24, 25
Hair (Cut for fast growth)	
Hair (Cut for slow growth)	24, 25
Hair (Cut for thicker hair)	
Harvest (Crops to dry)	1, 2, 22, 23, 28, 29
Job (Start new)	3, 7, 12, 16, 17, 22, 27
Legal (Gain damages or start proceeding)	6, 7, 12
Loan (Ask for)	1, 2
Massage (Relaxing)	1, 2, 22, 23, 28, 29
Mushrooms (Pick)	15, 16, 17
Promotion (Ask for)	12, 16, 17, 22
Prune to Promote Healing	
Prune to Retard Growth	
Sauerkraut (Make)	15, 16, 17
Spray Pests and Weeds	28, 29
Wean Children	24, 25
Weight (Reduce)	24, 25, 28, 29, 30

Activity	September
Advertise in Print	1, 6, 12, 21, 26
Automobile (Buy)	1, 4, 9, 12, 27
Animals (Neuter or spay)	8, 9, 10, 11, 12
Animals (Sell or buy)	14, 15, 26, 27, 28
Build (Start excavation)	
Business (Start new)	9
Can Fruits and Vegetables	23, 24
Concrete (Pour)	18, 19
Consultants (Begin work with)	1, 4, 12, 18, 25, 27
Contracts (Bid on)	10, 21
Copyrights/Patents (Apply for)	1, 4, 12, 21, 27
Cultivate	16, 17, 20, 21, 25, 26
Cut Wood	18, 19, 20, 21, 22
Entertain Guests	2, 3, 25, 26, 29, 30
Fertilize and Compost (Chemical)	14, 15
Fertilize and Compost (Organic)	23, 24
Habits (Break)	27, 28
Hair (Cut for fast growth)	14, 15
Hair (Cut for slow growth)	16, 17, 20, 21
Hair (Cut for thicker hair)	
Harvest (Crops to dry)	20, 21, 22, 25, 26
Job (Start new)	1, 4, 6, 9, 12, 18, 21
Legal (Gain damages or start proceeding)	4, 9, 18, 22
Loan (Ask for)	18, 26
Massage (Relaxing)	18, 19, 24, 25, 26
Mushrooms (Pick)	14, 15, 16
Promotion (Ask for)	12, 25
Prune to Promote Healing	
Prune to Retard Growth	
Sauerkraut (Make)	14, 15, 16
Spray Pests and Weeds	25, 26
Wean Children	
Weight (Reduce)	20, 21, 22, 25, 26

Activity	October
Advertise in Print	3, 5, 7, 17, 27
Automobile (Buy)	2, 7, 12, 16, 20, 29
Animals (Neuter or spay)	5, 6, 7, 9, 11
Animals (Sell or buy)	11, 12, 24, 25
Build (Start excavation)	
Business (Start new)	6, 7, 8
Can Fruits and Vegetables	20, 21, 29, 30
Concrete (Pour)	
Consultants (Begin work with)	7, 8, 12, 16, 20
Contracts (Bid on)	7, 17
Copyrights/Patents (Apply for)	4, 7, 17, 20, 27, 29
Cultivate	18, 19, 22, 23
Cut Wood	18, 19, 24, 25
Entertain Guests	1, 22, 23, 26, 27
Fertilize and Compost (Chemical)	11, 12
Fertilize and Compost (Organic)	20, 21
Habits (Break)	22, 23
Hair (Cut for fast growth)	11, 12, 13
Hair (Cut for slow growth)	24, 25
Hair (Cut for thicker hair)	
Harvest (Crops to dry)	18, 19, 22, 23
Job (Start new)	7, 16, 20, 24, 29
Legal (Gain damages or start proceeding)	2, 7, 11
Loan (Ask for)	16, 21
Massage (Relaxing)	16, 17, 22, 23
Mushrooms (Pick)	13, 14, 15
Promotion (Ask for)	9, 17, 24, 29
Prune to Promote Healing	
Prune to Retard Growth	
Sauerkraut (Make)	13, 14, 15
Spray Pests and Weeds	22, 23
Wean Children	
Weight (Reduce)	18, 19, 22, 23

Activity	November
Advertise in Print	1, 2, 7, 16, 25, 27
Automobile (Buy)	3, 13, 16, 21, 26
Animals (Neuter or spay)	1, 2, 3, 4, 7, 8
Animals (Sell or buy)	7, 8, 9, 20, 21, 22
Build (Start excavation)	3, 4
Business (Start new)	3, 4
Can Fruits and Vegetables	16, 17, 25, 26, 27
Concrete (Pour)	5, 6
Consultants (Begin work with)	3, 7, 12, 16, 21, 25
Contracts (Bid on)	3, 12
Copyrights/Patents (Apply for)	7, 8, 12, 16, 25
Cultivate	14, 15, 18, 19
Cut Wood	20, 21, 22
Entertain Guests	18, 19, 23, 24
Fertilize and Compost (Chemical)	
Fertilize and Compost (Organic)	16, 17, 25, 26
Habits (Break)	14, 15, 18, 19
Hair (Cut for fast growth)	8, 9
Hair (Cut for slow growth)	14, 15, 21, 22
Hair (Cut for thicker hair)	
Harvest (Crops to dry)	14, 15, 18, 19
Job (Start new)	8, 11, 12, 25, 29
Legal (Gain damages or start proceeding)	3, 8, 12
Loan (Ask for)	18
Massage (Relaxing)	13, 14, 18, 19
Mushrooms (Pick)	12, 13, 14
Promotion (Ask for)	7, 12, 13
Prune to Promote Healing	
Prune to Retard Growth	
Sauerkraut (Make)	12, 13, 14
Spray Pests and Weeds	25, 26, 27
Wean Children	
Weight (Reduce)	14, 15, 18, 19

Activity	December
Advertise in Print	3, 7, 8, 17, 28
Automobile (Buy)	1, 2, 3, 10, 23, 28
Animals (Neuter or spay)	26
Animals (Sell or buy)	6, 18, 19
Build (Start excavation)	30, 31
Business (Start new)	28, 29, 30, 31
Can Fruits and Vegetables	14, 15, 22, 23
Concrete (Pour)	30, 31
Consultants (Begin work with)	1, 6, 7, 17, 31
Contracts (Bid on)	26, 28
Copyrights/Patents (Apply for)	1, 10, 23, 26
Cultivate	16, 17, 20, 21
Cut Wood	13, 14, 18, 19
Entertain Guests	16, 17, 20, 21
Fertilize and Compost (Chemical)	5, 6
Fertilize and Compost (Organic)	14, 15, 22, 23
Habits (Break)	
Hair (Cut for fast growth)	
Hair (Cut for slow growth)	18, 19
Hair (Cut for thicker hair)	11, 13
Harvest (Crops to dry)	15, 16, 25, 26, 30, 31
Job (Start new)	1, 6, 10, 20, 31
Legal (Gain damages or start proceeding)	1, 6, 10
Loan (Ask for)	16, 17
Massage (Relaxing)	10, 11, 16, 17
Mushrooms (Pick)	11, 12, 13
Promotion (Ask for)	1, 8, 10, 17, 20, 31
Prune to Promote Healing	
Prune to Retard Growth	22, 23, 24
Sauerkraut (Make)	11, 12, 13
Spray Pests and Weeds	16, 17
Wean Children	25, 26
Weight (Reduce)	13, 16, 17

Choose the Best Time for Your Activities

When rules for elections refer to "favorable" and "unfavorable" aspects to your Sun or other planets, please refer to the Favorable and Unfavorable Days Tables and Lunar Aspectarian for more information. You'll find instructions beginning on page 127 and the tables beginning on page 134.

The material in this section came from several sources including: *The New A to Z Horoscope Maker and Delineator* by Llewellyn George (Llewellyn, 1999), *Moon Sign Book* (Llewellyn, 1945), and *Electional Astrology* by Vivian Robson (Slingshot Publishing, 2000). Robson's book was originally published in 1937.

Advertise (Internet)

The Moon should be conjunct, sextile, or trine Mercury or Uranus; and in the sign of Gemini, Capricorn, or Aquarius.

Advertise (Print)

Write ads on a day favorable to your Sun. The Moon should be conjunct, sextile, or trine Mercury or Venus. Avoid hard aspects to Mars and Saturn. Ad campaigns produce the best results when the Moon is well aspected in Gemini (to enhance communication) or Capricorn (to build business).

Animals

Take home new pets when the day is favorable to your Sun, or when the Moon is trine, sextile, or conjunct Mercury, Venus, or Jupiter, or in the sign of Virgo or Pisces. However, avoid days when the Moon is either square or opposing the Sun, Mars, Saturn, Uranus, Neptune, or Pluto. When selecting a pet, have the Moon well aspected by the planet that rules the animal. Cats are ruled by the Sun, dogs by Mercury, birds by Venus, horses by Jupiter, and fish by Neptune. Buy large animals when the Moon is in Sagittarius or Pisces, and making favorable aspects to Jupiter or Mercury. Buy animals smaller than sheep when the Moon is in Virgo with favorable aspects to Mercury or Venus.

Animals (Breed)

Animals are easiest to handle when the Moon is in Taurus, Cancer, Libra, or Pisces, but try to avoid the Full Moon. To encourage healthy births, animals should be mated so births occur when the Moon is increasing in Taurus, Cancer, Pisces, or Libra. Those born during a semi-fruitful sign (Taurus and Capricorn) will produce leaner meat. Libra yields beautiful animals for showing and racing.

Animals (Declaw)

Declaw cats in the dark of the Moon. Avoid the week before and after the Full Moon and the sign of Pisces.

Animals (Neuter or spay)

Have livestock and pets neutered or spayed when the Moon is in Sagittarius, Capricorn, Aquarius, or Pisces; after it has passed through Scorpio, the sign that rules reproductive organs. Avoid the week before and after the Full Moon.

Animals (Sell or buy)

In either buying or selling, it is important to keep the Moon and Mercury free from any aspect to Mars. Aspects to Mars will create discord and increase the likelihood of wrangling over price and quality. The Moon should be passing from the first quarter to full and sextile or trine Venus or Jupiter. When buying racehorses, let the Moon be in an air sign. The Moon should be in air signs when you buy birds. If the birds are to be pets, let the Moon be in good aspect to Venus.

Animals (Train)

Train pets when the Moon is in Virgo or when the Moon trines Mercury.

Animals (Train dogs to hunt)

Let the Moon be in Aries in conjunction with Mars, which makes them courageous and quick to learn. But let Jupiter also be in aspect to preserve them from danger in hunting.

Automobiles

When buying an automobile, select a time when the Moon is conjunct, sextile, or trine to Mercury, Saturn, or Uranus; and in the sign Gemini or Capricorn.

Baking Cakes

Your cakes will have a lighter texture if you see that the Moon is in Gemini, Libra, or Aquarius, and in good aspect to Venus or Mercury. If you are decorating a cake or confections are being made, have the Moon placed in Libra.

Beauty Treatments (Massage, etc.)

See that the Moon is in Taurus, Cancer, Leo, Libra, or Aquarius, and in favorable aspect to Venus. In the case of plastic surgery, aspects to Mars should be avoided, and the Moon should not be in the sign ruling the part to be operated on.

Borrow (Money or goods)

See that the Moon is not placed between 15 degrees Libra and 15 degrees Scorpio. Let the Moon be waning and in Leo, Scorpio (16 to 30 degrees), Sagittarius, or Pisces. Venus should be in good aspect to the Moon, and the Moon should not be square, opposing, or conjunct either Saturn or Mars.

Brewing

Start brewing during the third or fourth quarter, when the Moon is in Cancer, Scorpio, or Pisces

Build (Start foundation)

Turning the first sod for the foundation marks the beginning of the building. For best results, excavate the site when the Moon is in the first quarter of a fixed sign and making favorable aspects to Saturn.

Business (Start new)

When starting a business, have the Moon be in Taurus, Virgo, or Capricorn, and increasing. The Moon should be sextile or trine Jupiter or Saturn, but avoid oppositions or squares. The planet ruling the business should be well aspected, too.

Buy Goods

Buy during the third quarter, when the Moon is in Taurus for quality, or in a mutable sign (Gemini, Sagittarius, Virgo, or Pisces) for savings. Good aspects to Venus or the Sun are desirable. If you are buying for yourself, it is good if the day is favorable for your Sun sign. You may also apply rules for buying specific items.

Canning

Can fruits and vegetables when the Moon is in either the third or fourth quarter, and in the water sign Cancer or Pisces. Preserves and jellies use the same quarters and the signs Cancer, Pisces, or Taurus.

Clothing

Buy clothing on a day that is favorable for your Sun sign, and when Venus or Mercury is well aspected. Avoid aspects to Mars and Saturn. Buy your clothing when the Moon is in Taurus if you want to remain satisfied. Do not buy clothing or jewelry when the Moon is in Scorpio or Aries. See that the Moon is sextile or trine the Sun during the first or second quarters.

Collections

Try to make collections on days when your Sun is well aspected. Avoid days when the Moon is opposing or square Mars or Saturn. If possible, the Moon should be in a cardinal sign (Aries, Cancer, Libra, or Capricorn). It is more difficult to collect when the Moon is in Taurus or Scorpio.

Concrete

Pour concrete when the Moon is in the third quarter of the fixed sign Taurus, Leo, or Aquarius.

Construction (Begin new)

The Moon should be sextile or trine Jupiter. According to Hermes, no building should be begun when the Moon is in Scorpio or Pisces. The best time to begin building is when the Moon is in Aquarius.

Consultants (Work with)

The Moon should be conjunct, sextile, or trine Mercury or Jupiter.

Contracts (Bid on)

The Moon should be in Gemini or Capricorn, and either the Moon or Mercury should be conjunct, sextile, or trine Jupiter.

Copyrights/Patents

The Moon should be conjunct, trine, or sextile either Mercury or Jupiter.

Coronations and Installations

Let the Moon be in Leo and in favorable aspect to Venus, Jupiter, or Mercury. The Moon should be applying to these planets.

Cultivate

Cultivate when the Moon is in a barren sign and waning, ideally the fourth quarter in Aries, Gemini, Leo, Virgo, or Aquarius. The third quarter in the sign of Sagittarius will also work.

Cut Timber

Timber cut during the waning Moon does not become worm-eaten; it will season well, and not warp, decay, or snap during burning. Cut when the Moon is in Taurus, Gemini, Virgo, or Capricorn—especially in August. Avoid the water signs. Look for favorable aspects to Mars.

Decorating or Home Repairs

Have the Moon waxing, and in the sign of Libra, Gemini, or Aquarius. Avoid squares or oppositions to either Mars or Saturn. Venus in good aspect to Mars or Saturn is beneficial.

Demolition

Let the waning Moon be in Leo, Sagittarius, or Aries.

Dental and Dentists

Visit the dentist when the Moon is in Virgo, or pick a day marked favorable for your Sun sign. Mars should be marked sextile, conjunct, or trine; and avoid squares or oppositions to Saturn, Uranus, or Jupiter.

Teeth are best removed when the Moon is in Gemini, Virgo, Sagittarius, or Pisces, and during the first or second quarter. Avoid the Full Moon! The day should be favorable for your lunar cycle, and Mars and Saturn should be marked conjunct, trine, or sextile. Fillings should be done in the third or fourth quarters in the sign of Taurus, Leo, Scorpio, or Pisces. The same applies for dentures.

Dressmaking

William Lilly wrote in 1676: "Make no new clothes, or first put them on when the Moon is in Scorpio or afflicted by Mars, for they will be apt to be torn and quickly worn out." Design, repair, and sew clothes in the first and second quarters of Taurus, Leo, or Libra on a day marked favorable for your Sun sign. Venus, Jupiter, and Mercury should be favorably aspected, but avoid hard aspects to Mars or Saturn.

Egg-setting

Eggs should be set so chicks will hatch during fruitful signs. To set eggs, subtract the number of days given for incubation or gestation from the fruitful dates. Chickens incubate in twenty-one days, turkeys and geese in twenty-eight days.

A freshly laid egg loses quality rapidly if it is not handled properly. Use plenty of clean litter in the nests to reduce the number of dirty or cracked eggs. Gather eggs daily in mild weather and at least two times daily in hot or cold weather. The eggs should be placed in a cooler immediately after gathering and stored at 50 to 55 degrees Fahrenheit. Do not store eggs with foods or products that give off pungent odors since eggs may absorb the odors.

Eggs saved for hatching purposes should not be washed. Only clean and slightly soiled eggs should be saved for hatching. Dirty eggs should not be incubated. Eggs should be stored in a cool place with the large ends up. It is not advisable to store the eggs longer than one week before setting them in an incubator.

Electricity and Gas (Install)

The Moon should be in a fire sign, and there should be no squares, oppositions, or conjunctions with Uranus (ruler of electricity), Neptune (ruler of gas), Saturn, or Mars. Hard aspects to Mars can cause fires.

Electronics (Buying)

Choose a day when the Moon is in an air sign (Gemini, Libra, Aquarius) and well aspected by Mercury and/or Uranus when buying electronics.

Electronics (Repair)

The Moon should be sextile or trine Mars or Uranus, and in a fixed sign (Taurus, Leo, Scorpio, Aquarius).

Entertain Friends

Let the Moon be in Leo or Libra and making good aspects to Venus. Avoid squares or oppositions to either Mars or Saturn by the Moon or Venus.

Eyes and Eyeglasses

Have your eyes tested and glasses fitted on a day marked favorable for your Sun sign, and on a day that falls during your favorable lunar cycle. Mars should not be in aspect with the Moon. The same applies for any treatment of the eyes, which should also be started during the Moon's first or second quarter.

Fence Posts

Set posts when the Moon is in the third or fourth quarter of the fixed sign Taurus or Leo.

Fertilize and Compost

Fertilize when the Moon is in a fruitful sign (Cancer, Scorpio, Pisces). Organic fertilizers are best when the Moon is waning. Use chemical fertilizers when the Moon is waxing. Start compost when the Moon is in the fourth quarter in a water sign.

Find Hidden Treasure

Let the Moon be in good aspect to Jupiter or Venus. If you erect a horoscope for this election, place the Moon in the Fourth House.

Find Lost Articles

Search for lost articles during the first quarter and when your Sun sign is marked favorable. Also check to see that the planet ruling the lost item is trine, sextile, or conjunct the Moon. The Moon rules household utensils; Mercury rules letters and books; and Venus rules clothing, jewelry, and money.

Fishing

During the summer months, the best time of the day to fish is from sunrise to three hours after, and from two hours before sunset until one hour after. Fish do not bite in cooler months until the air is warm, from noon to 3 pm. Warm, cloudy days are good. The most favorable winds are from the south and southwest. Easterly winds are unfavorable. The best days of the month for fishing are when the Moon changes quarters, especially if the change occurs on a day when the Moon is in a water sign (Cancer, Scorpio, Pisces). The best period in any month is the day after the Full Moon.

Friendship

The need for friendship is greater when the Moon is in Aquarius, or when Uranus aspects the Moon. Friendship prospers when Venus or Uranus is trine, sextile, or conjunct the Moon. The Moon in Gemini facilitates the chance meeting of acquaintances and friends.

Grafting or Budding

Grafting is the process of introducing new varieties of fruit on less desirable trees. For this process you should use the increasing phase of the Moon in fruitful signs such as Cancer, Scorpio, or Pisces. Capricorn may be used, too. Cut your grafts while trees are dormant, from December to March. Keep them in a cool, dark, not too dry or too damp place. Do the grafting before the sap starts to flow and while the Moon is waxing, and preferably while it is in Cancer, Scorpio, or Pisces. The type of plant should determine both cutting and planting times.

Habit (Breaking)

To end an undesirable habit, and this applies to ending everything from a bad relationship to smoking, start on a day when the Moon is in the fourth quarter and in the barren sign of Gemini, Leo, or Aquarius. Aries, Virgo, and Capricorn may be suitable as well, depending on the habit you want to be rid of. Make sure that your lunar cycle is favorable. Avoid lunar aspects to Mars or Jupiter. However, favorable aspects to Pluto are helpful.

Haircuts

Cut hair when the Moon is in Gemini, Sagittarius, Pisces, Taurus, or Capricorn, but not in Virgo. Look for favorable aspects to Venus. For faster growth, cut hair when the Moon is increasing in Cancer or Pisces. To make hair grow thicker, cut when the Moon is full in the signs of Taurus, Cancer, or Leo. If you want your hair to grow more slowly, have the Moon be decreasing in Aries, Gemini, or Virgo, and have the Moon square or opposing Saturn.

Permanents, straightening, and hair coloring will take well if the Moon is in Taurus or Leo and trine or sextile Venus. Avoid hair treatments if Mars is marked as square or in opposition, especially if heat is to be used. For permanents, a trine to Jupiter is helpful. The Moon also should be in the first quarter. Check the lunar cycle for a favorable day in relation to your Sun sign.

Harvest Crops

Harvest root crops when the Moon is in a dry sign (Aries, Leo, Sagittarius, Gemini, Aquarius) and waning. Harvest grain for storage just after the Full Moon, avoiding Cancer, Scorpio, or Pisces. Harvest in the third and fourth quarters in dry signs. Dry crops in the third quarter in fire signs.

Health

A diagnosis is more likely to be successful when the Moon is in Aries, Cancer, Libra, or Capricorn; and less so when in Gemini, Sagittarius, Pisces, or Virgo. Begin a recuperation program when the Moon is in a cardinal or fixed sign and the day is favorable to your Sun sign. Enter hospitals at these times, too. For surgery, see "Surgical Procedures." Buy medicines when the Moon is in Virgo or Scorpio.

Home (Buy new)

If you desire a permanent home, buy when the New Moon is in a fixed sign—Taurus or Leo—for example. Each sign will affect your decision in a different way. A house bought when the Moon is in Taurus is likely to be more practical and have a country look—right down to the split-rail fence. A house purchased when the Moon is in Leo will more likely be a real showplace.

If you're buying for speculation and a quick turnover, be certain that the Moon is in a cardinal sign (Aries, Cancer, Libra, Capricorn). Avoid buying when the Moon is in a fixed sign (Leo, Scorpio, Aquarius, Taurus).

Home (Make repairs)

In all repairs, avoid squares, oppositions, or conjunctions to the planet ruling the place or thing to be repaired. For example, bathrooms are ruled by Scorpio and Cancer. You would not want to start a project in those rooms when the Moon or Pluto is receiving hard aspects. The front entrance, hall, dining room, and porch are ruled by the Sun. So you would want to avoid times when Saturn or Mars are square, opposing, or conjunct the Sun. Also, let the Moon be waxing.

Home (Sell)

Make a strong effort to list your property for sale when the Sun is marked favorable in your sign and in good aspect to Jupiter. Avoid adverse aspects to as many planets as possible.

Home Furnishings (Buy new)

Saturn days (Saturday) are good for buying, and Jupiter days (Thursday) are good for selling. Items bought on days when Saturn is well aspected tend to wear longer and purchases tend to be more conservative.

Job (Start new)

Jupiter and Venus should be sextile, trine, or conjunct the Moon. A day when your Sun is receiving favorable aspects is preferred.

Legal Matters

Good Moon-Jupiter aspects improve the outcome in legal decisions. To gain damages through a lawsuit, begin the process during the increasing Moon. To avoid paying damages, a court date during the decreasing Moon is desirable. Good Moon-Sun aspects strengthen your chance of success. A well-aspected Moon in Cancer or Leo, making good aspects to the Sun, brings the best results in custody cases. In divorce cases, a favorable Moon-Venus aspect is best.

Loan (Ask for)

A first and second quarter phase favors the lender, the third and fourth quarters favor the borrower. Good aspects of Jupiter and

Venus to the Moon are favorable to both, as is having the Moon in Leo or Taurus.

Machinery, Appliances, or Tools (Buy)

Tools, machinery, and other implements should be bought on days when your lunar cycle is favorable and when Mars and Uranus are trine, sextile, or conjunct the Moon. Any quarter of the Moon is suitable. When buying gas or electrical appliances, the Moon should be in Aquarius.

Make a Will

Let the Moon be in a fixed sign (Taurus, Leo, Scorpio, or Aquarius) to ensure permanence. If the Moon is in a cardinal sign (Aries, Cancer, Libra, or Capricorn), the will could be altered. Let the Moon be waxing—increasing in light—and in good aspect to Saturn, Venus, or Mercury. In the case the will is made in an emergency during illness, and the Moon is slow in motion, void-of-course, combust, or under the Sun's beams, the testator will die and the will remain unaltered. There is some danger that it will be lost or stolen, however.

Marriage

The best time for marriage to take place is when the Moon is increasing, but not yet full. Good signs for the Moon to be in are Taurus, Cancer, Leo, or Libra.

The Moon in Taurus produces the most steadfast marriages, but if the partners later want to separate, they may have a difficult time. Make sure that the Moon is well aspected, especially to Venus or Jupiter. Avoid aspects to Mars, Uranus, or Pluto, and the signs Aries, Gemini, Virgo, Scorpio, or Aquarius.

The values of the signs are as follows:

- Aries is not favored for marriage
- Taurus from 0 to 19 degrees is good, the remaining degrees are less favorable

- Cancer is unfavorable unless you are marrying a widow
- Leo is favored, but it may cause one party to deceive the other as to his or her money or possessions
- Virgo is not favored except when marrying a widow
- Libra is good for engagements but not for marriage
- Scorpio from 0 to 15 degrees is good, but the last fifteen degrees are entirely unfortunate. The woman may be fickle, envious, and quarrelsome
- Sagittarius is neutral
- Capricorn, from 0 to 10 degrees, is difficult for marriage; however, the remaining degrees are favorable, especially when marrying a widow
- Aquarius is not favored
- Pisces is favored, although marriage under this sign can incline a woman to chatter a lot

These effects are strongest when the Moon is in the sign. If the Moon and Venus are in a cardinal sign, happiness between the couple may not continue long.

On no account should the Moon apply to Saturn or Mars, even by good aspect.

Medical Treatment for the Eyes

Let the Moon be increasing in light and motion and making favorable aspects to Venus or Jupiter, and be unaspected by Mars. Keep the Moon out of Taurus, Capricorn, or Virgo. If an aspect between the Moon and Mars is unavoidable, let it be separating.

Medical Treatment for the Head

If possible, have Mars and Saturn free of hard aspects. Let the Moon be in Aries or Taurus, decreasing in light, in conjunction or aspect with Venus or Jupiter, and free of hard aspects. The Sun should not be in any aspect to the Moon.

Medical Treatment for the Nose

Let the Moon be in Cancer, Leo, or Virgo, and not aspecting Mars or Saturn, and not in conjunction with a weak or retrograde planet.

Mining

Saturn rules mining. Begin work when Saturn is marked conjunct, trine, or sextile. Mine for gold when the Sun is marked conjunct, trine, or sextile. Mercury rules quicksilver, Venus rules copper, Jupiter rules tin, Saturn rules lead and coal, Uranus rules radioactive elements, Neptune rules oil, the Moon rules water. Mine for these items when the ruling planet is marked conjunct, trine, or sextile.

Move to New Home

If you have a choice, and sometimes we don't, make sure that Mars is not aspecting the Moon. Move on a day favorable to your Sun sign, or when the Moon is conjunct, sextile, or trine the Sun.

Mow Lawn

Mow in the first and second quarters (waxing phase) to increase growth and lushness, and in the third and fourth quarters (waning phase) to decrease growth.

Negotiate

When you are choosing a time to negotiate, consider what the meeting is about and what you want to have happen. If it is agreement or compromise between two parties that you desire, have the Moon be in the sign of Libra. When you are making contracts, it is best to have the Moon in the same element. For example, if your concern is communication, then elect a time when the Moon is in an air sign. If, on the other hand, your concern is about possessions, an earth sign would be more appropriate. Fixed signs are unfavorable, with the exception of Leo; so are cardinal signs, except for Capricorn. If you are negotiating the end of something, use the rules that apply to ending habits.

Occupational Training

When you begin training, see that your lunar cycle is favorable that day, and that the planet ruling your occupation is marked conjunct or trine.

Paint

Paint buildings during the waning Libra or Aquarius Moon. If the weather is hot, paint when the Moon is in Taurus. If the weather is cold, paint when the Moon is in Leo. Schedule the painting to start in the fourth quarter as the wood is drier and paint will penetrate wood better. Avoid painting around the New Moon, though, as the wood is likely to be damp, making the paint subject to scalding when hot weather hits it. If the temperature is below 70 degrees Fahrenheit, it is not advisable to paint while the Moon is in Cancer, Scorpio, or Pisces as the paint is apt to creep, check, or run.

Party (Host or attend)

A party timed so the Moon is in Gemini, Leo, Libra, or Sagittarius, with good aspects to Venus and Jupiter, will be fun and well attended. There should be no aspects between the Moon and Mars or Saturn.

Pawn

Do not pawn any article when Jupiter is receiving a square or opposition from Saturn or Mars, or when Jupiter is within 17 degrees of the Sun, for you will have little chance to redeem the items.

Pick Mushrooms

Mushrooms, one of the most promising traditional medicines in the world, should be gathered at the Full Moon.

Plant

Root crops, like carrots and potatoes, are best if planted in the sign Taurus or Capricorn. Beans, peas, tomatoes, peppers, and other fruit-bearing plants are best if planted in a sign that supports seed growth. Leaf plants, like lettuce, broccoli, or cauliflower, are best planted when the Moon is in a water sign.

It is recommended that you transplant during a decreasing Moon, when forces are streaming into the lower part of the plant. This helps root growth.

Promotion (Ask for)

Choose a day favorable to your Sun sign. Mercury should be marked conjunct, trine, or sextile. Avoid days when Mars or Saturn is aspected.

Prune

Prune during the third and fourth quarter of a Scorpio Moon to retard growth and to promote better fruit. Prune when the Moon is in cardinal Capricorn to promote healing.

Reconcile with People

If the reconciliation be with a woman, let Venus be strong and well aspected. If elders or superiors are involved, see that Saturn is receiving good aspects; if the reconciliation is between young people or between an older and younger person, see that Mercury is well aspected.

Romance

There is less control of when a romance starts, but romances begun under an increasing Moon are more likely to be permanent or satisfying, while those begun during the decreasing Moon tend to transform the participants. The tone of the relationship can be guessed from the sign the Moon is in. Romances begun with the Moon in Aries may be impulsive. Those begun in Capricorn will take greater effort to bring to a desirable conclusion, but they may be very rewarding. Good aspects between the Moon and Venus will have a positive influence on the relationship. Avoid unfavorable aspects to Mars, Uranus, and Pluto. A decreasing Moon, particularly the fourth quarter, facilitates ending a relationship, and causes the least pain.

Roof a Building

Begin roofing a building during the third or fourth quarter, when the Moon is in Aries or Aquarius. Shingles laid during the New Moon have a tendency to curl at the edges.

Sauerkraut

The best-tasting sauerkraut is made just after the Full Moon in the fruitful signs of Cancer, Scorpio, or Pisces.

Select a Child's Sex

Count from the last day of menstruation to the first day of the next cycle and divide the interval between the two dates in half. Pregnancy in the first half produces females, but copulation should take place with the Moon in a feminine sign. Pregnancy in the latter half, up to three days before the beginning of menstruation, produces males, but copulation should take place with the Moon in a masculine sign. The three-day period before the next period again produces females.

Sell or Canvas

Begin these activities during a day favorable to your Sun sign. Otherwise, sell on days when Jupiter, Mercury, or Mars is trine, sextile, or conjunct the Moon. Avoid days when Saturn is square or opposing the Moon, for that always hinders business and causes discord. If the Moon is passing from the first quarter to full, it is best to have the Moon swift in motion and in good aspect with Venus and/or Jupiter.

Sign Papers

Sign contracts or agreements when the Moon is increasing in a fruitful sign and on a day when the Moon is making favorable aspects to Mercury. Avoid days when Mars, Saturn, or Neptune are square or opposite the Moon.

Spray and Weed

Spray pests and weeds during the fourth quarter when the Moon is in the barren sign Leo or Aquarius, and making favorable aspects to Pluto. Weed during a waning Moon in a barren sign.

Staff (Fire)

Have the Moon in the third or fourth quarter, but not full. The Moon should not be square any planets.

Staff (Hire)

The Moon should be in the first or second quarter, and preferably in the sign of Gemini or Virgo. The Moon should be conjunct, trine, or sextile Mercury or Jupiter.

Stocks (Buy)

The Moon should be in Taurus or Capricorn, and there should be a sextile or trine to Jupiter or Saturn.

Surgical Procedures

Blood flow, like ocean tides, appears to be related to Moon phases. To reduce hemorrhage after a surgery, schedule it within one week before or after a New Moon. Schedule surgery to occur during the increase of the Moon if possible, as wounds heal better and vitality is greater than during the decrease of the Moon. Avoid surgery within one week before or after the Full Moon. Select a date when the Moon is past the sign governing the part of the body involved in the operation. For example, abdominal operations should be done when the Moon is in Sagittarius,

Capricorn, or Aquarius. The further removed the Moon sign is from the sign ruling the afflicted part of the body, the better.

For successful operations, avoid times when the Moon is applying to any aspect of Mars. (This tends to promote inflammation and complications.) See the Lunar Aspectarian on odd pages 135–157 to find days with negative Mars aspects and positive Venus and Jupiter aspects. Never operate with the Moon in the same sign as a person's Sun sign or Ascendant. Let the Moon be in a fixed sign and avoid square or opposing aspects. The Moon should not be void-of-course. Cosmetic surgery should be done in the increase of the Moon, when the Moon is not square or in opposition to Mars. Avoid days when the Moon is square or opposing Saturn or the Sun.

Travel (Air)

Start long trips when the Moon is making favorable aspects to the Sun. For enjoyment, aspects to Jupiter are preferable; for visiting, look for favorable aspects to Mercury. To prevent accidents, avoid squares or oppositions to Mars, Saturn, Uranus, or Pluto. Choose a day when the Moon is in Sagittarius or Gemini and well aspected to Mercury, Jupiter, or Uranus. Avoid adverse aspects of Mars, Saturn, or Uranus.

Visit

On setting out to visit a person, let the Moon be in aspect with any retrograde planet, for this ensures that the person you're visiting will be at home. If you desire to stay a long time in a place, let the Moon be in good aspect to Saturn. If you desire to leave the place quickly, let the Moon be in a cardinal sign.

Wean Children

To wean a child successfully, do so when the Moon is in Sagittarius, Capricorn, Aquarius, or Pisces—signs that do not rule vital human organs. By observing this astrological rule, much trouble for parents and child may be avoided.

Weight (Reduce)

If you want to lose weight, the best time to get started is when the Moon is in the third or fourth quarter, and in the barren sign of Virgo. Review the section on How to Use the Moon Tables and Lunar Aspectarian beginning on page 134 to help you select a date that is favorable to begin your weight-loss program.

Wine and Drink Other Than Beer

Start brewing when the Moon is in Pisces or Taurus. Sextiles or trines to Venus are favorable, but avoid aspects to Mars or Saturn.

Write

Write for pleasure or publication when the Moon is in Gemini. Mercury should be making favorable aspects to Uranus and Neptune.

How to Use the Moon Tables and Lunar Aspectarian

Timing activities is one of the most important things you can do to ensure success. In many eastern countries, timing by the planets is so important that practically no event takes place without first setting up a chart for it. Weddings have occurred in the middle of the night because the influences were best then. You may not want to take it that far, but you can still make use of the influences of the Moon whenever possible. It's easy and it works!

In the *Moon Sign Book* is information to help you plan just about any activity: weddings, fishing, making purchases, cutting your hair, traveling, and more. We provide the guidelines you need to pick the best day out of the several from which you have to choose. The Moon Tables are the *Moon Sign Book's* primary method for choosing dates. Following are instructions, examples, and directions on how to read the Moon Tables. More advanced information on using the tables containing the Lunar Aspectarian and favorable and unfavorable days (found on odd-numbered pages opposite the Moon Tables), Moon void-of-course and retrograde information to choose the dates best for you is also included.

The Five Basic Steps

Step 1: Directions for Choosing Dates

Look up the directions for choosing dates for the activity that you wish to begin, beginning on page 106, then go to step 2.

Step 2: Check the Moon Tables

You'll find two tables for each month of the year beginning on page 134. The Moon Tables (on the left-hand pages) include the day, date, and sign the Moon is in; the element and nature of the sign; the Moon's phase; and when it changes sign or phase. If there is a time listed after a date, that time is the time when the Moon moves into that zodiac sign. Until then, the Moon is considered to be in the sign for the previous day.

The abbreviation Full signifies Full Moon and New signifies New Moon. The times listed with dates indicate when the Moon changes sign. The times listed after the phase indicate when the Moon changes phase.

Turn to the month you would like to begin your activity. You will be using the Moon's sign and phase information most often when you begin choosing your own dates. Use the Time Zone Map on page 162 and the Time Zone Conversions table on page 163 to convert time to your own time zone.

When you find dates that meet the criteria for the correct Moon phase and sign for your activity, you may have completed the process. For certain simple activities, such as getting a haircut, the phase and sign information is all that is needed. If the directions for your activity include information on certain lunar aspects, however, you should consult the Lunar Aspectarian. An example of this would be if the directions told you not to perform a certain activity when the Moon is square (Q) Jupiter.

Step 3: Check the Lunar Aspectarian

On the pages opposite the Moon Tables you will find tables containing the Lunar Aspectarian and Favorable and Unfavorable Days. The Lunar Aspectarian gives the aspects (or angles) of the Moon to other planets. Some aspects are favorable, while others are not. To use the Lunar Aspectarian, find the planet that the directions list as favorable for your activity, and run down the column to the date desired. For example, you should avoid aspects to Mars if you are planning surgery. So you would look for Mars across the top and then run down that column looking for days where there are no aspects to Mars (as signified by empty boxes). If you want to find a favorable aspect (sextile (X) or trine (T)) to Mercury, run your finger down the column under Mercury until you find an X or T. Adverse aspects to planets are squares (Q) or oppositions (O). A conjunction (C) is sometimes beneficial, sometimes not, depending on the activity or planets involved.

Step 4: Favorable and Unfavorable Days

The tables listing favorable and unfavorable days are helpful when you want to choose your personal best dates because your Sun sign is taken into consideration. The twelve Sun signs are listed on the right side of the tables. Once you have determined which days meet your criteria for phase, sign, and aspects, you can determine whether or not those days are positive for you by checking the favorable and unfavorable days for your Sun sign.

To find out if a day is positive for you, find your Sun sign and then look down the column. If it is marked F, it is very favorable. The Moon is in the same sign as your Sun on a favorable day. If it is marked f, it is slightly favorable; U is very unfavorable; and u means slightly unfavorable. A day marked very unfavorable (U) indicates that the Moon is in the sign opposing your Sun.

Once you have selected good dates for the activity you are about to begin, you can go straight to "Using What You've

Learned," beginning on the next page. To learn how to fine-tune your selections even further, read on.

Step 5: Void-of-Course Moon and Retrogrades

This last step is perhaps the most advanced portion of the procedure. It is generally considered poor timing to make decisions, sign important papers, or start special activities during a Moon void-of-course period or during a Mercury retrograde. Once you have chosen the best date for your activity based on steps one through four, you can check the Void-of-Course tables, beginning on page 75, to find out if any of the dates you have chosen have void periods.

The Moon is said to be void-of-course after it has made its last aspect to a planet within a particular sign, but before it has moved into the next sign. Put simply, the Moon is "resting" during the void-of-course period, so activities initiated at this time generally don't come to fruition. You will notice that there are many void periods during the year, and it is nearly impossible to avoid all of them. Some people choose to ignore these altogether and do not take them into consideration when planning activities.

Next, you can check the Retrograde Planets tables on page 158 to see what planets are retrograde during your chosen date(s).

A planet is said to be retrograde when it appears to move backward in the sky as viewed from the Earth. Generally, the farther a planet is away from the Sun, the longer it can stay retrograde. Some planets will retrograde for several months at a time. Avoiding retrogrades is not as important in lunar planning as avoiding the Moon void-of-course, with the exception of the planet Mercury.

Mercury rules thought and communication, so it is advisable not to sign important papers, initiate important business or legal work, or make crucial decisions during these times. As with the Moon void-of-course, it is difficult to avoid all planetary retrogrades when beginning events, and you may choose to ignore this step of the process. Following are some examples using some or all of the steps outlined above.

Using What You've Learned

Let's say it's a new year and you want to have your hair cut. It's thin and you would like it to look fuller, so you find the directions for hair care and you see that for thicker hair you should cut hair while the Moon is Full and in the sign of Taurus, Cancer, or Leo. You should avoid the Moon in Aries, Gemini, or Virgo. Look at the January Moon Table on page 134. You see that the Full Moon is on January 22 at 8:35 am in the sign of Leo, and remains in Leo until January 24 at 9:48 am, so January 22–23 meets both the phase and sign criteria.

Let's move on to a more difficult example using the sign and phase of the Moon. You want to buy a permanent home. After checking the instructions for purchasing a house: "Home (Buy new)" on page 116, you see that you should buy a home when the Moon is in Taurus, Cancer, or Leo. You need to get a loan, so you should also look under "Loan (Ask for)" on page 117. Here it says that the third and fourth quarters favor the borrower (you). You are going to buy the house in October so go to page 152. The Moon is in the third quarter October 15–21. The Moon is in Taurus from 5:31 am on October 15 until 6:25 am on October 17. The best days for obtaining a loan would be October 15–16, while the Moon is in Taurus.

Just match up the best sign and phase (quarter) to come up with the best date. With all activities, be sure to check the favorable and unfavorable days for your Sun sign in the table adjoining the Lunar Aspectarian. If there is a choice between several dates, pick the one most favorable for you. Because buying a home is an important business decision, you may also wish to see if the Moon is void or if Mercury is retrograde during these dates.

Now let's look at an example that uses signs, phases, and aspects. Our example is starting new home construction. We will use the month of April. Look under "Build (Start foundation)" on page 109 and you'll see that the Moon should be in the first quarter of Taurus or Leo. You should select a time when the Moon is not making unfavorable aspects to Saturn. (Conjunctions are usually considered good if they are not to Mars, Saturn, or Neptune.) Look in the April Moon Table. You will see that the Moon is in the first quarter April 8–14. The Moon is in Taurus from 7:38 pm on April 10 at 12:13 pm until April 12 at 1:54 pm. Now, look to the Lunar Aspectarian for April. We see that there are no squares or oppositions to either Mercury or Saturn on these dates. These are good dates to start a foundation.

A Note About Time and Time Zones

All tables in the *Moon Sign Book* use Eastern Time. You must calculate the difference between your time zone and the Eastern Time Zone. Please refer to the Time Zone Conversions chart on 165 for help with time conversions. The sign the Moon is in at midnight is the sign shown in the Aspectarian and Favorable and Unfavorable Days tables.

How Does the Time Matter?

Due to the three-hour time difference between the east and west coasts of the United States, those of you living on the East Coast may be, for example, under the influence of a Virgo Moon, while those of you living on the West Coast will still have a Leo Moon influence.

The Sign the Moon Is in at Midnight

We follow a commonly held belief among astrologers: whatever sign the Moon is in at the start of a day—12:00 am Eastern Time—is considered the dominant influence of the day. That sign is indicated in the Moon Tables. If the date you select for an activity shows the Moon changing signs, you can decide how important the sign change may be for your specific election and adjust your election date and time accordingly.

Use Common Sense

Some activities depend on outside factors. Obviously, you can't go out and plant when there is a foot of snow on the ground. You should adjust to the conditions at hand. If the weather was bad during the first quarter, when it was best to plant crops, do it during the second quarter while the Moon is in a fruitful sign. If the Moon is not in a fruitful sign during the first or second quarter, choose a day when it is in a semi-fruitful sign. The best advice is to choose either the sign or phase that is most favorable, when the two don't coincide.

To Summarize

First, look up the activity under the proper heading, then look for the information given in the tables. Choose the best date considering the number of positive factors in effect. If most of the dates are favorable, there is no problem choosing the one that will fit your schedule. However, if there aren't any really good dates, pick the ones with the least number of negative influences. Please keep in mind that the information found here applies in the broadest sense to the events you want to plan or are considering. To be the most effective, when you use electional astrology, you should also consider your own birth chart in relation to a chart drawn for the time or times you have under consideration. The best advice we can offer you is: read the entire introduction to each section.

January Moon Table

Date	Sign	Element	Nature	Phase
1 Tue 8:32 pm	Scorpio	Water	Fruitful	4th
2 Wed	Scorpio	Water	Fruitful	4th
3 Thu	Scorpio	Water	Fruitful	4th
4 Fri 9:13 am	Sagittarius	Fire	Barren	4th
5 Sat	Sagittarius	Fire	Barren	4th
6 Sun 8:43 pm	Capricorn	Earth	Semi-fruitful	4th
7 Mon	Capricorn	Earth	Semi-fruitful	4th
8 Tue	Capricorn	Earth	Semi-fruitful	New 6:37 am
9 Wed 6:13 am	Aquarius	Air	Barren	1st
10 Thu	Aquarius	Air	Barren	1st
11 Fri 1:44 pm	Pisces	Water	Fruitful	1st
12 Sat	Pisces	Water	Fruitful	1st
13 Sun 7:23 pm	Aries	Fire	Barren	1st
14 Mon	Aries	Fire	Barren	1st
15 Tue 11:13 pm	Taurus	Earth	Semi-fruitful	2nd 2:46 pm
16 Wed	Taurus	Earth	Semi-fruitful	2nd
17 Thu	Taurus	Earth	Semi-fruitful	2nd
18 Fri 1:30 am	Gemini	Air	Barren	2nd
19 Sat	Gemini	Air	Barren	2nd
20 Sun 3:05 am	Cancer	Water	Fruitful	2nd
21 Mon	Cancer	Water	Fruitful	2nd
22 Tue 5:20 am	Leo	Fire	Barren	Full 8:35 am
23 Wed	Leo	Fire	Barren	3rd
24 Thu 9:48 am	Virgo	Earth	Barren	3rd
25 Fri	Virgo	Earth	Barren	3rd
26 Sat 5:35 pm	Libra	Air	Semi-fruitful	3rd
27 Sun	Libra	Air	Semi-fruitful	3rd
28 Mon	Libra	Air	Semi-fruitful	3rd
29 Tue 4:35 am	Scorpio	Water	Fruitful	3rd
30 Wed	Scorpio	Water	Fruitful	4th 12:03 am
31 Thu 5:08 pm	Sagittarius	Fire	Barren	4th

Aspectarian/Favorable & Unfavorable Days

Date	Sun	Mercury	Venus	Mars	Jupiter	Saturn	Uranus	Neptune	Pluto	Aries	Taurus	Gemini	Cancer	Leo	Virgo	Libra	Scorpio	Sagittarius	Capricorn	Aquarius	Pisces
1			T					T	X	U		f	u	f		F		f	u	f	
2	X				X	X				U		f	u	f		F		f	u	f	f
3		X				T	Q			U		f	u	f		F		f	u	f	f
4			C							U		f	u	f		F		f	u	f	f
5					Q	Q				f		U		f	u	f		F		f	u
6			0					X	C	f		U		f	u	f		F		f	u
7				C	T					u	f		U		f	u	f	F			f
8	C					X				u	f		U		f	u	f	F			f
9		C								u	f		U		f	u	f	F			f
10			X					C		f	u	f		U		f	u	f		F	
11			T	X					X	f	u	f		U		f	u	f		F	
12		Q			0	C					f	u	f		U		f	u	f		F
13	X		Q						Q		f	u	f		U		f	u	f		F
14		X		Q						F		f	u	f		U		f	u	f	
15		T	X					X	T	F		f	u	f		U		f	u	f	
16		Q		T	T					F		f	u	f		U		f	u	f	f
17	T							X	Q	F		f	u	f		U		f	u	f	f
18						Q				F		f	u	f		U		f	u	f	
19		T	0	C		Q	T			f		F		f	u	f		U		f	u
20					0	X			0	f		F		f	u	f		U		f	u
21					T					u	f		F		f	u	f		U		f
22	0									u	f		F		f	u	f		U		f
23		0	X			0				f	u	f		F		f	u	f		U	
24		T			C				T	f	u	f		F		f	u	f		U	
25				T	0						f	u	f		F		f	u	f		U
26			Q						Q		f	u	f		F		f	u	f		U
27	T	Q		Q						U		f	u	f		F		f	u	f	
28		T	T					T		U		f	u	f		F		f	u	f	
29		X		X	X				X	U		f	u	f		F		f	u	f	
30	Q					T	Q			U		f	u	f		F		f	u	f	f
31		Q								U		f	u	f		F		f	u	f	f

February Moon Table

Date	Sign	Element	Nature	Phase
1 Fri	Sagittarius	Fire	Barren	4th
2 Sat	Sagittarius	Fire	Barren	4th
3 Sun 4:52 am	Capricorn	Earth	Semi-fruitful	4th
4 Mon	Capricorn	Earth	Semi-fruitful	4th
5 Tue 2:10 pm	Aquarius	Air	Barren	4th
6 Wed	Aquarius	Air	Barren	New 10:44 pm
7 Thu 8:46 pm	Pisces	Water	Fruitful	1st
8 Fri	Pisces	Water	Fruitful	1st
9 Sat	Pisces	Water	Fruitful	1st
10 Sun 1:17 am	Aries	Fire	Barren	1st
11 Mon	Aries	Fire	Barren	1st
12 Tue 4:34 am	Taurus	Earth	Semi-fruitful	1st
13 Wed	Taurus	Earth	Semi-fruitful	2nd 10:33 pm
14 Thu 7:19 am	Gemini	Air	Barren	2nd
15 Fri	Gemini	Air	Barren	2nd
16 Sat 10:12 am	Cancer	Water	Fruitful	2nd
17 Sun	Cancer	Water	Fruitful	2nd
18 Mon 1:51 pm	Leo	Fire	Barren	2nd
19 Tue	Leo	Fire	Barren	2nd
20 Wed 7:06 pm	Virgo	Earth	Barren	Full 10:30 pm
21 Thu	Virgo	Earth	Barren	3rd
22 Fri	Virgo	Earth	Barren	3rd
23 Sat 2:44 am	Libra	Air	Semi-fruitful	3rd
24 Sun	Libra	Air	Semi-fruitful	3rd
25 Mon 1:05 pm	Scorpio	Water	Fruitful	3rd
26 Tue	Scorpio	Water	Fruitful	3rd
27 Wed	Scorpio	Water	Fruitful	3rd
28 Thu 1:22 am	Sagittarius	Fire	Barren	4th 9:18 pm
29 Fri	Sagittarius	Fire	Barren	4th

Aspectarian/Favorable & Unfavorable Days

Date	Sun	Mercury	Venus	Mars	Jupiter	Saturn	Uranus	Neptune	Pluto	Aries	Taurus	Gemini	Cancer	Leo	Virgo	Libra	Scorpio	Sagittarius	Capricorn	Aquarius	Pisces
1	X					Q				f		U		f	u	f		F		f	u
2		X		0		Q	X			f		U		f	u	f		F		f	u
3						T			C	f		U		f	u	f		F		f	u
4			C		C		X			u	f		U		f	u	f		F		f
5										u	f		U		f	u	f		F		f
6	C	C								f	u	f		U		f	u	f		F	
7						T		C	X	f	u	f		U		f	u	f		F	
8					X	0					f	u	f		U		f	u	f		F
9			X	Q			C				f	u	f		U		f	u	f		F
10		X		Q					Q		f	u	f		U		f	u	f		F
11			Q	X				X		F		f	u	f		U		f	u	f	
12		Q				T			T	F		f	u	f		U		f	u	f	
13	Q			T			X	Q		F		f	u	f		U		f	u	f	
14		T	T			Q					F		f	u	f		U		f	u	f
15						Q	T			f		F		f	u	f		U		f	u
16	T			C	X				0	f		F		f	u	f		U		f	u
17				0		T				u	f		F		f	u	f		U		f
18			0							u	f		F		f	u	f		U		f
19		0								f	u	f		F		f	u	f		U	
20	0			X				0	T	f	u	f		F		f	u	f		U	
21				T	C						f	u	f		F		f	u	f		U
22			Q			0					f	u	f		F		f	u	f		U
23		T	T						Q		f	u	f		F		f	u	f		U
24				Q				T		U		f	u	f		F		f	u	f	
25				T		X			X	U		f	u	f		F		f	u	f	
26	T	Q	Q		X						U		f	u	f		F		f	u	f
27						T	Q				U		f	u	f		F		f	u	f
28	Q				Q						U		f	u	f		F		f	u	
29		X	X					Q	X	f		U		f	u	f		F		f	u

137

March Moon Table

Date	Sign	Element	Nature	Phase
1 Sat 1:33 pm	Capricorn	Earth	Semi-fruitful	4th
2 Sun	Capricorn	Earth	Semi-fruitful	4th
3 Mon 11:24 pm	Aquarius	Air	Barren	4th
4 Tue	Aquarius	Air	Barren	4th
5 Wed	Aquarius	Air	Barren	4th
6 Thu 5:53 am	Pisces	Water	Fruitful	4th
7 Fri	Pisces	Water	Fruitful	New 12:14 pm
8 Sat 9:23 am	Aries	Fire	Barren	1st
9 Sun	Aries	Fire	Barren	1st
10 Mon 12:13 pm	Taurus	Earth	Semi-fruitful	1st
11 Tue	Taurus	Earth	Semi-fruitful	1st
12 Wed 1:54 pm	Gemini	Air	Barren	1st
13 Thu	Gemini	Air	Barren	1st
14 Fri 4:37 pm	Cancer	Water	Fruitful	2nd 6:45 am
15 Sat	Cancer	Water	Fruitful	2nd
16 Sun 9:04 pm	Leo	Fire	Barren	2nd
17 Mon	Leo	Fire	Barren	2nd
18 Tue	Leo	Fire	Barren	2nd
19 Wed 3:25 am	Virgo	Earth	Barren	2nd
20 Thu	Virgo	Earth	Barren	2nd
21 Fri 11:45 am	Libra	Air	Semi-fruitful	Full 2:40 pm
22 Sat	Libra	Air	Semi-fruitful	3rd
23 Sun 10:06 pm	Scorpio	Water	Fruitful	3rd
24 Mon	Scorpio	Water	Fruitful	3rd
25 Tue	Scorpio	Water	Fruitful	3rd
26 Wed 10:11 am	Sagittarius	Fire	Barren	3rd
27 Thu	Sagittarius	Fire	Barren	3rd
28 Fri 10:43 pm	Capricorn	Earth	Semi-fruitful	3rd
29 Sat	Capricorn	Earth	Semi-fruitful	4th 5:47 pm
30 Sun	Capricorn	Earth	Semi-fruitful	4th
31 Mon 9:34 am	Aquarius	Air	Barren	4th

Aspectarian/Favorable & Unfavorable Days

Date	Sun	Mercury	Venus	Mars	Jupiter	Saturn	Uranus	Neptune	Pluto	Aries	Taurus	Gemini	Cancer	Leo	Virgo	Libra	Scorpio	Sagittarius	Capricorn	Aquarius	Pisces
1			O		T		C			f		U		f	u	f		F		f	u
2	X			C						u	f		U		f	u	f		F		f
3							X			u	f		U		f	u	f		F		f
4										f	u	f		U		f	u	f		F	
5		C	C					C		f	u	f		U		f	u	f		F	
6				T		O			X	f	u	f		U		f	u	f		F	
7	C				X		C				f	u	f		U		f	u	f		F
8			Q					Q			f	u	f		U		f	u	f		F
9			Q							F		f	u	f		U		f	u	f	
10		X	X	X	T			X	T	F		f	u	f		U		f	u	f	
11					T		X				F		f	u	f		U		f	u	f
12	X	Q	Q		Q		Q				F		f	u	f		U		f	u	f
13						Q				f		F		f	u	f		U		f	u
14	Q	T	T	C		X		T	O	f		F		f	u	f		U		f	u
15					O					u	f		F		f	u	f		U		f
16	T						T			u	f		F		f	u	f		U		f
17										f	u	f		F		f	u	f		U	
18								O		f	u	f		F		f	u	f		U	
19		O	O	X		C		T		f	u	f		F		f	u	f		U
20				T		O					f	u	f		F		f	u	f		U
21	O								Q		f	u	f		F		f	u	f		U
22			Q							U		f	u	f		F		f	u	f	
23			Q					T		U		f	u	f		F		f	u	f	
24			T		X			X		U		f	u	f		F		f	u	f	
25		T	T		X	T	Q				U		f	u	f		F		f	u	f
26					Q						U		f	u	f		F		f	u	f
27	T									f		U		f	u	f		F		f	u
28		Q	Q			Q	X			f		U		f	u	f		F		f	u
29	Q		O		T				C	u	f		U		f	u	f		F		f
30			X	C			X			u	f		U		f	u	f		F		f
31		X								u	f		U		f	u	f		F		f

April Moon Table

Date	Sign	Element	Nature	Phase
1 Tue	Aquarius	Air	Barren	4th
2 Wed 4:55 pm	Pisces	Water	Fruitful	4th
3 Thu	Pisces	Water	Fruitful	4th
4 Fri 8:27 pm	Aries	Fire	Barren	4th
5 Sat	Aries	Fire	Barren	New 11:55 pm
6 Sun 9:19 pm	Taurus	Earth	Semi-fruitful	1st
7 Mon	Taurus	Earth	Semi-fruitful	1st
8 Tue 9:27 pm	Gemini	Air	Barren	1st
9 Wed	Gemini	Air	Barren	1st
10 Thu 10:43 pm	Cancer	Water	Fruitful	1st
11 Fri	Cancer	Water	Fruitful	1st
12 Sat	Cancer	Water	Fruitful	2nd 2:32 pm
13 Sun 2:29 am	Leo	Fire	Barren	2nd
14 Mon	Leo	Fire	Barren	2nd
15 Tue 9:06 am	Virgo	Earth	Barren	2nd
16 Wed	Virgo	Earth	Barren	2nd
17 Thu 6:10 pm	Libra	Air	Semi-fruitful	2nd
18 Fri	Libra	Air	Semi-fruitful	2nd
19 Sat	Libra	Air	Semi-fruitful	2nd
20 Sun 5:00 am	Scorpio	Water	Fruitful	Full 6:25 am
21 Mon	Scorpio	Water	Fruitful	3rd
22 Tue 5:07 pm	Sagittarius	Fire	Barren	3rd
23 Wed	Sagittarius	Fire	Barren	3rd
24 Thu	Sagittarius	Fire	Barren	3rd
25 Fri 5:47 am	Capricorn	Earth	Semi-fruitful	3rd
26 Sat	Capricorn	Earth	Semi-fruitful	3rd
27 Sun 5:27 pm	Aquarius	Air	Barren	3rd
28 Mon	Aquarius	Air	Barren	4th 10:12 am
29 Tue	Aquarius	Air	Barren	4th
30 Wed 2:11 am	Pisces	Water	Fruitful	4th

Aspectarian/Favorable & Unfavorable Days

Date	Sun	Mercury	Venus	Mars	Jupiter	Saturn	Uranus	Neptune	Pluto	Aries	Taurus	Gemini	Cancer	Leo	Virgo	Libra	Scorpio	Sagittarius	Capricorn	Aquarius	Pisces
1	X									f	u	f		U		f	u	f		F	
2						0		C	X	f	u	f		U		f	u	f		F	
3			T								f	u	f		U		f	u	f		F
4			C		X	C		Q			f	u	f		U		f	u	f		F
5	C	C		Q						F		f	u	f		U		f	u	f	
6					Q			X	T	F		f	u	f		U		f	u	f	
7			X		T						F		f	u	f		U		f	u	f
8			T				X	Q			F		f	u	f		U		f	u	f
9		X	X		Q					f		F		f	u	f		U		f	u
10	X						Q	T		f		F		f	u	f		U		f	u
11			Q		X				0	u	f		F		f	u	f		U		f
12	Q	Q		C	0	T				u	f		F		f	u	f		U		f
13			T							u	f		F		f	u	f		U		f
14		T						0		f	u	f		F		f	u	f		U	
15	T					C			T	f	u	f		F		f	u	f		U	
16			X								f	u	f		F		f	u	f		U
17				T		0		Q			f	u	f		F		f	u	f		U
18										U		f	u	f		F		f	u	f	
19			0	Q	Q			T		U		f	u	f		F		f	u	f	
20	0	0				X			X	U		f	u	f		F		f	u	f	
21				T		T					U		f	u	f		F		f	u	f
22				X	Q			Q			U		f	u	f		F		f	u	f
23										f		U		f	u	f		F		f	u
24			T			Q	X			f		U		f	u	f		F		f	u
25	T					T			C	f		U		f	u	f		F		f	u
26		T								u	f		U		f	u	f		F		f
27			Q	0	C		X			u	f		U		f	u	f		F		f
28	Q									f	u	f		U		f	u	f		F	
29		Q						C		f	u	f		U		f	u	f		F	
30			X		0				X	f	u	f		U		f	u	f		F	

May Moon Table

Date	Sign	Element	Nature	Phase
1 Thu	Pisces	Water	Fruitful	4th
2 Fri 6:51 am	Aries	Fire	Barren	4th
3 Sat	Aries	Fire	Barren	4th
4 Sun 7:58 am	Taurus	Earth	Semi-fruitful	4th
5 Mon	Taurus	Earth	Semi-fruitful	New 8:18 am
6 Tue 7:17 am	Gemini	Air	Barren	1st
7 Wed	Gemini	Air	Barren	1st
8 Thu 7:02 am	Cancer	Water	Fruitful	1st
9 Fri	Cancer	Water	Fruitful	1st
10 Sat 9:10 am	Leo	Fire	Barren	1st
11 Sun	Leo	Fire	Barren	2nd 11:47 pm
12 Mon 2:48 pm	Virgo	Earth	Barren	2nd
13 Tue	Virgo	Earth	Barren	2nd
14 Wed 11:46 pm	Libra	Air	Semi-fruitful	2nd
15 Thu	Libra	Air	Semi-fruitful	2nd
16 Fri	Libra	Air	Semi-fruitful	2nd
17 Sat 10:59 am	Scorpio	Water	Fruitful	2nd
18 Sun	Scorpio	Water	Fruitful	2nd
19 Mon 11:18 pm	Sagittarius	Fire	Barren	Full 10:11 pm
20 Tue	Sagittarius	Fire	Barren	3rd
21 Wed	Sagittarius	Fire	Barren	3rd
22 Thu 11:55 am	Capricorn	Earth	Semi-fruitful	3rd
23 Fri	Capricorn	Earth	Semi-fruitful	3rd
24 Sat 11:51 pm	Aquarius	Air	Barren	3rd
25 Sun	Aquarius	Air	Barren	3rd
26 Mon	Aquarius	Air	Barren	3rd
27 Tue 9:38 am	Pisces	Water	Fruitful	4th 10:56 pm
28 Wed	Pisces	Water	Fruitful	4th
29 Thu 3:52 pm	Aries	Fire	Barren	4th
30 Fri	Aries	Fire	Barren	4th
31 Sat 6:18 pm	Taurus	Earth	Semi-fruitful	4th

Aspectarian/Favorable & Unfavorable Days

Date	Sun	Mercury	Venus	Mars	Jupiter	Saturn	Uranus	Neptune	Pluto	Aries	Taurus	Gemini	Cancer	Leo	Virgo	Libra	Scorpio	Sagittarius	Capricorn	Aquarius	Pisces
1				T	X		C				f	u	f		U		f	u	f		F
2		X							Q		f	u	f		U		f	u	f		F
3				Q				X		F		f	u	f		U		f	u	f	
4			C	Q		T			T	F		f	u	f		U		f	u	f	
5	C				T		X	Q			F		f	u	f		U		f	u	f
6		C		X	Q						F		f	u	f		U		f	u	f
7						Q	T			f		F		f	u	f		U		f	u
8						X			O	f		F		f	u	f		U		f	u
9			X		O	T				u	f		F		f	u	f		U		f
10			C							u	f		F		f	u	f		U		f
11		X	Q							f	u	f		F		f	u	f		U	
12						C	O	T		f	u	f		F		f	u	f		U	
13		Q	T								f	u	f		F		f	u	f		U
14	T				T	O					f	u	f		F		f	u	f		U
15				X				Q		U		f	u	f		F		f	u	f	
16		T		Q		T				U		f	u	f		F		f	u	f	
17			Q		X			X		U		f	u	f		F		f	u	f	
18											U		f	u	f		F		f	u	f
19	O		O	X		T	Q				U		f	u	f		F		f	u	f
20			T		Q					f		U		f	u	f		F		f	u
21	O				Q					f		U		f	u	f		F		f	u
22					T		X	C		f		U		f	u	f		F		f	u
23										u	f		U		f	u	f		F		f
24				C		X				u	f		U		f	u	f		F		f
25	T		T	O						f	u	f		U		f	u	f		F	
26		T					C			f	u	f		U		f	u	f		F	
27	Q		Q		O			X		f	u	f		U		f	u	f		F	
28											f	u	f		U		f	u	f		F
29		Q		X	C			Q			f	u	f		U		f	u	f		F
30	X		X	T						F		f	u	f		U		f	u	f	
31		X			Q	T		X	T	F		f	u	f		U		f	u	f	

June Moon Table

Date	Sign	Element	Nature	Phase
1 Sun	Taurus	Earth	Semi-fruitful	4th
2 Mon 6:06 pm	Gemini	Air	Barren	4th
3 Tue	Gemini	Air	Barren	New 3:22 pm
4 Wed 5:16 pm	Cancer	Water	Fruitful	1st
5 Thu	Cancer	Water	Fruitful	1st
6 Fri 6:00 pm	Leo	Fire	Barren	1st
7 Sat	Leo	Fire	Barren	1st
8 Sun 10:01 pm	Virgo	Earth	Barren	1st
9 Mon	Virgo	Earth	Barren	1st
10 Tue	Virgo	Earth	Barren	2nd 11:03 am
11 Wed 5:55 am	Libra	Air	Semi-fruitful	2nd
12 Thu	Libra	Air	Semi-fruitful	2nd
13 Fri 4:53 pm	Scorpio	Water	Fruitful	2nd
14 Sat	Scorpio	Water	Fruitful	2nd
15 Sun	Scorpio	Water	Fruitful	2nd
16 Mon 5:19 am	Sagittarius	Fire	Barren	2nd
17 Tue	Sagittarius	Fire	Barren	2nd
18 Wed 5:51 pm	Capricorn	Earth	Semi-fruitful	Full 1:30 pm
19 Thu	Capricorn	Earth	Semi-fruitful	3rd
20 Fri	Capricorn	Earth	Semi-fruitful	3rd
21 Sat 5:33 am	Aquarius	Air	Barren	3rd
22 Sun	Aquarius	Air	Barren	3rd
23 Mon 3:32 pm	Pisces	Water	Fruitful	3rd
24 Tue	Pisces	Water	Fruitful	3rd
25 Wed 10:49 pm	Aries	Fire	Barren	3rd
26 Thu	Aries	Fire	Barren	4th 8:10 am
27 Fri	Aries	Fire	Barren	4th
28 Sat 2:50 am	Taurus	Earth	Semi-fruitful	4th
29 Sun	Taurus	Earth	Semi-fruitful	4th
30 Mon 4:03 am	Gemini	Air	Barren	4th

Aspectarian/Favorable & Unfavorable Days

Date	Sun	Mercury	Venus	Mars	Jupiter	Saturn	Uranus	Neptune	Pluto	Aries	Taurus	Gemini	Cancer	Leo	Virgo	Libra	Scorpio	Sagittarius	Capricorn	Aquarius	Pisces
1				Q							F		f	u	f		U		f	u	f
2					T	Q	X	Q			F		f	u	f		U		f	u	f
3	C		C	X						f		F		f	u	f		U		f	u
4		C			X	Q	T	O		f		F		f	u	f		U		f	u
5										u	f		F		f	u	f		U		f
6				O		T				u	f		F		f	u	f		U		f
7		X	X	C						f	u	f		F		f	u	f		U	
8	X							O	T	f	u	f		F		f	u	f		U	
9					C						f	u	f		F		f	u	f		U
10	Q	Q	Q		T		O				f	u	f		F		f	u	f		U
11								Q			f	u	f		F		f	u	f		U
12		T		X	Q					U		f	u	f		F		f	u	f	
13	T		T		X			T	X	U		f	u	f		F		f	u	f	
14											U		f	u	f		F		f	u	f
15			Q	X		T	Q				U		f	u	f		F		f	u	f
16						Q					U		f	u	f		F		f	u	f
17		O								f		U		f	u	f		F		f	u
18	O		O	T			Q	X	C	f		U		f	u	f		F		f	u
19						T				u	f		U		f	u	f		F		f
20				C		X				u	f		U		f	u	f		F		f
21										u	f		U		f	u	f		F		f
22		T								f	u	f		U		f	u	f		F	
23	T			O	O			C	X	f	u	f		U		f	u	f		F	
24		Q	T								f	u	f		U		f	u	f		F
25				X		C		Q			f	u	f		U		f	u	f		F
26	Q		Q							F		f	u	f		U		f	u	f	
27		X		T	Q			X		F		f	u	f		U		f	u	f	
28	X					T		T		F		f	u	f		U		f	u	f	
29			X			T		X	Q		F		f	u	f		U		f	u	f
30				Q	Q						F		f	u	f		U		f	u	f

July Moon Table

Date	Sign	Element	Nature	Phase
1 Tue	Gemini	Air	Barren	4th
2 Wed 3:53 am	Cancer	Water	Fruitful	New 10:18 pm
3 Thu	Cancer	Water	Fruitful	1st
4 Fri 4:15 am	Leo	Fire	Barren	1st
5 Sat	Leo	Fire	Barren	1st
6 Sun 7:04 am	Virgo	Earth	Barren	1st
7 Mon	Virgo	Earth	Barren	1st
8 Tue 1:31 pm	Libra	Air	Semi-fruitful	1st
9 Wed	Libra	Air	Semi-fruitful	1st
10 Thu 11:35 pm	Scorpio	Water	Fruitful	2nd 12:35 am
11 Fri	Scorpio	Water	Fruitful	2nd
12 Sat	Scorpio	Water	Fruitful	2nd
13 Sun 11:50 am	Sagittarius	Fire	Barren	2nd
14 Mon	Sagittarius	Fire	Barren	2nd
15 Tue	Sagittarius	Fire	Barren	2nd
16 Wed 12:20 am	Capricorn	Earth	Semi-fruitful	2nd
17 Thu	Capricorn	Earth	Semi-fruitful	2nd
18 Fri 11:40 am	Aquarius	Air	Barren	Full 3:59 am
19 Sat	Aquarius	Air	Barren	3rd
20 Sun 9:07 pm	Pisces	Water	Fruitful	3rd
21 Mon	Pisces	Water	Fruitful	3rd
22 Tue	Pisces	Water	Fruitful	3rd
23 Wed 4:22 am	Aries	Fire	Barren	3rd
24 Thu	Aries	Fire	Barren	3rd
25 Fri 9:14 am	Taurus	Earth	Semi-fruitful	4th 2:41 pm
26 Sat	Taurus	Earth	Semi-fruitful	4th
27 Sun 11:55 am	Gemini	Air	Barren	4th
28 Mon	Gemini	Air	Barren	4th
29 Tue 1:11 pm	Cancer	Water	Fruitful	4th
30 Wed	Cancer	Water	Fruitful	4th
31 Thu 2:21 pm	Leo	Fire	Barren	4th

Aspectarian/Favorable & Unfavorable Days

Date	Sun	Mercury	Venus	Mars	Jupiter	Saturn	Uranus	Neptune	Pluto	Aries	Taurus	Gemini	Cancer	Leo	Virgo	Libra	Scorpio	Sagittarius	Capricorn	Aquarius	Pisces
1		C					Q	T		f		F		f	u	f		U		f	u
2	C			X		X			O	f		F		f	u	f		U		f	u
3			C	O		T				u	f		F		f	u	f		U		f
4										u	f		F		f	u	f		U		f
5		X						O		f	u	f		F		f	u	f		U	
6			C		C			T		f	u	f		F		f	u	f		U	
7				T			O				f	u	f		F		f	u	f		U
8		Q	X					Q			f	u	f		F		f	u	f		U
9				Q						U		f	u	f		F		f	u	f	
10	Q		Q					T	X	U		f	u	f		F		f	u	f	
11		T		X		X					U		f	u	f		F		f	u	f
12	T			X		T	Q				U		f	u	f		F		f	u	f
13			T			Q					U		f	u	f		F		f	u	f
14			Q							f		U		f	u	f		F		f	u
15						Q	X	C		f		U		f	u	f		F		f	u
16		O		T		T				f		U		f	u	f		F		f	u
17				C		X				u	f		U		f	u	f		F		f
18	O									u	f		U		f	u	f		F		f
19			O							f	u	f		U		f	u	f		F	
20							C	X		f	u	f		U		f	u	f		F	
21			O		O					f	u	f			U		f	u	f		F
22		T		X		C				f	u	f			U		f	u	f		F
23	T							Q		f	u	f			U		f	u	f		F
24			T	Q			X			F		f	u	f		U		f	u	f	
25	Q	Q				T			T	F		f	u	f		U		f	u	f	
26		Q	T	T		X					F		f	u	f		U		f	u	f
27	X	X				Q	Q				F		f	u	f		U		f	u	f
28			X	Q						f		F		f	u	f		U		f	u
29					Q	T	O			f		F		f	u	f		U		f	u
30			X	O	X					u	f		F		f	u	f		U		f
31						T				u	f		F		f	u	f		U		f

August Moon Table

Date	Sign	Element	Nature	Phase
1 Fri	Leo	Fire	Barren	New 6:12 am
2 Sat 4:59 pm	Virgo	Earth	Barren	1st
3 Sun	Virgo	Earth	Barren	1st
4 Mon 10:28 pm	Libra	Air	Semi-fruitful	1st
5 Tue	Libra	Air	Semi-fruitful	1st
6 Wed	Libra	Air	Semi-fruitful	1st
7 Thu 7:26 am	Scorpio	Water	Fruitful	1st
8 Fri	Scorpio	Water	Fruitful	2nd 4:20 pm
9 Sat 7:10 pm	Sagittarius	Fire	Barren	2nd
10 Sun	Sagittarius	Fire	Barren	2nd
11 Mon	Sagittarius	Fire	Barren	2nd
12 Tue 7:42 am	Capricorn	Earth	Semi-fruitful	2nd
13 Wed	Capricorn	Earth	Semi-fruitful	2nd
14 Thu 6:56 pm	Aquarius	Air	Barren	2nd
15 Fri	Aquarius	Air	Barren	2nd
16 Sat	Aquarius	Air	Barren	Full 5:16 pm
17 Sun 3:46 am	Pisces	Water	Fruitful	3rd
18 Mon	Pisces	Water	Fruitful	3rd
19 Tue 10:10 am	Aries	Fire	Barren	3rd
20 Wed	Aries	Fire	Barren	3rd
21 Thu 2:38 pm	Taurus	Earth	Semi-fruitful	3rd
22 Fri	Taurus	Earth	Semi-fruitful	3rd
23 Sat 5:48 pm	Gemini	Air	Barren	4th 7:49 pm
24 Sun	Gemini	Air	Barren	4th
25 Mon 8:18 pm	Cancer	Water	Fruitful	4th
26 Tue	Cancer	Water	Fruitful	4th
27 Wed 10:51 pm	Leo	Fire	Barren	4th
28 Thu	Leo	Fire	Barren	4th
29 Fri	Leo	Fire	Barren	4th
30 Sat 2:18 am	Virgo	Earth	Barren	New 3:58 pm
31 Sun	Virgo	Earth	Barren	1st

Aspectarian/Favorable & Unfavorable Days

Date	Sun	Mercury	Venus	Mars	Jupiter	Saturn	Uranus	Neptune	Pluto	Aries	Taurus	Gemini	Cancer	Leo	Virgo	Libra	Scorpio	Sagittarius	Capricorn	Aquarius	Pisces
1	C	C								f	u	f	.	F		f	u	f		U	
2			C					O	T	f	u	f		F		f	u	f		U	
3					T	C					f	u	f		F		f	u	f		U
4			C					O	Q		f	u	f		F		f	u	f		U
5										U		f	u	f		F		f	u	f	
6	X	X			Q			T		U		f	u	f		F		f	u	f	
7			X						X	U		f	u	f		F		f	u	f	
8	Q				X	X					U		f	u	f		F		f	u	f
9		Q		X		T	Q				U		f	u	f		F		f	u	f
10			Q		Q					f		U		f	u	f		F		f	u
11	T			Q		Q	X			f		U		f	u	f		F		f	u
12		T							C	f		U		f	u	f		F		f	u
13			T		C	T				u	f		U		f	u	f		F		f
14			T				X			u	f		U		f	u	f		F		f
15										f	u	f		U		f	u	f		F	
16	O						C			f	u	f		U		f	u	f		F	
17					O			X		f	u	f		U		f	u	f		F	
18		O	O	X		C					f	u	f		U		f	u	f		F
19			O						Q		f	u	f		U		f	u	f		F
20					Q					F		f	u	f		U		f	u	f	
21	T							X	T	F		f	u	f		U		f	u	f	
22					T	T					F		f	u	f		U		f	u	f
23	Q	T	T	T			X	Q			F		f	u	f		U		f	u	f
24					Q					f		F		f	u	f		U		f	u
25		Q	Q			Q	T	O		f		F		f	u	f		U		f	u
26	X			Q	O	X				u	f		F		f	u	f		U		f
27		X	X				T			u	f		F		f	u	f		U		f
28			X							f	u	f		F		f	u	f		U	
29								O	T	f	u	f		F		f	u	f		U	
30	C				C					f	u	f		F		f	u	f		U	
31					T	O					f	u	f		F		f	u	f			U

September Moon Table

Date	Sign	Element	Nature	Phase
1 Mon 7:44 am	Libra	Air	Semi-fruitful	1st
2 Tue	Libra	Air	Semi-fruitful	1st
3 Wed 4:02 pm	Scorpio	Water	Fruitful	1st
4 Thu	Scorpio	Water	Fruitful	1st
5 Fri	Scorpio	Water	Fruitful	1st
6 Sat 3:11 am	Sagittarius	Fire	Barren	1st
7 Sun	Sagittarius	Fire	Barren	2nd 10:04 am
8 Mon 3:45 pm	Capricorn	Earth	Semi-fruitful	2nd
9 Tue	Capricorn	Earth	Semi-fruitful	2nd
10 Wed	Capricorn	Earth	Semi-fruitful	2nd
11 Thu 3:19 am	Aquarius	Air	Barren	2nd
12 Fri	Aquarius	Air	Barren	2nd
13 Sat 12:04 pm	Pisces	Water	Fruitful	2nd
14 Sun	Pisces	Water	Fruitful	2nd
15 Mon 5:39 pm	Aries	Fire	Barren	Full 5:13 am
16 Tue	Aries	Fire	Barren	3rd
17 Wed 8:56 pm	Taurus	Earth	Semi-fruitful	3rd
18 Thu	Taurus	Earth	Semi-fruitful	3rd
19 Fri 11:17 pm	Gemini	Air	Barren	3rd
20 Sat	Gemini	Air	Barren	3rd
21 Sun	Gemini	Air	Barren	3rd
22 Mon 1:48 am	Cancer	Water	Fruitful	4th 1:04 am
23 Tue	Cancer	Water	Fruitful	4th
24 Wed 5:13 am	Leo	Fire	Barren	4th
25 Thu	Leo	Fire	Barren	4th
26 Fri 9:52 am	Virgo	Earth	Barren	4th
27 Sat	Virgo	Earth	Barren	4th
28 Sun 4:05 pm	Libra	Air	Semi-fruitful	4th
29 Mon	Libra	Air	Semi-fruitful	New 4:12 am
30 Tue	Libra	Air	Semi-fruitful	1st

Aspectarian/Favorable & Unfavorable Days

Date	Sun	Mercury	Venus	Mars	Jupiter	Saturn	Uranus	Neptune	Pluto	Aries	Taurus	Gemini	Cancer	Leo	Virgo	Libra	Scorpio	Sagittarius	Capricorn	Aquarius	Pisces
1		C	C	C					Q		f	u	f		F		f	u	f		U
2			Q							U		f	u	f		F		f	u	f	
3						T	X			U		f	u	f		F		f	u	f	
4	X				X	X					U		f	u	f		F		f	u	f
5						T	Q				U		f	u	f		F		f	u	f
6			X								U		f	u	f		F		f	u	f
7		X		X		Q	Q			f		U		f	u	f		F		f	u
8								X	C	f		U		f	u	f		F		f	u
9		Q	Q	Q	C	T				u	f		U		f	u	f		F		f
10	T						X			u	f		U		f	u	f		F		f
11										u	f		U		f	u	f		F		f
12		T	T	T				C		f	u	f		U		f	u	f		F	
13									X	f	u	f		U		f	u	f		F	
14					X	O					f	u	f		U		f	u	f		F
15	O					C		Q			f	u	f		U		f	u	f		F
16			Q							F		f	u	f		U		f	u	f	
17		O	O	O				X	T	F		f	u	f		U		f	u	f	
18					T	T				F		f	u	f		U		f	u	f	
19	T						X	Q		F		f	u	f		U		f	u	f	
20						Q					F		f	u	f		U		f	u	f
21		T	T	T		Q	T	O			F		f	u	f		U		f	u	f
22	Q			O						f		F		f	u	f		U		f	u
23		Q		Q	X	T				u	f		F		f	u	f		U		f
24	X	Q								u	f		F		f	u	f		U		f
25		X						O		f	u	f		F		f	u	f		U	
26			X	X					T	f	u	f		F		f	u	f		U	
27					T	C	O				f	u	f		F		f	u	f		U
28								Q			f	u	f		F		f	u	f		U
29	C			Q						U		f	u	f		F		f	u	f	
30		C		C				T	X	U		f	u	f		F		f	u	f	

151

October Moon Table

Date	Sign	Element	Nature	Phase
1 Wed 12:26 am	Scorpio	Water	Fruitful	1st
2 Thu	Scorpio	Water	Fruitful	1st
3 Fri 11:14 am	Sagittarius	Fire	Barren	1st
4 Sat	Sagittarius	Fire	Barren	1st
5 Sun 11:48 pm	Capricorn	Earth	Semi-fruitful	1st
6 Mon	Capricorn	Earth	Semi-fruitful	1st
7 Tue	Capricorn	Earth	Semi-fruitful	2nd 5:04 am
8 Wed 12:03 pm	Aquarius	Air	Barren	2nd
9 Thu	Aquarius	Air	Barren	2nd
10 Fri 9:31 pm	Pisces	Water	Fruitful	2nd
11 Sat	Pisces	Water	Fruitful	2nd
12 Sun	Pisces	Water	Fruitful	2nd
13 Mon 3:07 am	Aries	Fire	Barren	2nd
14 Tue	Aries	Fire	Barren	Full 4:02 pm
15 Wed 5:31 am	Taurus	Earth	Semi-fruitful	3rd
16 Thu	Taurus	Earth	Semi-fruitful	3rd
17 Fri 6:25 am	Gemini	Air	Barren	3rd
18 Sat	Gemini	Air	Barren	3rd
19 Sun 7:40 am	Cancer	Water	Fruitful	3rd
20 Mon	Cancer	Water	Fruitful	3rd
21 Tue 10:35 am	Leo	Fire	Barren	4th 7:54 am
22 Wed	Leo	Fire	Barren	4th
23 Thu 3:40 pm	Virgo	Earth	Barren	4th
24 Fri	Virgo	Earth	Barren	4th
25 Sat 10:47 pm	Libra	Air	Semi-fruitful	4th
26 Sun	Libra	Air	Semi-fruitful	4th
27 Mon	Libra	Air	Semi-fruitful	4th
28 Tue 7:47 am	Scorpio	Water	Fruitful	New 7:14 pm
29 Wed	Scorpio	Water	Fruitful	1st
30 Thu 6:41 pm	Sagittarius	Fire	Barren	1st
31 Fri	Sagittarius	Fire	Barren	1st

Aspectarian/Favorable & Unfavorable Days

Date	Sun	Mercury	Venus	Mars	Jupiter	Saturn	Uranus	Neptune	Pluto	Aries	Taurus	Gemini	Cancer	Leo	Virgo	Libra	Scorpio	Sagittarius	Capricorn	Aquarius	Pisces
1		C								U		f	u	f		F		f	u	f	
2				X	X	T	Q				U		f	u	f		F		f	u	f
3											U		f	u	f		F		f	u	f
4	X	X			Q					f		U		f	u	f		F		f	u
5						Q	X	C		f		U		f	u	f		F		f	u
6			X							u	f		U		f	u	f		F		f
7	Q	Q	X		C	T	X			u	f		U		f	u	f		F		f
8			Q							u	f		U		f	u	f		F		f
9	T	T								f	u	f		U		f	u	f		F	
10		Q						C	X	f	u	f		U		f	u	f		F	
11				T	X						f	u	f		U		f	u	f		F
12			T		O	C					f	u	f		U		f	u	f		F
13		O							Q		f	u	f		U		f	u	f		F
14	O				Q			X		F		f	u	f		U		f	u	f	
15			O					T		F		f	u	f		U		f	u	f	
16				T	T	X	Q				F		f	u	f		U		f	u	f
17		T	O								F		f	u	f		U		f	u	f
18					Q	Q	T			f		F		f	u	f		U		f	u
19	T	Q							O	f		F		f	u	f		U		f	u
20				T	O	X	T			u	f		F		f	u	f		U		f
21	Q	T								u	f		F		f	u	f		U		f
22		X		Q						f	u	f		F		f	u	f		U	
23	X					O	T			f	u	f		F		f	u	f		U	
24			Q	X	T						f	u	f		F		f	u	f		U
25						C	O		Q		f	u	f		F		f	u	f		U
26			X							U		f	u	f		F		f	u	f	
27		C		Q			T			U		f	u	f		F		f	u	f	
28	C							X		U		f	u	f		F		f	u	f	
29				C	X	X	T				U		f	u	f		F		f	u	f
30							Q				U		f	u	f		F		f	u	f
31										f		U		f	u	f		F		f	u

November Moon Table

Date	Sign	Element	Nature	Phase
1 Sat	Sagittarius	Fire	Barren	1st
2 Sun 6:13 am	Capricorn	Earth	Semi-fruitful	1st
3 Mon	Capricorn	Earth	Semi-fruitful	1st
4 Tue 7:01 pm	Aquarius	Air	Barren	1st
5 Wed	Aquarius	Air	Barren	2nd 11:03 pm
6 Thu	Aquarius	Air	Barren	2nd
7 Fri 5:43 am	Pisces	Water	Fruitful	2nd
8 Sat	Pisces	Water	Fruitful	2nd
9 Sun 12:26 pm	Aries	Fire	Barren	2nd
10 Mon	Aries	Fire	Barren	2nd
11 Tue 3:05 pm	Taurus	Earth	Semi-fruitful	2nd
12 Wed	Taurus	Earth	Semi-fruitful	2nd
13 Thu 3:11 pm	Gemini	Air	Barren	Full 1:17 am
14 Fri	Gemini	Air	Barren	3rd
15 Sat 2:52 pm	Cancer	Water	Fruitful	3rd
16 Sun	Cancer	Water	Fruitful	3rd
17 Mon 4:07 pm	Leo	Fire	Barren	3rd
18 Tue	Leo	Fire	Barren	3rd
19 Wed 8:12 pm	Virgo	Earth	Barren	4th 4:31 pm
20 Thu	Virgo	Earth	Barren	4th
21 Fri	Virgo	Earth	Barren	4th
22 Sat 3:20 am	Libra	Air	Semi-fruitful	4th
23 Sun	Libra	Air	Semi-fruitful	4th
24 Mon 12:54 pm	Scorpio	Water	Fruitful	4th
25 Tue	Scorpio	Water	Fruitful	4th
26 Wed	Scorpio	Water	Fruitful	4th
27 Thu 12:14 am	Sagittarius	Fire	Barren	New 11:54 am
28 Fri	Sagittarius	Fire	Barren	1st
29 Sat 12:48 pm	Capricorn	Earth	Semi-fruitful	1st
30 Sun	Capricorn	Earth	Semi-fruitful	1st

Aspectarian/Favorable & Unfavorable Days

Date	Sun	Mercury	Venus	Mars	Jupiter	Saturn	Uranus	Neptune	Pluto	Aries	Taurus	Gemini	Cancer	Leo	Virgo	Libra	Scorpio	Sagittarius	Capricorn	Aquarius	Pisces
1		X	C			Q	Q	X		F		U		f	u	f		F		f	u
2									C	f		U		f	u	f		F		f	u
3	X				C	T	X			u	f		U	f	u	f			F		f
4		Q		X						u	f		U	f	u	f			F		f
5	Q									f	u	f		U		f	u	f		F	
6			X	Q				C		f	u	f		U		f	u	f		F	
7		T							X	f	u	f		U		f	u	f		F	
8	T				X	O	C				f	u	f		U		f	u	f		F
9			Q	T					Q		f	u	f		U		f	u	f		F
10				Q						F		f	u	f		U		f	u	f	
11			T					X	T	F		f	u	f		U		f	u	f	
12		O			T	T	X				F	f	u	f		U		f	u	f	
13	O			O				Q			F	f	u	f		U		f	u	f	
14					Q	Q				f		F	f	u	f		U		f	u	f
15			O				T	O		f		F	f	u	f		U		f	u	f
16		T			O	X	T			u	f		F	f	u	f		U		f	
17	T			T						u	f		F	f	u	f		U		f	
18										f	u	f		F		f	u	f		U	
19	Q	Q						O	T	f	u	f		F		f	u	f		U	
20			T	Q							f	u	f		F		f	u	f		U
21					T	C	O				f	u	f		F		f	u	f		U
22		X		X					Q		f	u	f		F		f	u	f		U
23			Q		Q			T		U		f	u	f		F		f	u	f	
24								X		U		f	u	f		F		f	u	f	
25			X								U	f	u	f		F		f	u	f	
26				X	X	T	Q				U	f	u	f		F		f	u	f	
27	C	C		C							U	f	u	f		F		f	u	f	
28					Q	Q	X			f		U		f	u	f		F		f	u
29									C	f		U		f	u	f		F		f	u
30										u	f		U		f	u	f			F		f

December Moon Table

Date	Sign	Element	Nature	Phase
1 Thu	Capricorn	Earth	Semi-fruitful	1st
2 Tue 1:44 am	Aquarius	Air	Barren	1st
3 Wed	Aquarius	Air	Barren	1st
4 Thu 1:23 pm	Pisces	Water	Fruitful	1st
5 Fri	Pisces	Water	Fruitful	2nd 4:25 pm
6 Sat 9:44 pm	Aries	Fire	Barren	2nd
7 Sun	Aries	Fire	Barren	2nd
8 Mon	Aries	Fire	Barren	2nd
9 Tue 1:52 am	Taurus	Earth	Semi-fruitful	2nd
10 Wed	Taurus	Earth	Semi-fruitful	2nd
11 Thu 2:33 am	Gemini	Air	Barren	2nd
12 Fri	Gemini	Air	Barren	Full 11:37 am
13 Sat 1:39 am	Cancer	Water	Fruitful	3rd
14 Sun	Cancer	Water	Fruitful	3rd
15 Mon 1:22 am	Leo	Fire	Barren	3rd
16 Tue	Leo	Fire	Barren	3rd
17 Wed 3:35 am	Virgo	Earth	Barren	3rd
18 Thu	Virgo	Earth	Barren	3rd
19 Fri 9:23 am	Libra	Air	Semi-fruitful	4th 5:29 am
20 Sat	Libra	Air	Semi-fruitful	4th
21 Sun 6:36 pm	Scorpio	Water	Fruitful	4th
22 Mon	Scorpio	Water	Fruitful	4th
23 Tue	Scorpio	Water	Fruitful	4th
24 Wed 6:13 am	Sagittarius	Fire	Barren	4th
25 Thu	Sagittarius	Fire	Barren	4th
26 Fri 6:56 pm	Capricorn	Earth	Semi-fruitful	4th
27 Sat	Capricorn	Earth	Semi-fruitful	New 7:22 am
28 Sun	Capricorn	Earth	Semi-fruitful	1st
29 Mon 7:42 am	Aquarius	Air	Barren	1st
30 Tue	Aquarius	Air	Barren	1st
31 Wed 7:27 pm	Pisces	Water	Fruitful	1st

Aspectarian/Favorable & Unfavorable Days

Date	Sun	Mercury	Venus	Mars	Jupiter	Saturn	Uranus	Neptune	Pluto	Aries	Taurus	Gemini	Cancer	Leo	Virgo	Libra	Scorpio	Sagittarius	Capricorn	Aquarius	Pisces
1		C	X	C	T	X				u	f		U		f	u	f		F		f
2										u	f		U		f	u	f		F		f
3	X	X		X					C	f	u	f		U		f	u	f		F	
4								X		f	u	f		U		f	u	f		F	
5			Q								f	u	f		U		f	u	f		F
6		Q	X		X	0	C		Q		f	u	f		U		f	u	f		F
7										F		f	u	f		U		f	u	f	
8	T	T		T	Q			X		F		f	u	f		U		f	u	f	
9		Q							T		F		f	u	f		U		f	u	f
10				T	T	X	Q				F		f	u	f		U		f	u	f
11			T								F		f	u	f		U		f	u	f
12	0			0	Q	Q	T			f		F		f	u	f		U		f	u
13	0								0	f		F		f	u	f		U		f	u
14				0	X	T				u	f		F		f	u	f		U		f
15			0							u	f		F		f	u	f		U		f
16	T			T				0		f	u	f		F		f	u	f		U	
17		T						T		f	u	f		F		f	u	f		U	
18			Q		C	0					f	u	f		F		f	u	f		U
19	Q			T					Q		f	u	f		F		f	u	f		U
20		Q	T							U		f	u	f		F		f	u	f	
21	X			X	Q			T	X	U		f	u	f		F		f	u	f	
22											U		f	u	f		F		f	u	f
23		X	Q		X	T	Q				U		f	u	f		F		f	u	f
24				X							U		f	u	f		F		f	u	f
25						Q				f		U		f	u	f		F		f	u
26			X	C	Q		X	C		f		U		f	u	f		F		f	u
27	C									u	f		U		f	u	f		F		f
28		C				T	X			u	f		U		f	u	f		F		f
29			C							u	f		U		f	u	f		F		f
30										f	u	f		U		f	u	f		F	
31			C					C	X	f	u	f		U		f	u	f		F	

2008 Retrograde Planets

Planet	Begin	Eastern	Pacific	End	Eastern	Pacific
Mars	11/15/07	3:24 am	**12:24 am**	01/30/08	5:33 pm	**2:33 pm**
Saturn	12/19/07	9:09 am	**6:09 am**	05/02/08	11:07 pm	**8:07 pm**
Mercury	01/28/08	3:31 pm	**12:31 pm**	02/18/08	9:57 pm	**6:57 pm**
Pluto	04/02/08	5:23 am	**2:23 am**	09/09/08	11:14 pm	**8:14 pm**
Jupiter	05/09/08	8:11 am	**5:11 am**	09/07/08		**9:16 pm**
				09/08/08	12:16 am	
Mercury	05/26/08	11:48 am	**8:48 am**	06/19/08	10:31 am	**7:31 am**
Neptune	05/26/08	12:14 pm	**9:14 am**	11/01/08	·	**11:38 pm**
				11/02/08	1:38 am	
Uranus	06/26/08	8:01 pm	**5:01 pm**	11/27/08	11:08 am	**8:08 am**
Mercury	09/24.08	3:17 am	**12:17 am**	10/15/08	4:06 pm	**1:06 pm**
Saturn	12/31/08	1:08 pm	**10:08 am**	05/16/09	10:06 pm	**7:06 pm**

Eastern Time in plain type, **Pacific Time in bold type**

	07 Dec	08 Jan	Feb	Mar	Apr	May	Jun	Jul	Aug	Sep	Oct	Nov	Dec	09 Jan
☿			■				■			■				
♀														
♂	■	■												
♃						■	■	■	■					
♄	■	■	■	■	■									■
♅							■	■	■	■	■	■		
♆						■	■	■	■	■	■	■		
♇					■	■	■	■	■	■				

Note: Venus does not turn retrograde in 2008

Egg-setting Dates

Dates to be Born	Sign	Qtr.	Set Eggs
Jan 11 1:44 pm-Jan 13 7:23 pm	Pisces	1st	Dec 21
Jan 15 11:13 pm-Jan 17	Taurus	1st	Dec 25
Jan 20 3:05 am-Jan 22 5:20 am	Cancer	1st	Dec 30
Feb 12 4:34 am-Feb 14 7:19 am	Taurus	1st	Jan 23
Feb 16 10:12 am-Feb 18 1:51 pm	Cancer	1st	Jan 26
Mar 7 12:14 pm-Mar 8 9:23 am	Pisces	1st	Feb 15
Mar 10 11:13 am-Mar 12 12:54 pm	Taurus	1st	Feb 19
Mar 14 3:37 pm-Mar 16 8:04 pm	Cancer	1st	Feb 22
Mar 21 10:45 am-Mar 21 1:40 pm	Libra	1st	Feb 29
Apr 6 9:19 pm-Apr 8 9:27 pm	Taurus	1st	Mar 17
Apr 10 10:43 pm-Apr 13 2:29 am	Cancer	1st	Mar 19
Apr 17 6:10 pm-Apr 20 5:00 am	Libra	1st	Mar 27
May 5 8:18 am-May 6 7:17 am	Taurus	1st	Apr 14
May 8 7:02 am-May 10 9:10 am	Cancer	1st	Apr 17
May 14 11:46 pm-May 17 10:59 am	Libra	1st	Apr 23
Jun 4 5:16 pm-Jun 6 6:00 pm	Cancer	1st	May 15
Jun 11 5:55 am-Jun 13 4:53 pm	Libra	1st	May 17
Jul 2 10:18 pm-Jul 4 4:15 am	Cancer	1st	Jun 11
Jul 8 1:31 pm-Jul 10 11:35 pm	Libra	1st	Jun 20
Aug 4 10:28 pm-Aug 7 7:26 am	Libra	1st	Jul 14
Aug 17 3:46 am-Aug 19 10:10 am	Pisces	1st	Jul 27
Aug 21 2:38 pm-Aug 23 5:48 pm	Taurus	1st	Jul 31
Aug 25 8:18 pm-Aug 27 10:51 pm	Cancer	1st	Aug 4
Sep 1 7:44 am-Sep 3 4:02 pm	Libra	1st	Aug 11
Sep 13 12:04 pm-Sep 15 2:13 am	Pisces	1st	Aug 23
Sep 29 1:12 am-Sep 30	Libra	1st	Sep 8
Oct 10 9:31 pm-Oct 13 3:07 am	Pisces	1st	Sep 19
Nov 7 5:43 am-Nov 9 12:26 pm	Pisces	1st	Oct 19
Nov 11 3:05 pm-Nov 12 10:17 pm	Taurus	1st	Oct 21
Dec 4 1:23 pm-Dec 6 9:44 pm	Pisces	1st	Nov 13
Dec 8 -Dec 9 1:52 am	Taurus	1st	Nov 17

Dates to Hunt or Fish

Jan 1, 8:32 pm-Jan 4, 9:13 am	4th	Scorpio
Jan 11, 1:44 pm-Jan 13, 7:23 pm	1st	Pisces
Jan 20, 3:05 am-Jan 22, 5:20 am	2nd	Cancer
Jan 29, 4:35 am-Jan 31, 5:08 pm	3rd	Scorpio
Feb 16, 10:12 am-Feb 18, 1:51 pm	2nd	Cancer
Feb 25, 1:05 pm-Feb 27,	3rd	Scorpio
Feb 28, 1:22 am-March 1, 1:33 pm	3rd	Sagittarius
March 6, 5:53 am-March 8, 9:23 am	4th	Pisces
March 14, 3:37 pm-March 16, 8:04 pm	2nd	Cancer
March 23, 10:06 pm-March 26, 10:11 am	3rd	Scorpio
March 26, 10:11 am-March 28, 10:43 pm	3rd	Sagittarius
Apr 2, 3:55 pm-Apr 4, 7:27 pm	4th	Pisces
Apr 10, 10:43 pm-Apr 13, 2:29 am	1st	Cancer
Apr 20, 5:00 am-Apr 22, 5:07 pm	2nd	Scorpio
Apr 22, 5:07 pm-Apr 25, 5:47 am	3rd	Sagittarius
Apr 29, 5:27 pm-Apr 30, 2:11 am	4th	Pisces
Apr 30, 2:11 am-May 2, 6:51 am	4th	Pisces
May 8, 7:02 am-May 10, 9:10 am	1st	Cancer
May 17, 10:59 am-May 19, 11:18 pm	2nd	Scorpio
May 19, 11:18 pm-May 22, 11:55 am	3rd	Sagittarius
May 27, 9:38 am-May 29, 3:52 pm	3rd	Pisces
Jun 4, 5:16 pm-Jun 6, 6:00 pm	1st	Cancer
Jun 13, 4:53 pm-Jun 16, 5:19 am	2nd	Scorpio
Jun 16, 5:19 am-Jun 18, 5:51 pm	2nd	Sagittarius
Jun 23, 3:32 pm-Jun 25, 10:49 pm	3rd	Pisces
Jun 25, 10:49 pm-Jun 28, 2:50 am	3rd	Aries

Jul 2, 3:53 am-Jul 4, 4:15 am	4th	Cancer
Jul 10, 11:35 pm-Jul 13, 11:50 am	2nd	Scorpio
Jul 13, 11:50 am-Jul 16, 12:20 am	2nd	Sagittarius
Jul 20, 9:07 pm-Jul 23, 4:22 am	3rd	Pisces
Jul 23, 4:22 am-Jul 25, 9:14 am	3rd	Aries
Jul 29, 1:11 pm-Jul 31, 2:21 pm	4th	Cancer
Aug 7, 7:26 am-Aug 9, 7:10 pm	1st	Scorpio
Aug 9, 7:10 pm-Aug 12, 7:42 am	2nd	Sagittarius
Aug 17, 3:46 am-Aug 19, 10:10 am	2nd	Pisces
Aug 19, 10:10 am-Aug 21, 2:38 pm	2nd	Aries
Aug 25, 8:18 pm-Aug 27, 10:51 pm	4th	Cancer
Sep 3, 4:02 pm-Sep 6, 3:11 am	1st	Scorpio
Sep 13, 12:04 pm-Sep 15, 5:39 pm	2nd	Pisces
Sep 15, 5:39 pm-Sep 17, 8:56 pm	3rd	Aries
Sep 21, 1:48 am-Sep 22, 1:48 am	4th	Cancer
Sep 22, 1:48 am-Sep 24, 5:13 am	4th	Cancer
Oct 1, 12:26 am-Oct 3, 11:14 am	1st	Scorpio
Oct 10, 9:31 pm-Oct 13, 3:07 am	2nd	Pisces
Oct 13, 3:07 am-Oct 15, 5:31 am	2nd	Aries
Oct 19, 7:40 am-Oct 21, 10:35 am	3rd	Cancer
Oct 28, 7:47 am-Oct 30, 6:41 pm	4th	Scorpio
Nov 7, 5:43 am-Nov 9, 12:26 pm	2nd	Pisces
Nov 9, 12:26 pm-Nov 11, 3:05 pm	2nd	Aries
Nov 15, 2:52 pm-Nov 17, 4:07 pm	3rd	Cancer
Nov 24, 12:54 pm-Nov 27, 12:14 am	4th	Scorpio
Dec 4, 1:23 pm-Dec 6, 9:44 pm	1st	Pisces
Dec 6, 9:44 pm-Dec 8, 4:35 pm	2nd	Aries
Dec 13, 1:39 am-Dec 15, 1:22 am	3rd	Cancer

Fire signs Aries, Leo, and Sagittarius are best for hunting.
Water signs Cancer, Scorpio, and Pisces are best for fishing.

Time Zone Map

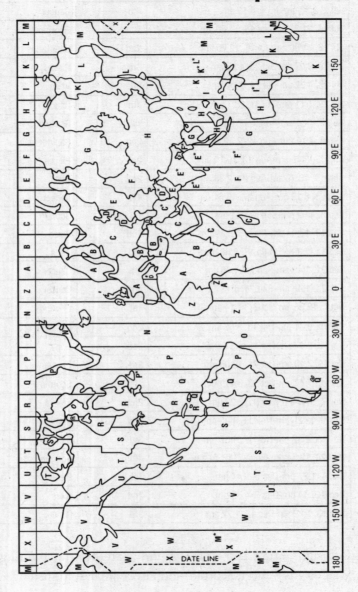

Time Zone Conversions

World Time Zones Compared to Eastern Time

(R) EST—Used in book
(S) CST—Subtract 1 hour
(T) MST—Subtract 2 hours
(U) PST—Subtract 3 hours
(V) Subtract 4 hours
(V*) Subtract 4½ hours
(U*) Subtract 3½ hours
(W) Subtract 5 hours
(X) Subtract 6 hours
(Y) Subtract 7 hours
(Q) Add 1 hour
(P) Add 2 hours
(P*) Add 2½ hours
(O) Add 3 hours
(N) Add 4 hours
(Z) Add 5 hours
(A) Add 6 hours
(B) Add 7 hours
(C) Add 8 hours
(C*) Add 8½ hours

(D) Add 9 hours
(D*) Add 9½ hours
(E) Add 10 hours
(E*) Add 10½ hours
(F) Add 11 hours
(F*) Add 11½ hours
(G) Add 12 hours
(H) Add 13 hours
(I) Add 14 hours
(I*) Add 14½ hours
(K) Add 15 hours
(K*) Add 15½ hours
(L) Add 16 hours
(L*) Add 16½ hours
(M) Add 17 hours
(M*) Add 18 hours
(P*) Add 2½ hours

Important!

All times given in the *Moon Sign Book* are set in Eastern Time. The conversions shown here are for standard times only. Use the time zone conversions map and table to calculate the difference in your time zone. You must make the adjustment for your time zone and adjust for Daylight Saving Time where applicable.

Weather Forecasting

By Kris Brandt Riske

Astrometeorology—astrological weather forecasting—reveals seasonal and weekly weather trends based on the cardinal ingresses (Summer and Winter Solstices, and Spring and Autumn Equinoxes) and the four monthly lunar phases. The planetary alignments and the longitudes and latitudes they influence have the strongest effect, but the zodiacal signs are also involved in creating weather conditions.

The components of a thunderstorm, for example, are heat, wind, and electricity. A Mars-Jupiter configuration generates the necessary heat and Mercury adds wind and electricity. A severe thunderstorm, and those that produce tornados, usually involve Mercury, Mars, Uranus, or Neptune. The zodiacal signs add their energy to the planetary mix to increase or decrease the chance of weather phenomena and their severity.

In general, the fire signs (Aries, Leo, Sagittarius) indicate heat and dryness, both of which peak when Mars, the planet with a similar nature, is in these signs. Water signs (Cancer, Scorpio, Pisces) are conducive to precipitation, and air signs (Gemini, Libra, Aquarius) to cool temperatures and wind. Earth signs (Taurus, Virgo, Capricorn) vary from wet to dry, heat to cold. The signs and their prevailing weather conditions are listed here:

Aries: Heat, dry, wind
Taurus: Moderate temperatures, precipitation
Gemini: Cool temperatures, wind, dry
Cancer: Cold, steady precipitation
Leo: Heat, dry, lightning
Virgo: Cold, dry, windy
Libra: Cool, windy, fair
Scorpio: Extreme temperatures, abundant precipitation
Sagittarius: Warm, fair, moderate wind
Capricorn: Cold, wet, damp
Aquarius: Cold, dry, high pressure, lightning
Pisces: Wet, cool, low pressure

Take note of the Moon's sign at each lunar phase. It reveals the prevailing weather conditions for the next six to seven days. The same is true of Mercury and Venus. These two influential weather planets transit the entire zodiac each year, unless retrograde patterns add their influence.

Planetary Influences

People relied on astrology to forecast weather for thousands of years. They were able to predict drought, floods, and temperature variations through interpreting planetary alignments. In recent years there has been a renewed interest in astrometeorology. A weather forecast can be composed for any date—tomorrow, next week, or a thousand years in the future. Astrometeorology reveals seasonal and weekly weather trends based on the cardinal ingresses (Summer and Winter Solstices, and Spring and Fall Equinoxes) and the four lunar phases that occur monthly in combination with the transiting planets. According to astrometeorology, each planet governs certain weather phenomena. When certain planets are aligned with other planets, weather—precipitation, cloudy or clear skies, tornados, hurricanes, and other conditions—are generated.

Sun and Moon

The Sun governs the constitution of the weather and, like the Moon, it serves as a trigger for other planetary configurations that result in weather events. When the Sun is prominent in a cardinal ingress or lunar phase chart, the area is often warm and sunny. The Moon can bring or withhold moisture, depending upon its sign placement.

Mercury

Mercury is also a triggering planet, but its main influence is wind direction and velocity. In its stationary periods, Mercury reflects high winds, and its influence is always prominent in major weather events, such as hurricanes and tornados, when it tends to lower the temperature.

Venus

Venus governs moisture, clouds, and humidity. It brings warming trends that produce sunny, pleasant weather if in positive aspect to other planets. In some signs—Libra, Virgo, Gemini, Sagittarius—Venus is drier. It is at its wettest when placed in Cancer, Scorpio, Pisces, or Taurus.

Mars

Mars is associated with heat, drought, and wind, and can raise the temperature to record-setting levels when in a fire sign (Aries, Leo, Sagittarius). Mars also provides the spark that generates thunderstorms and is prominent in tornado and hurricane configurations.

Jupiter

Jupiter, a fair-weather planet, tends toward higher temperatures when in Aries, Leo, or Sagittarius. It is associated with high-pressure systems and is a contributing factor at times to dryness. Storms are often amplified by Jupiter.

Saturn

Saturn is associated with low-pressure systems, cloudy to overcast skies, and excessive precipitation. Temperatures drop when Saturn is involved. Major winter storms always have a strong Saturn influence, as do storms that produce a slow, steady downpour for hours or days.

Uranus

Like Jupiter, Uranus indicates high-pressure systems. It reflects descending cold air and, when prominent, is responsible for a jet stream that extends far south. Uranus can bring drought in winter, and it is involved in thunderstorms, tornados, and hurricanes.

Neptune

Neptune is the wettest planet. It signals low-pressure systems and is dominant when hurricanes are in the forecast. When Neptune is strongly placed, flood danger is high. It's often associated with winter thaws. Temperatures, humidity, and cloudiness increase where Neptune influences weather.

Pluto

Pluto is associated with weather extremes, as well as unseasonably warm temperatures and drought. It reflects the high winds involved in major hurricanes, storms, and tornados.

Severe Weather Forecast for 2008

By Kris Brandt Riske

Winter

The western third of the continental U.S. can expect temperatures below normal and significant precipitation, especially in Washington, Oregon, southern California, and throughout the Rocky Mountains and foothills. Temperatures will be coldest, however, from Wisconsin south to Louisiana. Michigan and areas to the south also can expect abundant downfall. Although the Plains will be more temperate, these states will also see significant precipitation at times. Significant winter weather events include:

- Abundant downfall in the eastern third of the continental United States and California, and a storm front that advances across the Plains.

- The second week of January features another front moving into California before advancing into Nevada, Utah, and Arizona, and abundant downfall in the Plains later in the week.
- The Plains states should prepare for potential blizzard conditions the week of January 22.
- The front that moves through the Plains will advance into areas to the east at the end of January and early February, when another system brings abundant precipitation to the western Plains.
- Temperatures dip throughout most of the continental U.S. the week of February 20.
- The central Plains, especially more southern areas, see abundant precipitation the second and third weeks of March, along with the potential for flooding and tornados.

Spring

There is potential for very severe tornados in 2008. Areas from the Plains to Michigan and points south can expect a colder than normal spring, along with thunderstorms with tornado conditions. The western third of the continental U.S. continues to see abundant downfall, along with cool temperatures in many areas and flood potential throughout the mountain west, foothills, and the central and southern Plains. The northeastern U.S. also sees abundant downfall at times. Weather highlights during the spring season include:

- Severe thunderstorms with tornado potential in the southern Plains and southeastern U.S. the week of March 21.
- Possible tornados along with abundant precipitation in the Plains at the end of March and into early April, while Eastern areas are stormy.
- The severe thunderstorm/tornado trend continues into the second week of April in the Plains and from Indiana and Ohio south, along with abundant precipitation, with the most severe weather occurring in the southern Plains.

- Severe thunderstorms with abundant precipitation and tornado potential pop up again the end of April and early May throughout the Plains and areas to the east from Ohio south.
- The weeks of May 12 and 19 also feature severe thunderstorms with tornado potential, with weather centering in the Plains the first week, and throughout much of the eastern two-thirds of the U.S. the second week.

Summer

Severe tornado potential continues into the summer season, along with an above average potential for hurricanes in the Gulf and southeastern coastal areas. Temperatures range from below to above normal throughout much of the Rocky Mountain west, the Plains, Mississippi River Valley, northeast, and southeast, along with significant precipitation and flood potential in many of these areas. Potential weather patterns include:

- Severe thunderstorms with tornado potential from mid-June into early July in the Plains and areas from Ohio and Indiana south, as well as in the southeastern states, and again the weeks of July 10 and 25.
- High potential for hurricanes throughout July on the East Coast and in the Gulf the weeks of July 2 and 18, and again on the East Coast the end of July.
- Hurricane potential is high the week of August 30 and September 7 for the Gulf States, as is the week of September 15 for the southeastern U.S.
- Severe thunderstorms with tornado potential pop up across the Plains and throughout much of the eastern third of the U.S. the weeks of August 1 and 8, and again in the Plains the weeks of August 23 and 30.

Autumn

Cooler conditions, along with significant precipitation, continue to dominate in the Rocky Mountain region, Plains states, and much of the eastern third of the U.S. Severe weather potential will include:

- High flood potential in the Mississippi River Valley, as well as areas from Michigan to Alabama.
- High hurricane potential the week of September 22 for the Gulf States, and the weeks of October 7 and 14 for the East Coast and Gulf.
- The central Plains and Mississippi River Valley areas are prone to flooding from significant precipitation the week of October 7.
- The Plains see the season's first major winter storm with abundant downfall and cold temperatures the week of October 14.
- Storm conditions prevail the week of November 13 in the northeastern U.S.

More Weather in 2008

A more complete weather forecast by Kris Brandt Riske begins on the next page.

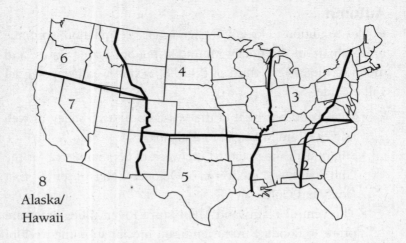

2008 Weather Forecast

By Kris Brandt Riske

Winter

Zone 1: Temperatures and precipitation are average.

Zone 2: Temperatures are seasonal and precipitation is average to below.

Zone 3: Abundant precipitation west could trigger flooding, and central and eastern areas see average downfall. Temperatures are seasonal.

Zone 4: The zone is windy with temperatures seasonal to below, and precipitation average to abundant in eastern areas with flood potential.

Zone 5: The zone is windy with major storms, but precipitation is average to below.

Zone 6: Cloudy and stormy east and central, while western areas see average precipitation. Temperatures are seasonal.

Zone 7: Western and central areas are cloudy with above average precipitation, and zonal temperatures are average. Eastern areas are dry south, with more downfall north.

Zone 8: Alaska's precipitation is average to above, and temperatures are seasonal to below. Hawaii is seasonal and windy.

3rd Quarter Moon, December 31, 2007

Zone 1: Northern areas are fair to partly cloudy, and southern parts of the zone are cloudy with abundant precipitation. Temperatures are seasonal to below.

Zone 2: Much of the zone is windy with precipitation; heaviest downfall north, where conditions are stormy. Temperatures are seasonal to below.

Zone 3: Temperatures dip, especially north, and the zone is windy and cloudy with heaviest downfall east.

Zone 4: Western and central areas are windy with precipitation as a front moves through the area, followed by colder temperatures. Eastern areas are cold with variable cloudiness and scattered precipitation.

Zone 5: Much of the south-central zone is cold, windy, and cloudy with precipitation.

Zone 6: Central and eastern areas are cold with precipitation, and seasonal but windy conditions prevail to the west.

Zone 7: Western areas are mostly fair and cool with scattered precipitation north. Central and eastern parts of the zone see precipitation.

Zone 8: Western and central Alaska see precipitation, with drier, colder weather east. Central and eastern Hawaii are overcast and wet, with significant precipitation in some areas. Temperatures are seasonal, and western areas see scattered showers.

New Moon, January 8

Zone 1: The zone is windy and seasonal, with precipitation primarily north.

Zone 2: Northern areas are windy with scattered precipitation. Increasing clouds south bring precipitation later in the week.

Zone 3: Western and central areas are partly cloudy with scattered precipitation, while the east sees more cloudiness and wind with precipitation.

Zone 4: The zone is variably cloudy with a chance for precipitation east. Storms later in the week in Western areas will advance into the Plains.

Zone 5: Eastern areas are cloudy with scattered precipitation, and western and central areas are stormy and very windy.

Zone 6: Western and central areas are seasonal, and eastern areas colder. Skies across the zone are partly cloudy to cloudy with precipitation, the heaviest downfall occurring central and east.

Zone 7: Conditions are cloudy and wet as a front travels across the zone, bringing more precipitation north. Temperatures are seasonal to below.

Zone 8: Central and eastern Alaska are very windy as a front advances, bringing precipitation. Increasing clouds west later in the week bring precipitation. Hawaii is cool and windy with scattered precipitation.

First Quarter Moon, January 15

Zone 1: Temperatures are seasonal to below and cloudy skies yield scattered precipitation.

Zone 2: Northern areas are partly cloudy, and central and southern areas windy with precipitation. Temperatures are seasonal to below.

Zone 3: Western and central areas are cloudy with precipitation, and fair and windy skies prevail to the east.

Zone 4: Western areas are mostly fair and seasonal as a front moves into central areas of the zone bringing high winds and precipitation. Eastern areas, especially north, are cloudy with scattered precipitation and then clearing. Temperatures are seasonal to below.

Zone 5: Western areas see scattered precipitation, and central parts of the zone are windy with more downfall. Eastern parts of the zone are mostly fair, windy, and seasonal.

Zone 6: The zone is windy and fair to partly cloudy with a chance for precipitation central and east.

Zone 7: The zone is fair to partly cloudy with more cloudiness south and in the central mountains. Eastern areas see precipitation. Temperatures are seasonal to below.

Zone 8: Alaska is stormy and cold central and east, and mostly fair and seasonal west. Hawaii sees showers central and east, where temperatures are cooler than to the west, which is mostly fair.

Full Moon, January 22

Zone 1: Northern areas are windy and cold with precipitation, while skies are fair to partly cloudy south.

Zone 2: Much of the zone is cloudy with precipitation.

Zone 3: Western and central areas are mostly fair to partly cloudy with a chance for precipitation. Eastern areas are cloudy with precipitation.

Zone 4: Much of the zone sees precipitation, with the heaviest downfall and blizzard potential to the east.

Zone 5: Precipitation in western areas moves into central and eastern areas of the zone, bringing cooler temperatures. Heaviest downfall occurs east, possibly a blizzard.

Zone 6: Temperatures are seasonal to below with scattered precipitation west. Central and eastern areas are windy and fair to partly cloudy.

Zone 7: Central and eastern areas are fair to partly cloudy and windy with a chance for precipitation. Eastern areas are partly cloudy to cloudy with precipitation. Temperatures range from seasonal to below.

Zone 8: Alaska is cold, windy, and variably cloudy with precipitation west and east. Hawaii is seasonal, mostly fair, and breezy.

Third Quarter Moon, January 30

Zone 1: The zone is windy and cold with precipitation.

Zone 2: Much of the southeast coast is cold and windy with scattered precipitation.

Zone 3: Western and central areas are cloudy and windy with significant downfall in some areas, and eastern parts of the zone are partly cloudy and cold with scattered precipitation.

Zone 4: Precipitation moves across much of the zone, and is heaviest to the west. Eastern areas are fair to partly cloudy and windy.

Zone 5: Clouds increase across the zone, bringing heavy downfall to much of the zone. Temperatures are seasonal to below.

Zone 6: Western and central parts of the zone are windy with precipitation, and areas to the east are colder and fair to partly cloudy.

Zone 7: The zone is windy and fair to partly cloudy with temperatures ranging from seasonal to below.

Zone 8: Much of Alaska is cloudy and wet, with abundant downfall central. Hawaii is cloudy with precipitation, some abundant, central and east, and fair to partly cloudy west.

New Moon, February 6

Zone 1: The zone is cold, windy, and fair.

Zone 2: Partly cloudy skies north bring scattered precipitation. Central and southern areas are cloudy with precipitation, some abundant, and then clearing and colder.

Zone 3: Temperatures are seasonal to below, and western skies are mostly fair. Cloudy skies prevail central and east with abundant downfall in some areas.

Zone 4: Western and eastern areas are mostly fair and seasonal, and central parts of the zone are windy with precipitation.

Zone 5: The zone is windy and variably cloudy with temperatures seasonal to below and precipitation central and east.

Zone 6: Central areas are mostly fair and cold with a chance for precipitation, and eastern areas are cloudy with precipitation later in the week. Western parts of the zone are windy with

precipitation, fog, and potential for thawing at higher elevations.

Zone 7: Most of the zone is fair and seasonal, but the desert is hot. Clouds developing later in the week bring precipitation to western and central areas.

Zone 8: Much of Alaska is wet, with heaviest downfall east. Hawaii sees scattered showers, mostly east, seasonal temperatures, and variable cloudiness.

First Quarter Moon, February 13

Zone 1: The zone is cold and fair to partly cloudy.

Zone 2: Much of the zone is windy, with precipitation north and fair to partly cloudy skies central and south. Temperatures are seasonal to below.

Zone 3: Western areas are fair to partly cloudy, and eastern parts of the zone see precipitation. Temperatures range from seasonal to below.

Zone 4: Skies are windy and partly cloudy west and central and fair to the east. Temperatures are seasonal to below.

Zone 5: Much of the zone is windy, and western areas are partly cloudy and cold. Central and eastern areas are fair to partly cloudy and seasonal.

Zone 6: Western parts of the zone are windy and partly cloudy with scattered precipitation. Skies are mostly fair central and east, which are cold, with scattered precipitation east.

Zone 7: Coastal and mountain areas are mostly fair with a chance for precipitation. Eastern areas are partly cloudy and windy with scattered precipitation. Temperatures range from seasonal to below.

Zone 8: Eastern and western Alaska see precipitation, and central areas are mostly fair. Colder weather prevails west and central. Hawaii is windy and stormy west, and windy and fair to partly cloudy central and east, with temperatures seasonal to below.

Full Moon, February 20

Zone 1: The zone is wet, cold, and windy.

Zone 2: Northern areas are cold with precipitation, and central and southern parts of the zone are windy with scattered precipitation and temperatures seasonal to below.

Zone 3: Skies are partly cloudy west and fair and windy central, and eastern areas see precipitation. Temperatures range from seasonal to below.

Zone 4: Partly cloudy to cloudy skies west yield scattered precipitation. Central and eastern areas are fair to partly cloudy with a chance for precipitation east. Temperatures are seasonal to below.

Zone 5: Temperatures are seasonal to below, and partly cloudy to cloudy skies west signal precipitation. Central areas are fair, and eastern areas partly cloudy.

Zone 6: Eastern parts of the zone are mostly fair, windy, and cold. Central areas are windy and cloudy with precipitation that moves in from the west.

Zone 7: Coastal and central areas are windy with precipitation. Eastern areas are cold, partly cloudy, and very windy.

Zone 8: Variable cloudiness brings precipitation across Alaska, along with a new storm front west later in the week. Hawaii is cloudy with precipitation central and east, and mostly fair west.

Third Quarter Moon, February 28

Zone 1: Most of the zone is windy and partly cloudy, cold north and more seasonal south.

Zone 2: The zone is fair to partly cloudy with temperatures ranging from seasonal to below.

Zone 3: Western and central areas are cloudy with precipitation, some abundant, and fair skies prevail to the east. Temperatures are seasonal.

Zone 4: Precipitation moves across the zone with heaviest downfall in central areas.

Zone 5: Much of the zone is cloudy, wet, and windy with abundant downfall east.

Zone 6: The zone is fair to partly cloudy with a chance for precipitation east, and temperatures ranging from seasonal to below.

Zone 7: The zone is fair to partly cloudy with a chance for precipitation central and east, and temperatures seasonal to below.

Zone 8: Overcast skies yield significant downfall in central and eastern Alaska, and western areas are fair to partly cloudy. In

Hawaii, skies are fair to partly cloudy west and central, and eastern areas are cooler with precipitation.

New Moon, March 7

Zone 1: Temperatures are seasonal to below and skies fair to partly cloudy with a chance for precipitation.

Zone 2: The zone is fair with temperatures ranging from seasonal to below.

Zone 3: Western areas are cloudy and windy with precipitation, central areas are mostly fair, and cold, wet weather prevails to the east.

Zone 4: Conditions are stormy west and central with abundant precipitation in the western Plains. Eastern areas are cloudy with windy and precipitation.

Zone 5: Western areas are windy with scattered precipitation, and central and eastern parts of the zone are stormy with flood potential. Tornados are possible.

Zone 6: Eastern areas are fair and seasonal. Western and central parts of the zone are partly cloudy, cold, and windy with scattered precipitation.

Zone 7: Coastal precipitation advances into central areas, where downfall is heaviest under cloudy skies. Eastern areas are fair and windy.

Zone 8: Western and central Alaska are stormy and cold with high winds, and eastern areas see precipitation. Hawaii is mostly fair and seasonal with scattered precipitation.

First Quarter Moon, March 14

Zone 1: The zone is fair to partly cloudy and seasonal, with increasing clouds and precipitation north later in the week.

Zone 2: Fair and seasonal weather prevails across the zone.

Zone 3: Central and eastern areas are mostly fair, while western parts of the zone see precipitation, some abundant. Temperatures are seasonal to below.

Zone 4: Overcast skies across much of the zone yield abundant precipitation and elevate flood potential. Temperatures are seasonal to below.

Zone 5: Conditions are cloudy and windy with precipitation, which is heaviest to the east.

Zone 6: Cloudy, windy, wet weather west moves into central parts of the zone.

Eastern areas are mostly fair. Temperatures are seasonal to below.

Zone 7: Variable cloudiness produces scattered precipitation west and abundant downfall in some central areas. Eastern parts of the zone are fair and windy, and the desert is hot.

Zone 8: Western Alaska is stormy and cold, and central and eastern parts of the state are fair to partly cloudy. Hawaii is windy and mostly fair with scattered precipitation in some areas.

Spring

Zone 1: Precipitation is average to below, with severe storms north, and temperatures are seasonal to above.

Zone 2: Severe storms across the zone yield average precipitation, and temperatures are seasonal to above.

Zone 3: Precipitation is average to below, but central and eastern areas see severe thunderstorms. Temperatures are seasonal to above.

Zone 4: The zone is seasonal to cool with above average precipitation west, dry to average downfall in the western Plains, and average precipitation east with severe thunderstorms.

Zone 5: Western areas receive abundant precipitation, which is below average central, and eastern areas see severe thunderstorms. Temperatures are seasonal to cool.

Zone 6: Cloudy skies and average to above precipitation accompany cool temperatures.

Zone 7: Temperatures and precipitation are seasonal to above, and cloudiness prevails.

Zone 8: Alaska is windy with temperatures seasonal to below, and cloudy with precipitation average to above. Hawaii is fair to partly cloudy with temperatures and precipitation average to below.

Full Moon, March 21

Zone 1: The zone is windy with increasing clouds and precipitation, and temperatures ranging from seasonal to below.

Zone 2: Temperatures dip across much of the zone. Northern areas have a chance for precipitation, and central and southern areas see downfalls later in the week. Tornados are possible.

Zone 3: Western skies are partly cloudy with scattered precipitation, and central and eastern areas are cool and cloudy with precipitation east.

Zone 4: The zone is fair to partly cloudy and windy, and eastern areas have a chance for precipitation.

Zone 5: Skies are fair to partly cloudy across the zone with a chance for thunderstorms, some severe with tornado potential, to the east, which is more cloudy.

Zone 6: Windy, cloudy skies yield precipitation across the zone, which is heaviest west.

Zone 7: Western areas are overcast with precipitation, which moves into central and eastern areas, where clouds increase and temperatures dip.

Zone 8: Alaska is fair to partly cloudy with scattered precipitation and temperatures seasonal to below. Hawaii is fair to partly cloudy, windy, and seasonal with a chance for precipitation east.

Third Quarter Moon, March 29

Zone 1: There is precipitation across the zone, some abundant, and seasonal temperatures. It's windy and stormy to the south.

Zone 2: Northern parts of the zone are stormy, and fair weather prevails central and south. Temperatures are seasonal.

Zone 3: The zone is fair to partly cloudy and seasonal except for eastern areas, which are stormy with high winds and precipitation.

Zone 4: The zone is cloudy with precipitation, some abundant central and west, and temperatures seasonal to below. Tornados are possible.

Zone 5: Variable cloudiness brings precipitation to much of the zone, with heavy downfall west, and tornado potential.

Zone 6: Western areas are cloudy and cool with scattered precipitation. Central parts of the zone see precipitation, which moves into eastern areas, which are very windy.

Zone 7: Western, central, and northernmost eastern areas see variable cloudiness and scattered precipitation. The desert is fair.

Zone 8: Much of Alaska sees precipitation, some abundant to the east, which is windy. Temperatures are cold west and seasonal central and east. Hawaii is windy with precipitation across the zone as a front advances. Temperatures are seasonal to above.

New Moon, April 5

Zone 1: The zone is partly cloudy to cloudy with showers, severe thunderstorms, and seasonal temperatures.

Zone 2: Northern areas see precipitation, and central and southern areas are mostly fair with scattered precipitation south.

Zone 3: Eastern areas are cloudy with precipitation, and western and central parts of the zone are windy with scattered thunderstorms, some severe. Temperatures are seasonal to below.

Zone 4: Western and central skies are cloudy with precipitation, some abundant, and severe thunderstorms are possible central and east. Temperatures are seasonal to below.

Zone 5: Eastern areas are fair to partly cloudy and breezy. Western areas see scattered precipitation, and central parts of the zone are cloudy with abundant downfall and severe thunderstorms.

Zone 6: Western areas are windy and mostly fair, and central and eastern areas are variably cloudy with scattered precipitation. Temperatures are seasonal to below.

Zone 7: Much of the zone sees precipitation, which is heaviest to the east, and temperatures are seasonal to below.

Zone 8: Alaska is stormy and windy with some areas receiving abundant downfall. Temperatures are seasonal to below. Hawaii is warm, fair, and windy east with precipitation west and central.

First Quarter Moon, April 12

Zone 1: Northern areas are cloudy with showers, severe thunderstorms, and significant downfall, and southern areas are fair to partly cloudy. Temperatures range from seasonal to below.

Zone 2: Northern skies are mostly fair and windy, but some areas see severe thunderstorms. Southern parts of the zone are windy and mostly fair with scattered showers.

Zone 3: Western areas are partly cloudy to cloudy with precipitation later in the week. Central and eastern areas are partly cloudy and windy with scattered showers and thunderstorms.

Zone 4: Tornados are possible with stormy conditions and significant downfall west and central. Eastern areas are fair to partly cloudy with a chance for showers.

Zone 5: Eastern areas are fair, and western and central parts of the zone are windy with scattered precipitation.

Zone 6: The zone is fair to partly cloudy, with showers and thunderstorms east.

Zone 7: Western and central areas see precipitation later in the week, and cloudy eastern skies yield precipitation before becoming fair. Temperatures rise in the desert.

Zone 8: Central and eastern Alaska are cloudy with precipitation, and western areas are mostly fair. Eastern Hawaii sees showers, some with abundant downfall, and western and central areas are fair to partly cloudy.

Full Moon, April 20

Zone 1: Rising temperatures spark thunderstorms, some severe, across the zone.

Zone 2: Central and southern areas are fair to partly cloudy, and northern parts of the zone see thunderstorms, some severe. Temperatures are seasonal to above.

Zone 3: Western and central areas are mostly fair and humid with a chance for thunderstorms, which are severe to the east. Temperatures range from seasonal to above.

Zone 4: Eastern parts of the zone are windy with scattered thunderstorms, and western and central areas see thunderstorms, some severe.

Zone 5: Central and eastern areas are humid and fair to partly cloudy with scattered thunderstorms and high winds, and western areas see thunderstorms. Temperatures are seasonal to above.

Zone 6: Cloudy skies yield significant precipitation west before the weather front advances to bring showers to central and eastern areas, which are initially fair to partly cloudy. Temperatures are seasonal to below.

Zone 7: Northern coastal areas are cloudy with precipitation, southern coastal and central parts of the zone are fair to partly cloudy. Northern areas to the east see scattered showers and precipitation, and the desert is fair to partly cloudy.

Zone 8: Much of Alaska is windy and cloudy with precipitation. Hawaii is windy and cloudy with precipitation east, and fair to partly cloudy central and west with scattered thunderstorms. Temperatures range from seasonal to above.

Third Quarter Moon, April 28

Zone 1: Variable cloudiness brings scattered showers and thunderstorms across the zone.

Zone 2: Northern areas see scattered thunderstorms, and areas to the south are fair with a chance for showers.

Zone 3: Thunderstorms, some severe with tornado potential, occur to the west, and central and eastern areas have a chance for showers and thunderstorms.

Zone 4: Much of the zone sees thunderstorms, the most severe with tornado potential in western and central areas, along with significant downfall.

Zone 5: Showers and thunderstorms west yield heavy downfall in some areas, and central parts of the zone see scattered showers and thunderstorms. Eastern areas are fair to partly cloudy with high winds and scattered thunderstorms, some severe with tornado potential, later in the week.

Zone 6: The zone is variably cloudy and seasonal, with precipitation, some abundant, central and east.

Zone 7: Much of the zone is fair to partly cloudy with temperatures seasonal to above. Northern coastal areas and central mountains see showers.

Zone 8: Alaska is cloudy with precipitation central and east, and fair west. Temperatures are seasonal to below. Hawaii is windy with precipitation east, and fair to partly cloudy west and central with scattered showers.

New Moon, May 5

Zone 1: The zone is windy, cloudy, and cool with scattered precipitation.

Zone 2: Northern areas are cloudy and windy, and central and southern areas are humid with scattered thunderstorms and temperatures seasonal to above.

Zone 3: Temperatures are seasonal to above west and central, and cooler but cloudy and humid with scattered showers and thunderstorms east.

Zone 4: Skies clear to the west and temperatures rise as precipitation advances into central and eastern parts of the zone.

Zone 5: Western parts of the zone are warm and fair, and central and eastern areas are mostly fair with scattered showers.

Zone 6: Conditions are fair to partly cloudy west, with increasing clouds, cooler temperatures, showers, and thunderstorms central and east.

Zone 7: Western and central areas are cloudy with scattered precipitation, and eastern areas have a chance for thunderstorms. The desert is hot.

Zone 8: Alaska is windy and fair to partly cloudy west and central with scattered precipitation, and stormy east and cooler. Hawaii is windy, seasonal, and fair to partly cloudy.

First Quarter Moon, May 11

Zone 1: The zone is fair to partly cloudy with scattered thunderstorms and temperatures ranging from seasonal to above.

Zone 2: Much of the zone is fair to partly cloudy and windy with scattered thunderstorms. Central and southern areas are hot and humid.

Zone 3: The zone is fair to partly cloudy with temperatures seasonal to above, and a chance for showers and thunderstorms east.

Zone 4: Western skies are fair to partly cloudy and windy with scattered showers, and central areas see precipitation later in the week, some abundant. Eastern areas are fair to partly cloudy with thunderstorms, some severe with tornado potential.

Zone 5: Temperatures rise and much of the zone sees showers and thunderstorms, some severe with tornado potential.

Zone 6: The zone is variably cloudy, and western and central areas are windy with precipitation, some abundant.

Zone 7: The zone is fair to partly cloudy with scattered precipitation north and central, and showers and thunderstorms east, some severe.

Zone 8: Eastern Alaska sees precipitation, some abundant, and western and central areas are mostly fair. Temperatures range from seasonal to below. Hawaii is fair, windy, and seasonal.

Full Moon, May 19

Zone 1: The zone is fair to partly cloudy, humid, and seasonal with showers and thunderstorms. Some areas see significant downfall.

Zone 2: Scattered thunderstorms across the zone are more severe central and south, with significant downfall and tornado potential.

Zone 3: The zone is humid, fair to partly cloudy, and windy with scattered showers and thunderstorms, some severe with abundant precipitation and tornado potential. Temperatures are seasonal to above.

Zone 4: Western areas are fair to partly cloudy, and central parts of the zone are stormy with severe thunderstorms with tornado potential. Eastern areas are fair to partly cloudy, windy, and warmer.

Zone 5: Scattered showers accompany fair to partly cloudy skies west, and central and eastern parts of the zone are humid with thunderstorms, some severe with tornado potential.

Zone 6: Much of the zone is cloudy with precipitation, some abundant with flood potential, and temperatures are seasonal to below.

Zone 7: Cloudy skies yield significant precipitation in coastal and central areas of the zone. Eastern areas are cloudy with showers, and the desert is hot with a chance for thunderstorms.

Zone 8: Western and central Alaska see precipitation, some abundant, and eastern areas are fair and warmer. Hawaii is fair to partly cloudy, humid, and seasonal with scattered showers.

Third Quarter Moon, May 27

Zone 1: The zone is fair to partly cloudy with temperatures seasonal to above and strong thunderstorms.

Zone 2: Much of the zone is cloudy and humid with scattered showers and thunderstorms.

Zone 3: Humidity rises west and central, where rising temperatures spark scattered thunderstorms, some severe. Eastern areas see more clouds and precipitation.

Zone 4: The zone is fair to partly cloudy, and humid with scattered precipitation and temperatures seasonal to above.

Zone 5: The zone is fair to partly cloudy with temperatures seasonal to above and scattered showers and thunderstorms, some severe.

Zone 6: Western areas are fair, and central and eastern areas see thunderstorms, some severe.

Zone 7: Northern coastal areas are fair to partly cloudy with scattered precipitation. Southern coastal and central parts of the zone are cloudy with showers, with severe thunderstorms central. Fair to partly cloudy skies dominate to the east. Temperatures are seasonal to above.

Zone 8: Alaska is windy west and central and much of the zone sees scattered precipitation. Hawaii is windy and mostly fair with scattered thunderstorms and temperatures seasonal to above.

New Moon, June 3

Zone 1: The zone is fair to partly cloudy and seasonal with a chance for precipitation.

Zone 2: Northern areas are fair, and southern and central parts of the zone are humid and cloudy with thunderstorms, some severe.

Zone 3: The zone is variably cloudy, seasonal, and humid, with scattered showers and thunderstorms.

Zone 4: Skies are mostly fair, with more cloudiness east, and temperatures seasonal to above. Western and central areas see scattered thunderstorms.

Zone 5: The zone is humid, hot, and fair to partly cloudy with scattered thunderstorms.

Zone 6: Much of the zone is cloudy with temperatures seasonal to above. Precipitation centers east and central.

Zone 7: The zone is variably cloudy and windy with temperatures seasonal to above, and precipitation east.

Zone 8: Western and central Alaska are windy with precipitation, and eastern areas see mostly scattered precipitation. Much of Hawaii is windy, with precipitation and seasonal temperatures.

First Quarter Moon, June 10

Zone 1: The zone is cloudy, humid, and seasonal with scattered showers.

Zone 2: Much of the zone is humid and seasonal with scattered thunderstorms, some severe.

Zone 3: Showers and thunderstorms across the zone, some severe, yield significant downfall east.

Zone 4: Western and central areas are hot with a chance for scattered thunderstorms, and eastern areas are cooler with a chance for precipitation.

Zone 5: Western and central areas are windy with scattered thunderstorms, as humidity and temperature rise. Eastern areas see more cloudiness and showers.

Zone 6: Much of the zone sees scattered showers and thunderstorms, and temperatures seasonal to above. Conditions are mostly fair to partly cloudy and dry east.

Zone 7: Northern coastal areas are stormy and windy, southern coastal and central areas are fair, and eastern parts of the zone are windy with scattered thunderstorms. Temperatures are seasonal to above.

Zone 8: Alaska is windy with precipitation east, cloudy central, and fair to partly cloudy west. Temperatures are seasonal to above. Hawaii is cloudy east, and fair to partly cloudy and humid west and central with scattered precipitation. Temperatures are seasonal to above.

Full Moon, June 18

Zone 1: Temperatures are seasonal to below and conditions are cloudy with precipitation.

Zone 2: Northern areas are cloudy and cool with precipitation, and central and southern parts of the zone are variably cloudy, windy, and warm with showers and thunderstorms.

Zone 3: Rising temperatures spark severe thunderstorms with tornado potential across much of the zone. Areas to the east are cooler and cloudy with precipitation.

Zone 4: Temperatures are seasonal to above, western skies are cloudy, and central areas are windy. Scattered thunderstorms to the east are severe with tornado potential.

Zone 5: The zone is fair to partly cloudy and windy with temperatures seasonal to above.

Zone 6: Western and central areas are windy with showers and thunderstorms, some severe with significant downfall. Eastern areas are cloudy with showers.

Zone 7: Central parts of the zone see abundant precipitation from showers and severe thunderstorms. Eastern areas are cloudy with scattered showers.

Zone 8: Western Alaska is cloudy with precipitation, some abundant, and fair to partly cloudy skies prevail central and east. Hawaii is breezy, seasonal, and fair to partly cloudy.

Summer

Zone 1: Precipitation is average and temperatures seasonal, but cloudy days prevail.

Zone 2: Mostly fair, dry, and windy with high temperatures and humidity, the zone sees some severe thunderstorms.

Zone 3: Western and central areas see abundant precipitation and severe thunderstorms, and temperatures are average to below.

Zone 4: The zone is windy and seasonal to cool with average to below precipitation and some severe thunderstorms in the Plains.

Zone 5: Severe thunderstorms and temperatures seasonal to below accompany precipitation average to below.

Zone 6: Precipitation is average to above, and temperatures seasonal to below.

Zone 7: Cloudiness prevails, and temperatures are seasonal to below with average to above precipitation.

Zone 8: Alaska is seasonal to below with average precipitation. Hawaii's precipitation and temperatures are average to below.

Third Quarter Moon, June 26

Zone 1: The zone is variably cloudy, humid, windy, and seasonal with showers and thunderstorms, especially south.

Zone 2: Partly cloudy to cloudy skies and humidity yield showers and thunderstorms, and northern areas are windy.

Zone 3: Central and western areas sees showers and thunderstorms, some severe with tornado potential and abundant downfall. Eastern areas are cloudy, cooler, and windy with scattered precipitation.

Zone 4: Areas to the west are fair and cool with a chance for precipitation. Central portions of the zone are partly cloudy with a chance for showers, and areas to the east are windy with thunderstorms, some severe with tornado potential.

Zone 5: Temperatures are seasonal to above across the zone, with fair to partly cloudy skies and a chance for precipitation west and central. Severe thunderstorms with tornado potential are possible to the east.

Zone 6: Western and central areas are cloudy and cool with precipitation, while eastern parts of the zone are fair and windy.

Zone 7: Northern coastal and central areas of the zone are cloudy with precipitation, some abundant, and eastern areas are windy and fair. The desert is hot.

Zone 8: Alaska is fair to partly cloudy and windy with scattered precipitation and temperatures seasonal to below. Hawaii is seasonal, fair, and windy.

New Moon, July 2

Zone 1: Stormy skies yield abundant precipitation, possibly from a tropical storm or hurricane.

Zone 2: Much of the zone is stormy, possibly from a tropical storm or hurricane, with abundant downfall and flood and tornado potential.

Zone 3: Western areas see scattered thunderstorms, and central and eastern parts of the zone are cloudy with thunderstorms and showers, some with abundant downfall, possibly from a tropical storm or hurricane.

Zone 4: The zone is fair to partly cloudy, and central and eastern areas see scattered thunderstorms, some strong with tornado potential.

Zone 5: Thunderstorms in central areas could be severe with tornado potential, while other parts of the zone are fair to partly cloudy. Temperatures are seasonal to above.

Zone 6: Western areas are fair, eastern areas are fair to partly cloudy, and some central parts of the zone see abundant precipitation and severe thunderstorms.

Zone 7: Showers and thunderstorms, some strong, visit western and central areas; eastern parts of the zone are fair to partly cloudy, while the desert is hot and humid.

Zone 8: Alaska is stormy west with some abundant downfall, and central and eastern areas are mostly fair with scattered precipitation. Hawaii is cloudy with severe thunderstorms west and scattered precipitation in central areas.

First Quarter Moon, July 10

Zone 1: The zone is fair to partly cloudy and seasonal, with humidity and scattered thunderstorms south.

Zone 2: Much of the zone is humid and partly cloudy with scattered thunderstorms.

Zone 3: Western and central areas see strong thunderstorms, some with tornado potential, and areas to the east are windy and fair to partly cloudy. Temperatures are seasonal.

Zone 4: A weather front that brings precipitation, some abundant, to western areas advances into the Plains, which see thunderstorms, some severe with tornado potential; eastern areas are partly cloudy with scattered thunderstorms.

Zone 5: Tornados could accompany severe thunderstorms east, and western and central areas see thunderstorms and showers.

Zone 6: Much of the zone is cloudy, with abundant precipitation west, and stormy with thunderstorms central and east.

Zone 7: Western skies are fair to partly cloudy, while central and eastern parts of the zone see thunderstorms, some with abundant downfall. Temperatures are seasonal to above.

Zone 8: Central Alaskan areas are stormy with high winds and abundant precipitation. Fair skies prevail to the west, and eastern areas see precipitation. Much of Hawaii sees precipitation, some abundant, and central and eastern areas are cloudy, windy, and stormy.

Full Moon, July 18

Zone 1: The zone is fair and windy north, and cloudy and windy with thunderstorms, some severe with abundant precipitation, to the south, possibly from a tropical storm or hurricane.

Zone 2: Much of the zone is cloudy and wet and some areas see abundant downfall from severe thunderstorms, a tropical storm, or a hurricane.

Zone 3: Thunderstorms, some strong with high winds, high humidity, and cloudy skies prevail west and central, and eastern areas are cloudy and windy with precipitation, some abundant, possibly from a tropical storm or hurricane.

Zone 4: Western and central areas see scattered thunderstorms, some strong with high winds, and the eastern Plains are mostly fair. Areas to the east are humid with a chance for showers, especially north. Temperatures are seasonal to above.

Zone 5: Western areas are cloudy with showers, and central areas see increasing clouds with scattered showers and thunderstorms later in the week. Areas to the east are humid with scattered thunderstorms. Temperatures are seasonal to above.

Zone 6: Temperatures are seasonal to above, central and eastern areas are fair to partly cloudy and windy, and western parts of the zone are cloudy with showers.

Zone 7: Southern coastal areas are fair to partly cloudy, while showers and cloudy skies prevail in northern coastal and central areas of the zone. Eastern areas see showers. Temperatures are seasonal to above.

Zone 8: Western Alaska is windy, central areas are stormy with significant downfall, and eastern areas are fair. Temperatures are seasonal to above. Central and eastern parts of Hawaii see showers and thunderstorms, and areas to the west are mostly fair. High humidity accompanies seasonal temperatures.

Third Quarter Moon, July 25

Zone 1: The zone is seasonal with scattered precipitation and mostly fair skies north. Cloudy skies produce abundant precipitation south, possibly from a tropical storm or hurricane.

Zone 2: Significant precipitation accompanies cloudy skies across the zone, possibly from a hurricane or tropical storm; there is potential for severe thunderstorms and tornados.

Zone 3: Western and central areas see scattered showers and thunderstorms, accompanied by high winds. To the east, skies are cloudy and downfall significant. The zone is humid with temperatures seasonal to above.

Zone 4: Temperatures are seasonal to above across the zone, and windy and partly cloudy west and central. Central and eastern areas see thunderstorms, some severe with tornado potential, later in the week.

Zone 5: Some western areas see abundant precipitation, and western and central areas are windy. Severe thunderstorms east could produce tornados. Temperatures are seasonal to above.

Zone 6: Cloudy skies in western areas yield significant precipitation later in the week. Windy central and eastern areas are fair to partly cloudy, with showers primarily east. Temperatures are seasonal.

Zone 7: Northern coastal and central parts of the zone are cloudy with precipitation, some abundant, and eastern areas are partly cloudy with scattered precipitation.

Zone 8: Central and eastern Alaska are cloudy and windy with precipitation, and western areas are fair; temperatures are seasonal. Eastern Hawaii is fair, while cloudy skies produce showers central and west; temperatures are seasonal to above.

New Moon, August 1

Zone 1: The zone is seasonal and partly cloudy, with strong thunderstorms in some areas.

Zone 2: Northern areas have a chance for precipitation. Central and southern areas are cloudy and humid with thunderstorms, some severe with tornado potential, and heavy downfall in some locations. Temperatures are seasonal to above.

Zone 3: Tornado potential accompanies scattered thunderstorms west and central, where clouds are more prevalent. Eastern areas are mostly fair with a chance for precipitation. Temperatures range from seasonal to above

Zone 4: Western areas are windy and partly cloudy with a chance for showers and thunderstorms. Central and eastern areas see showers and scattered thunderstorms, some severe with tornado potential. Temperatures are seasonal.

Zone 5: Much of the zone is partly cloudy with temperatures seasonal to above and showers and thunderstorms, some severe with tornado potential.

Zone 6: Western areas are cloudy with precipitation, central areas are fair to partly cloudy with scattered precipitation, and eastern parts of the zone see thunderstorms, some severe with significant downfall. Temperatures are seasonal to above.

Zone 7: Southern coastal and central parts of the zone are fair, and northern coastal areas are cloudy with showers. Strong thunderstorms bring significant precipitation to some central and eastern areas. Temperatures range from seasonal to above across the zone.

Zone 8: Central Alaska is wet and windy, and eastern areas see significant precipitation later in the week. Western parts of the state are mostly fair. Temperatures are seasonal to below. Hawaii is windy with some strong thunderstorms and temperatures seasonal to above.

First Quarter Moon, August 8

Zone 1: Northern areas are fair with a chance for thunderstorms, and partly cloudy to cloudy skies bring showers south.

Zone 2: Temperatures are seasonal to above, with partly cloudy to cloudy skies north and showers. Central and southern areas are windy with a chance for showers.

Zone 3: Eastern parts of the zone are fair to partly cloudy with scattered precipitation, while western and central areas see thunderstorms, some severe with tornado potential.

Zone 4: Western parts of the zone are cloudy with some areas receiving abundant precipitation. The eastern Plains are mostly fair, and eastern areas see thunderstorms, some severe with tornado potential.

Zone 5: A weather front advances from western to central parts of the zone, bringing cloudy skies and abundant precipitation to some areas. Fair skies prevail east.

Zone 6: Eastern areas are fair and windy, while central parts of the zone are cloudy with precipitation, some abundant, later in the week. Western areas are fair to partly cloudy with a chance for showers.

Zone 7: Fair and windy weather prevails in northern coastal areas, and southern coastal and central parts of the zone see scattered precipitation. Eastern areas are fair and windy. Temperatures are seasonal to above.

Zone 8: Eastern areas of Alaska see precipitation, some abundant, while western and central parts of the state of mostly fair. Hawaii is fair to partly cloudy and breezy with a chance for showers. Temperatures are seasonal to above.

Full Moon, August 16

Zone 1: Temperatures are seasonal to above under fair to partly cloudy skies, with scattered precipitation south.

Zone 2: The zone is humid and windy with scattered showers and thunderstorms. Temperatures are seasonal to above.

Zone 3: Skies are fair to partly cloudy and temperatures seasonal to above, with a chance for precipitation east.

Zone 4: Central and eastern areas are fair to partly cloudy and humid with scattered precipitation and thunderstorms north. High winds and precipitation dominate the west. Zonal temperatures are seasonal to above.

Zone 5: Western areas are stormy, and humid central and eastern parts of the zone are partly cloudy with scattered precipitation. Temperatures are seasonal to above.

Zone 6: The zone is variably cloudy with precipitation and seasonal temperatures. Eastern areas see thunderstorms, some severe.

Zone 7: Coastal and central areas see showers, and eastern areas are fair to partly cloudy with scattered thunderstorms. The desert is hot and humid.

Zone 8: Eastern Alaska is fair, and western and central areas are windy with precipitation. Hawaii is fair to partly cloudy with scattered showers west and central. Temperatures are seasonal to below.

Third Quarter Moon, August 23

Zone 1: Southern areas are mostly fair and humid, and abundant downfall accompanies thunderstorms, some severe, to the north.

Zone 2: Fair skies dominate to the north, and central and southern areas are humid and cloudy with precipitation.

Zone 3: Rising temperatures trigger scattered thunderstorms, some severe, west and central, and eastern areas are cloudy with precipitation.

Zone 4: Much of the zone sees scattered thunderstorms, some severe with tornado potential in central areas. Fair skies prevail to the east. Temperatures are seasonal to above.

Zone 5: The zone is mostly fair and humid with scattered thunderstorms, some of which could be severe with tornado potential.

Zone 6: Western areas are fair to partly cloudy, while central and eastern parts of the zone are windy with showers and thunderstorms, some severe.

Zone 7: Scattered showers and thunderstorms, some severe, dominate to the west. Central and eastern areas are windy with scattered precipitation later in the week.

Zone 8: Stormy weather advances from western Alaska into central areas of the state, and mostly fair weather prevails to the east. Hawaii is windy with precipitation, and western and central areas see thunderstorms, some severe.

New Moon, August 30

Zone 1: The zone is fair to partly cloudy and seasonal, with scattered showers north.

Zone 2: Variable cloudiness, seasonal temperatures, and humidity prevail, along with scattered showers and thunderstorms.

Zone 3: Western areas see severe thunderstorms with tornado potential, possibly from a tropical storm or hurricane. Central and eastern areas are humid with scattered showers and thunderstorms.

Zone 4: The zone is humid and windy, with temperatures seasonal to above and strong scattered thunderstorms with tornado potential.

Zone 5: Humidity and temperatures rise, and much of the zone sees thunderstorms, some severe with tornado potential.

Zone 6: Eastern and western areas are fair to partly cloudy, and increasing cloudiness in central parts of the zone signals precipitation, some abundant. Temperatures are seasonal, but much cooler in the mountains.

Zone 7: Northern coastal areas are partly cloudy with scattered showers, while cloudiness and precipitation, some abundant, dominate southern coastal and central areas. Eastern parts of the zone are fair, and the desert is hot.

Zone 8: Alaska is fair west and central, with precipitation, some abundant, east. Hawaii is fair to partly cloudy and seasonal.

First Quarter Moon, September 7

Zone 1: The zone sees showers and thunderstorms alter in the week, along with falling temperatures.

Zone 2: Increasing cloudiness signals showers and thunderstorms later in the week, and the zone is seasonal and humid.

Zone 3: Western parts of the zone see thunderstorms, some severe, and central and eastern skies are fair to partly cloudy with scattered precipitation.

Zone 4: Conditions are fair, hot, and dry west, then become cooler with clouds, wind, and precipitation. Central and eastern areas are cloudy with showers and thunderstorms, some severe.

Zone 5: Western areas are fair, and cloudy skies and precipitation central and east could be triggered by a tropical storm or hurricane.

Zone 6: Cloudy skies yield precipitation west, which moves into central areas. Eastern areas are fair to partly cloudy and windy.

Zone 7: Much of the zone sees precipitation, but eastern areas remain mostly fair and dry.

Zone 8: Alaska is fair west and central with scattered precipitation, and some eastern areas see abundant downfall. Temperatures are seasonal to below. Hawaii is partly cloudy and windy with a chance for precipitation.

Full Moon, September 15

Zone 1: The zone is windy and cloudy with showers and thunderstorms.

Zone 2: Fair to partly cloudy skies prevail north, and central and southern areas are humid with precipitation, some abundant, possibly from a tropical storm or hurricane.

Zone 3: Western and central areas see scattered showers and thunderstorms. Eastern areas are humid and cloudy with scattered showers.

Zone 4: The zone is variably cloudy and windy with scattered showers and thunderstorms.

Zone 5: The zone is fair to partly cloudy with a chance for precipitation, especially north.

Zone 6: Western areas are partly cloudy with scattered showers, and central and eastern parts of the zone are windy with precipitation, some abundant, and temperatures seasonal to below.

Zone 7: Wind and clouds increase across the zone, bringing showers, thunderstorms, and abundant precipitation to some areas. Temperatures are seasonal.

Zone 8: Alaska is stormy central and east, and then clearing and colder. Fair to partly cloudy skies dominate to the west.

Autumn

Zone 1: The zone is cold and cloudy with above average precipitation.

Zone 2: Precipitation is average to below, windy days are prominent, with seasonal temperatures.

Zone 3: Temperatures are seasonal to below, with average precipitation except in eastern areas, where downfall is abundant.

Zone 4: The zone is cold, with average precipitation west and central and abundant precipitation east.

Zone 5: Windy conditions accompany temperatures and precipitation average to below.

Zone 6: Temperatures are seasonal to below and precipitation average except in central areas, which receive above average downfall.

Zone 7: Western and central areas are cloudy and cool with significant precipitation, and areas to the east are dry with temperatures seasonal to below.

Zone 8: Alaska is windy, with temperatures seasonal to below and precipitation average to above. Hawaii is windy with significant storms, and average temperatures and precipitation.

Third Quarter Moon, September 22

Zone 1: The zone is mostly fair, and temperatures rise with a warming trend.

Zone 2: A chance for precipitation accompanies warm temperatures, fair to partly cloudy skies, and wind.

Zone 3: The zone is humid with temperatures seasonal to above. Eastern skies are fair, and western and central areas cloudy with severe thunderstorms and significant precipitation, possibly from a tropical storm or hurricane.

Zone 4: Western and central parts of the zone are hot with showers and thunderstorms. Eastern areas are cooler and cloudy with thunderstorms, some severe.

Zone 5: Central and eastern areas are hot and humid with severe thunderstorms and significant precipitation, possibly from a tropical storm or hurricane. Western parts of the zone are fair to partly cloudy.

Zone 6: Western and central areas are windy, partly cloudy, and cool with scattered precipitation that advances into eastern parts of the zone.

Zone 7: Skies are fair to partly cloudy and windy west, central areas see precipitation, and eastern parts of the zone are cloudy with significant downfall and thunderstorms. Temperatures are seasonal to above.

Zone 8: Alaska is fair west and central, and stormy with significant downfall and windy to the east. Temperatures are seasonal to below. Hawaii is fair to partly cloudy and seasonal, with scattered showers east.

New Moon, September 29

Zone 1: Scattered precipitation accompanies wind and seasonal temperatures.

Zone 2: The zone is windy with scattered showers and thunderstorms. Central and southern areas are humid, and temperatures seasonal.

Zone 3: Variable cloudiness across the zone produces showers west, and windy weather with scattered thunderstorms central and east.

Zone 4: Western and central areas are windy and stormy with significant downfall, and areas to the east are partly cloudy to cloudy with scattered precipitation.

Zone 5: The zone is windy and seasonal with showers and thunderstorms.

Zone 6: Western areas are windy and partly cloudy, and central and eastern parts of the zone are fair to partly cloudy with a chance for precipitation east.

Zone 7: Much of the zone is fair to partly cloudy with a chance for precipitation in northern coastal areas. Eastern areas are windy with precipitation north.

Zone 8: Eastern Alaska is stormy, and central and western parts of the state are windy and fair to partly cloudy with scattered precipitation. Hawaii is windy west with scattered showers, and mostly fair and seasonal.

First Quarter Moon, October 7

Zone 1: The zone is wet, stormy, and cloudy with seasonal temperatures. A tropical storm or hurricane is possible.

Zone 2: The zone is cloudy and conditions are stormy north. Central areas see severe thunderstorms with tornado potential, and southern areas are wet with showers and thunderstorms. A tropical storm or hurricane is possible.

Zone 3: Western areas are fair, and central parts of the zone are partly cloudy and windy. Stormy conditions east with severe thunderstorms could be due to a tropical storm or hurricane.

Zone 4: Western and central areas see significant precipitation with flood potential, and areas to the east are windy and fair to partly cloudy with scattered precipitation.

Zone 5: Downfall is significant to the west, and fair skies central and east become increasingly cloudy, bringing precipitation.

Zone 6: Much of the zone is windy and stormy as a front advances, bringing significant downfall to some areas.

Zone 7: The zone is cloudy and windy with thunderstorms, some severe, and showers, with some areas seeing abundant precipitation.

Zone 8: Central and eastern Alaska are very windy with precipitation, and western areas are stormy. Hawaii is fair, windy, and seasonal with scattered showers west.

Full Moon, October 14

Zone 1: Northern areas are cloudy with precipitation, and southern parts of the zone are partly cloudy and windy with precipitation.

Zone 2: Variable cloudiness accompanies wet weather across much of the zone, with some areas receiving abundant downfall.

Zone 3: Central and eastern areas are fair and windy, and western parts of the zone are cloudy with precipitation, abundant in some areas.

Zone 4: The zone is variably cloudy with temperatures seasonal to below, and windy west. Central and eastern areas are wet, with abundant downfall in some locations.

Zone 5: Western and central areas are fair to partly cloudy with scattered precipitation, and eastern parts of the zone see more downfall, some significant. Temperatures are seasonal to below.

Zone 6: Eastern areas are wet and windy, and central and western areas, partly cloudy with scattered precipitation.

Zone 7: The zone is mostly fair to partly cloudy with scattered precipitation, but stormy east with more precipitation north.

Zone 8: Central Alaska is stormy and cold, and western and eastern areas are fair to partly cloudy, windy, and seasonal. Hawaii is cloudy with precipitation in all but eastern areas, and temperatures are seasonal to below.

Third Quarter Moon, October 21

Zone 1: The zone is windy and partly cloudy, with temperatures seasonal to below and scattered precipitation.

Zone 2: Chilly weather and wind accompany fair to partly cloudy skies and scattered precipitation.

Zone 3: Skies are fair to partly cloudy west, with more cloudiness central and east, which are colder and windy with precipitation.

Zone 4: Conditions are windy, cloudy, and cool as a front advances across the zone.

Zone 5: Western and central areas are windy with scattered thunderstorms, some strong, and variable cloudiness east yields scattered precipitation.

Zone 6: The zone is windy, with cloudy skies and precipitation central and east.

Zone 7: Western and central areas are fair and windy, and eastern skies are windy and partly cloudy with scattered precipitation north.

Zone 8: Cloudy skies and precipitation, some abundant, prevail across Alaska, which is windy and seasonal. Hawaii is fair to partly cloudy, and windy with scattered showers.

New Moon, October 28

Zone 1: Southern areas are fair to partly cloudy with scattered precipitation, and areas to the north are windy with abundant downfall in some locations.

Zone 2: Precipitation dominates across the zone, with some areas receiving significant downfall. Central and southern areas are stormy, and zonal temperatures are seasonal to below.

Zone 3: Western skies are fair to partly cloudy, and central and eastern areas see precipitation, some abundant, later in the week. Temperatures are seasonal to below.

Zone 4: The zone is variably cloudy with temperatures seasonal to below. Central and eastern areas are windy with precipitation.

Zone 5: Western areas are mostly fair, and central and eastern areas are cloudy with precipitation.

Zone 6: Central and eastern areas are windy and cloudy with precipitation, and western parts of the zone are stormy later in the week. Temperatures are seasonal to below.

Zone 7: The zone is windy and seasonal with precipitation, especially central and east.

Zone 8: Alaska is windy and seasonal with variable cloudiness and precipitation, which is heaviest in central parts of the state. Hawaii is seasonal, windy west and central, and partly cloudy to cloudy with showers.

First Quarter Moon, November 5

Zone 1: Cloudy skies yield precipitation, some abundant, across the zone, which is windy and seasonal.

Zone 2: Northern areas are cold with abundant downfall, and central and southern areas are partly cloudy and seasonal with scattered precipitation.

Zone 3: Variable cloudiness brings precipitation across the zone. Eastern areas are very windy, and zonal temperatures are seasonal to below.

Zone 4: Western areas are wet and windy, central parts of the zone are partly cloudy, and eastern areas are windy and cloudy with scattered precipitation. Temperatures are seasonal to below.

Zone 5: The zone is windy and seasonal, with precipitation west and central.

Zone 6: Temperatures range from seasonal to below, as stormy skies bring precipitation to central and eastern parts of the zone. Western areas are fair.

Zone 7: Western and central areas are stormy, and eastern areas see precipitation. The zone is windy and cold.

Zone 8: Western Alaska is fair to partly cloudy and seasonal, and central and eastern areas are stormy and cold. Hawaii is windy with showers and temperatures seasonal to below.

Full Moon, November 13

Zone 1: Northern areas are cloudy with significant downfall, and southern parts of the zone are partly cloudy to cloudy with scattered precipitation. Temperatures are seasonal to below.

Zone 2: Seasonal temperatures accompany scattered precipitation north, which is windy, and fair to partly cloudy skies prevail central and south.

Zone 3: Western areas are windy with scattered precipitation, and central and eastern areas are mostly fair.

Zone 4: Cloudy, windy skies yield precipitation across the zone and abundant downfall west and central. Temperatures are seasonal to below.

Zone 5: A front advances across the zone, bringing cloudy skies, wind, and precipitation, which is heaviest east; temperatures are dropping.

Zone 6: The zone is cloudy and wet.

Zone 7: Partly cloudy to cloudy skies yield scattered precipitation west and central, and areas to the east are fair to partly cloudy with a chance for precipitation.

Zone 8: Alaska is cold, windy, and stormy central and east, and fair to partly cloudy west. Hawaii is cloudy, windy, and cool with abundant downfall in some areas.

Third Quarter Moon, November 19

Zone 1: Skies are fair to partly cloudy north, and windy with more cloudiness and scattered precipitation south.

Zone 2: Northern areas are cloudy with scattered precipitation, and central and southern areas are fair and seasonal.

Zone 3: Western areas are cloudy and cool with scattered precipitation; eastern parts of the zone are fair to partly cloudy with scattered precipitation, with windy conditions and temperatures from seasonal to below.

Zone 4: Precipitation in western areas advances into central parts of the zone. Eastern areas see scattered precipitation, and the zone is windy with temperatures seasonal to below.

Zone 5: Temperatures are seasonal to below, and variable cloudiness produces precipitation across the zone.

Zone 6: Eastern areas are fair and windy, and cloudy skies produce scattered precipitation west and central.

Zone 7: Western and central parts of the zone see scattered precipitation, and eastern areas are mostly fair and windy.

Zone 8: Western Alaska is fair, and central and eastern areas are cloudy with precipitation. Hawaii is mostly fair to partly cloudy with a chance for precipitation, but cloudy and windy east with showers.

New Moon, November 27

Zone 1: Northern areas are fair, and southern parts of the zone are windy and cloudy with precipitation.

Zone 2: Precipitation accompanies windy, cloudy skies north, and central and southern areas are fair to partly cloudy and seasonal.

Zone 3: Variably cloudy skies produce precipitation across the zone, which is windy.

Zone 4: The zone is fair to partly cloudy with temperatures seasonal to below, and scattered precipitation central.

Zone 5: Fair to partly cloudy skies prevail across the zone, with scattered precipitation west and a chance for downfall central and east.

Zone 6: Western and central areas are cloudy with precipitation as a front advances, and eastern areas are fair and colder.

Zone 7: Northern coastal and central areas see precipitation, and southern coastal and eastern parts of the zone are partly cloudy. Temperatures are cooler east.

Zone 8: Alaska is stormy east and cold, and western and central areas are windy with precipitation. Temperatures are seasonal to below. Hawaii is cloudy east with showers, and fair and seasonal west and central with increasing cloudiness and showers later in the week.

First Quarter Moon, December 5

Zone 1: The zone is cloudy and seasonal with precipitation, some abundant.

Zone 2: Scattered precipitation accompanies windy, partly cloudy skies and seasonal temperatures.

Zone 3: The zone is partly cloudy and windy, with precipitation and temperatures seasonal to below.

Zone 4: Variable cloudiness produces precipitation across the zone, and temperatures are seasonal to below.

Zone 5: Central and eastern areas are windy with precipitation, and western parts of the zone are partly cloudy with scattered precipitation.

Zone 6: The zone is mostly fair and windy, with scattered precipitation east.

Zone 7: Conditions are seasonal and skies fair to partly cloudy.

Zone 8: Alaska is stormy east with high winds and abundant downfall, and western and central areas are fair to partly cloudy. Temperatures are seasonal to below. Hawaii is seasonal and breezy.

Full Moon, December 12

Zone 1: The zone is cloudy, stormy, and cold with abundant downfall.

Zone 2: Northern areas are stormy and cold, and central and southern areas are mostly fair and seasonal.

Zone 3: Western and central areas are seasonal with scattered precipitation, and eastern parts of the zone are stormy and cold.

Zone 4: The zone is mostly fair to partly cloudy, seasonal, and windy with scattered precipitation.

Zone 5: Conditions are seasonal and skies variably cloudy, with scattered precipitation west and central.

Zone 6: Western areas are fair and windy, and central and eastern areas see precipitation, which is more significant central. Temperatures are seasonal to below.

Zone 7: Coastal and central areas are windy, with precipitation that advances into eastern areas. Temperatures are seasonal to below.

Zone 8: Western and central Alaska are stormy with significant downfall, and eastern Alaska is windy with scattered precipitation. Temperatures are seasonal to below.

Third Quarter Moon, December 19

Zone 1: The zone is windy, cloudy, and cold with precipitation.

Zone 2: Northern areas are cloudy and cold with precipitation; conditions are more seasonal central and south, where partly cloudy skies and scattered precipitation prevail.

Zone 3: The zone is fair west, partly cloudy central, and cloudy and colder east, with precipitation.

Zone 4: Much of the zone is cold, windy, and fair to partly cloudy with scattered precipitation, while eastern areas are more seasonal and windy.

Zone 5: The zone is partly cloudy to cloudy and cold with scattered precipitation.

Zone 6: Western skies are fair, and central and eastern areas are partly cloudy to cloudy with precipitation. Much of the zone is cold.

Zone 7: The zone is windy with temperatures seasonal to below. Central and eastern areas are cloudy with precipitation, and western parts of the zone are mostly fair.

Zone 8: Western Alaska is fair to partly cloudy and windy, and central and eastern areas see precipitation. Temperatures are seasonal to below. Hawaii is windy with showers, followed by a warming trend.

New Moon, December 27

Zone 1: Temperatures are seasonal to below, and skies are windy and fair to partly cloudy with scattered precipitation.

Zone 2: The zone is partly cloudy, seasonal, and windy with scattered precipitation.

Zone 3: Western skies are fair, and central and eastern areas are windy and partly cloudy with scattered precipitation.

Zone 4: Eastern parts of the zone are cloudy with precipitation, some abundant, and western and central areas are windy with scattered precipitation.

Zone 5: Precipitation and clouds blanket the east, and western and central areas are windy with scattered precipitation.

Zone 6: Much of the zone sees precipitation, which is heaviest east, where conditions are cloudier and cooler.

Zone 7: Northern coastal areas are windy with scattered precipitation, and southern coastal and central parts of the zone are mostly fair. Cloudy, windy skies east yield scattered precipitation. Temperatures are seasonal to below.

Zone 8: Eastern and western Alaska are fair to partly cloudy and seasonal, and central areas of the state are windy with precipitation. Hawaii is partly cloudy, windy, and cool with scattered precipitation.

Global Warming: Is it Fact or Fiction?

By Kris Brandt Riske

Is global warming reality, or is it just opinion? Are the media and global warming's chief proponent, former Vice President Al Gore, of the film *An Inconvenient Truth*, just promoting a theory?

As with most theories, it all depends upon whom you listen to. Proponents and naysayers alike, however, agree that the concentration of greenhouse gases has increased, and that Earth is experiencing a warming trend. What they disagree on is the cause, and that is the crux of the issue. Is Earth's changing environment the result of human decisions and actions, or is it a naturally occurring phenomenon?

Gases present in Earth's atmosphere are nitrogen, oxygen, argon, carbon dioxide, water vapor, neon, helium, methane, krypton, and hydrogen. The chief culprit cited in the global warming debate is the carbon dioxide emitted by burning fossil

fuels. But carbon dioxide levels can rise from other emissions, such as erupting volcanoes. Water does the same thing when the cloud cover increases.

When carbon dioxide and water that is contained in the atmosphere increase, temperatures warm because the heat generated by sunlight becomes trapped in the atmosphere, creating a greenhouse effect. The trapped heat in turn triggers even more temperature increases because as Earth's surface warms, more carbon dioxide is released from the oceans.

Carbon dioxide levels are high during Earth's warm periods and low during cool periods, such as occurred during several ice ages. Other factors that contribute to shifts in Earth's atmosphere are periodic changes in its tilt and orbit, and changes in the Sun's intensity, both of which are believed to have contributed to the ice ages.

Greenhouse gas is therefore a natural part of Earth's cycle and, without it, there would be no life on the planet. At issue is artificial greenhouse gas, created by industry and our choice of lifestyles, that results in excess carbon dioxide, methane, nitrous oxide, and fluorinated gases being dumped into the atmosphere.

Global temperatures rose by 1 degree in the twentieth century, and speculation and scientific prediction estimate that if carbon dioxide levels continue to increase, the rise will be anywhere from 1 to 6 degrees in the twenty-first century. This has benefitted, and could conceivably continue to benefit, agriculture with longer growing seasons (which have already increased by eleven days in the past fifty years) and lower energy demands during colder months. But with it comes the risk of expanding the equatorial disease zone farther north and south, rising sea levels (estimated at 8–17 inches by 2100), stronger storms, intense but less frequent precipitation, and melting glaciers and ice sheets.

Global warming skeptics argue that emissions have been reduced in the United States by reducing power plant and car emissions. The pollution emitted by a new car today is about 1 percent of what was emitted by a 1970 model, and acid rain is no longer a danger in the Appalachian Mountains. But other countries, such as China, India, and Pakistan, are not so kind to the environment. Industry and more vehicles on the roads in developing countries produce large quantities of industrial soot and methane, both of which are contributors to greenhouse gas. The World Resources Institute reported that U.S. greenhouse emission rose 18 percent since 1990, while Chinese emissions rose 77 percent.

Dr. Robert Balling, director of the Office of Climatology at Arizona State University, noted that temperatures did not increase any more at the end of the twentieth century than they did at the beginning, when emissions were not controlled. He also says evidence suggests that Earth was warmer in the past, so today's rising temperatures are not as significant as they appear.

Forests and agriculture absorb some of the carbon dioxide, as do the oceans. But even though 75 percent of Earth's surface is water, the oceans are approaching the point where they can no longer contain the increasing emissions.

Some scientists believe the Arctic, Antarctic, and Greenland glaciers are melting at an alarming rate, while others say they began to grow in the 1970s. The Storbreen Glacier in Norway retreated between 1750 and 1961, before artificial greenhouse gas became an issue, and the Nisqually Glacier near Tacoma, Washington, thickened between 1931 and 1945 and again in the mid-1990s. Scientists also question the temperature increases cited by global warming proponents, noting that the urban heat island effect might be skewing the figures.

John Christy, University of Alabama climatologist, noted that the Arctic became increasingly warmer between 1917 and 1937, and the warmest recorded years were 1937 and 1938, after which the area cooled. His data also shows that the Arctic is warming faster today than is Earth as a whole, but that the Antarctic is cooling.

The most alarming factor associated with global warming, however, might be a shift in the Atlantic Ocean currents. This phenomenon would result in colder temperatures, not warmer ones.

Earth is currently in an interglacial period—when climatic conditions are relatively stable, or constant—that began about 12,000 years ago after the most recent ice age. But Earth experienced little ice ages between 1150 and 1460 and between 1560 and 1850. During these periods, the growing season in Europe changed by 15 to 20 percent. The summers were cool and wet, storms increased, glaciers advanced, crops failed, and illness and malnutrition increased.

The cause of these little ice ages in Europe might have been the same as what is happening today in the Atlantic Ocean: warm water from equatorial areas flows north, where it gradually cools, sinks, and returns to the equator to repeat the cycle.

This is why some coastal European countries, which are farther north than Maine, have a temperate climate.

But freshwater is increasing in the North Atlantic, possibly from glacial melt, and water in the tropics is becoming saltier. The result is an altering of the ocean currents because freshwater is lighter than saltwater and thus does not sink and return to the equator, which in turn effectively disrupts the hydrologic process.

A new little ice age might be in the near future, whether as a result of artificial greenhouse gasses and global warming, or because of natural climatic changes, such as have occurred in the past. Earth is in a constant state of change.

Astrometeorology

Astrometeorology (weather forecasting with astrology) offers some insight into this global warming controversy. Each planet and sign represents certain weather conditions—temperature, moisture, and wind. When these planets link forces, the astrometeorologist can predict, for example, a sunny day or a tornado.

Pluto, the slowest moving planet and therefore one of long-term influence, has been in Sagittarius, a hot (temperature) sign, for the past thirteen years. On January 26, 2008, Pluto will enter Capricorn, a cold sign. On its own, Pluto often signifies intense weather, the extremes of heat and cold, high winds, and significant storms.

When Pluto entered Sagittarius in 1995, it was closely aligned in the sky with Venus and Jupiter. When Pluto enters Capricorn in January 2008, it also will be closely aligned with Venus and Jupiter. An interesting coincidence? Or an indication of natural changes in the planet?

Venus represents moisture and warmth. Jupiter represents fair weather, but it also tends to amplify the effects of other planets, positively or negatively.

Venus, Jupiter, and Pluto aligned in hot Sagittarius equal rising temperatures and abundant moisture. The same planets aligned in cold Capricorn equal cooling temperatures and abundant moisture.

Possibly even more significant is the exact alignment of the three planets in Capricorn at the longitude of the North and South Poles. This means that the weather or climatic changes represented by these planets will surely impact conditions at the poles, which have been much publicized in the global warming debate. The longitudinal influence extends around the globe, with the strongest impact in Eastern Europe, Asia, and the Midwestern United States.

The three planets in Sagittarius will be aligned longitudinally in Australia, where there has been a severe drought, and in the eastern Atlantic Ocean and Greenland, where ocean conditions are undergoing significant changes as the flow of warm equatorial water is altered by freshwater.

But the shift of emphasis from Sagittarius to Capricorn could indicate a build-up of ice masses that have been receding. And that, of course, might be a reflection of a shift in Earth's climate, which is the norm, not the exception.

So global conditions could gradually shift from steamy, hot summers to cooler and wetter ones, and from temperate winters to very cold ones with heavy snowfall in many areas.

Will Earth see another little ice age? Or will the recent warming trends simply be reversed to the more stable climate of an interglacial period?

Time—and Earth—will tell.

Resources

Bailey, Ronald. "Two Sides to Global Warming." (10 November 2004). Retrieved from www.reason.com.

Balling, Robert. "The Increase in Global Temperature: What it Does and Does Not Tell Us," (September 2003). *Policy Outlook* from the George C. Marshall Institute.

Cartlidge, Edwin. "A Climate of Alarm." (February 2007). Retrieved from www.physicsweb.org.

Easterbrook, Gregg. "Case Closed: The Debate about Global Warming is Over." (June 2006). Retrieved from www.brook.edu/views/papers/easterbrook/20060517.htm.

Mandia, Scott A. "The Little Ice Age in Europe." (nd). Retrieved from www2.sunysoffolk.edu.

Economic Forecast for 2008

By Dorothy J. Kovach

There are three faithful friends—an old wife, an old dog, and ready money.

—BEN FRANKLIN

If we don't want to be caught out in the cold like Cinderella at midnight, we may want to batten down our financial hatches. There has been a great deal of momentum built up in the markets in recent years. Wise investors think like the "big boys," who know that when a lot of money is circulating, then real value in the markets is less. What this means for you and me at this time is that our risks may not bring us the rewards we've had in the past. Markets are subject to the law of supply and demand, not to mention gravity. What goes up really does, eventually, come down.

Regardless of whether we are playing the market or just trying to get through the day, it is time to get out of financial denial. In short, no person, company, or country ever borrowed and consumed their way to prosperity. Two wars and the ever-expanding federal debt have taken a severe toll on the economy. A wise government does not just print money, but in the years since George W. Bush took office, the dollar has lost more than 30 percent of its value. China has a trillion dollar surplus. On the other hand, the U.S. has a trillion dollar deficit. It doesn't take an economic genius to figure it out—trouble looms ahead. As long as those ships are leaving our ports empty, we are sitting on an economic time bomb, ready to blow up with one puff of geopolitical ill will.

Markets hate uncertainty, and we have no idea who will be sitting in the White House after the 2008 election. Currently we have a Republican president and a Democratic Congress, which means that Congress will not be passing a lot of laws. Markets also hate regulations, and they love gridlock. When we add uncertainty, gridlock, and regulation together, it's realistic to assume that there will be some wild market swings ahead. So fasten your seat belts and get ready for quite a ride.

You might say: "I'm not invested in the market. What does this have to do with me?" In a word: everything. When the markets are up, companies can afford to hire and there is plenty of work to go around. Where there is plenty of work, there is also plenty of money to go around, and everybody is happy. When markets turn downward, everybody worries. Some think the Wall Street "fat cats" control the market, but that's only partially true. The planets above form the structure of the market, and provide indications that show what we humans are predisposed to do. The markets change as the planets move through their cycles, and so do we.

Jupiter and Saturn

Diligence is the mother of good luck.
—BEN FRANKLIN

When it comes to making money, we need look no further than the fluctuations of the two Titans of the economy: Jupiter and Saturn. Jupiter makes us rich, while Saturn brings limitation and loss. Jupiter rules the principle of expansion of the markets. Saturn, on the other hand, brings the markets down. Knowing a little about these two planetary CEOs keeps wise business people two steps ahead of the competition.

Overview of Jupiter in Capricorn

The use of money is all the advantage there is in having it.
—BEN FRANKLIN

Jupiter is the kindest of the planets. When he is traveling unhindered in a favorable sign, things tend to flourish. It should come as no surprise, then, that Jupiter represents bull markets and all growth sectors. In recent years we have been very lucky, because Jupiter has brought us, not one, but two major bullish cycles. First, we had the tech boom. And, when the dot-com boom turned bust, rock bottom interest rates in turn created the real estate and commodity boom. This amounted to a cash windfall unprecedented in modern history. Loose lending practices made it possible for anybody who could breathe to qualify for a mortgage! Folks poured money into real estate. With so few risks, the speculators stepped in, and flipping houses became somewhat of a cottage industry. Home prices skyrocketed. In no time, we were in the midst of a second bubble.

When Jupiter runs the show, the subtle scent of euphoria permeates our surroundings. We believe dreams really can come true. Indeed they can, because the planet of luck has the Midas Touch. Whatever product is symbolized by the sign Jupiter is in will flourish, and in 2008, Jupiter is in Capricorn. He's out of his element in this sign because Capricorn is ruled by Saturn, so Saturn's conservative approach will cramp Jupiter's preferred approach to operations, which is, as you remember, expansion. This could result in more cutbacks in the workforce as management pares down on excess—again. Everybody will cut down on excess, except the government! Look for more red tape in 2008 as the Big Brother effect may make profits harder to come by. This could bring market stagnation later on in the second quarter.

The Bottom Line

Jupiter in Capricorn will like black, not red, on the bottom line, and efficient businesses, whose books mimic Jupiter's present color choice, will be rewarded. In general, we should expect to see a good supply of oil and energy-related substances on the market, and blue chips will be favored over emerging markets.

Senior Benefits

Jupiter in Capricorn will benefit seniors (who are ruled by Capricorn). America is graying at a rapid pace, and in a very short while there will be more seniors than teenagers. In this election year, we will probably see presidential hopefuls of both parties courting seniors. We will probably also be hearing of multiple breakthroughs in the treatment of geriatric illnesses, and businesses that cater to the elderly will benefit in one way or another.

Mergers and Acquisitions

Look for even more consolidation in the market as mergers and acquisitions continue, especially in the first few months of 2008. Mergers and acquisitions may be great for the big businesses, but they're not so great for the little guy. When companies consolidate, people lose jobs. The global technological miracle has left a larger gap between the rich and the poor in the U.S. We can expect companies that specialize in retraining to do well. Jupiter in Capricorn loves mining. With that in mind, we like United States Gypsum stocks. Jupiter in Capricorn will help keep the flagging real-estate market afloat, but for how long is anyone's guess.

Real-Estate Markets

George W. Bush has not been good for the war in Iraq, but he has been great for real estate (for more details, see my article in Llewellyn's *2004 Moon Sign Book*). With the sub-prime lenders on the verge of collapse, and defaults climbing, let's hope the next president-elect has an exceptional chart for real estate (as President Bush has), because if he or she does not, the real-estate market could drop precipitously, taking over 750 billion dollars out of circulation. With Jupiter in Capricorn, the Democrats have the edge in the upcoming elections because the Democratic Party is the older of the two parties and thus is favored by Jupiter in Capricorn. This year, lucky Jupiter smiles on age.

Overview of Saturn in Virgo

Experience keeps a dear school, but fools will learn in no other.
—BEN FRANKLIN

Where Jupiter elevates, Saturn takes down. Saturn represents the 80 percent of new businesses that fail, that ugly pink slip, and bear markets. In a perfect world, the days are never dark and all markets go up. Unfortunately, this is not a perfect world, but Saturn teaches us what we need to know so we can face the music in hard times. Saturn is short on compliments, but is long on endurance.

Virgo is the most discerning of all the signs. Saturn in Virgo teaches us to read the fine print. This is no time to take a quick glance at the numbers, because when Saturn is in Virgo, the numbers rarely tell the entire story. Make certain you do your homework before you invest. Make sure your books are in order. Saturn is not nice to tax cheats. With all the litigation that is going to come down, it will be a great time for both lawyers and CPAs, with one caveat. The Sarbanes-Oxley Act has made auditors vulnerable to prosecution. Hedge funds may be the next to see regulations.

Virgo gives Saturn a mercurial nature, which demands that we heed the adage: "Buy on the rumor and sell on the news." It is exactly when financial pundits are forecasting a rosy future that we need to prepare ourselves. Some say that the market was created to impart the greatest amount of pain to the greatest number of people. Don't follow that line of thinking. Before buying into this market, do your homework.

Technology

The computer industry, as a whole, stagnates under Saturn in Virgo, but even in this beat-up sector, there are some beams of light, especially for the little computers. A cheap laptop has been developed for distribution to children in third world countries. It is set to come to market in the fall of 2008. Created without costly liquid crystal display, it's priced to sell for under $200. We can expect Taiwan-based manufacturer Quanta to reap a huge bonanza. But overall, computer orders may be down, and we may want to pare down our investments in the tech-heavy NASDAQ. Watch for the war of the mobile phones as competition looms large in the telecommunications industry.

Pharmaceuticals

Since Saturn will be in opposition to Uranus, which is in the sign designated for drugs, investors should continue to avoid the big pharmaceuticals. The Medicare prescription bill of a few years back wasn't much more than a financial bonanza for the giant pharmaceutical companies. Today, the big pharmaceuticals are involved in a detrimental combination of litigation and expiring patents. We may want to wait for the rubble to clear before returning to this sector. There are still some bright spots in the biotech industry. One of the major winners will continue to be Genentech, a good company with several great products, like Avastin, which has shown great promise in cancer studies and treatment of macular degeneration. The stock itself is pricey, but we may want to consider buying when it dips down.

Insurance

Take one aging electorate, add bankrupt hospitals, roll in a corrupt healthcare industry, and you have a recipe for disaster. Forty million people do not have medical insurance. In an election year, this will be *the* issue people want to talk about. Anybody who wants to be elected president in 2008 had better give some serious thought to our broken healthcare system. Despite the demographics, Saturn in Virgo opposite Uranus in Pisces really makes this a sector investors will want to avoid.

Agriculture

Where Saturn goes, shortages follow. Look for a rise in wheat and corn prices as a result of crop failures worldwide.

Real Estate

Saturn is transiting the nation's Fourth House. It will be a long time before salaries catch up to home prices.

Overview of Pluto in Capricorn
By failing to prepare, you are preparing to fail.
—BEN FRANKLIN

Have you ever wanted to get in on the beginning of the next big thing? There is a buying opportunity every time one of the great planets changes signs, and with the advent of Pluto entering Capricorn, an opportunity just dropped in our lap. This is because whatever sector is symbolized by the sign a planet enters is in the running to become the dark horse stock in the decade ahead.

We must always remember that we will be investing for the long haul, ten years out. Simply put, Pluto means change. Whatever sector is indicated by the sign a planet is entering will grow steadily hotter, while the sign the planet has left will cool. We will begin to see restriction of religious fanaticism and the global economy; and country and western is about to become passé (Sagittarius is a man on a horse) as Pluto leaves Sagittarius behind.

Credit and Interest Rates

Unfortunately, Sagittarius is both the most risk-oriented and the most optimistic of the signs. In the eighteen years that Pluto was in gambling-lovin' Sag, the market soared! The advent of Pluto to Capricorn may bring the longest period of easy credit in history to an end. It also marks the beginning of a rather conservative trend in banking. Those of us who used home equity like a credit card had better be prepared to tighten our belts. If we cannot or will not live within our means, there will be troubled times ahead. Those who believe we are in the midst of a "Goldilock's Economy," where the market is neither too hot not too cold, may be in for a rude awakening by the big bad bear market.

Trade Deficits

Pluto in Capricorn demands accountability. Most of our energy comes from foreign sources. Because of this dependence, our indebtedness to international suppliers has gone up some five trillion dollars in the last five years alone. Sixty-eight percent of that money is spent on transportation, so it can't be much of a surprise that we are involved in costly foreign wars over this commodity. Governmental policies are shaped by need. Thirty consecutive years of trade deficits have made us the largest debtor nation in the world. Given our trade imbalances, it is no wonder that the politicians do not want to bring this thorny issue up. There are few ways to deal with this without raising taxes, and politicians don't get elected on such a platform. It is time that we do something about our addiction to oil.

We will begin to feel the pain of depending on China like a child begging at his mother's breast. It is never wise to be blasé about the dwindling value of our dollar. As more money is printed up without substance to back it up, our quality of life will suffer. Buying in this climate is only for the strong of stomach.

Banking and Business

Capricorn is often associated with management in big business. During the years when Pluto has been in Sagittarius, the banking houses have made a great deal of money on mortgages and on investing for the burgeoning baby-boomer generation. That, along with the industry-wide slow down and the potential adjustments in foreign markets, indicates that we may want to seek investment groups with less exposure to emerging markets. Remember that your investment banker may not always have your personal interests in mind. Do you know what you own, and what your funds manager is doing with them? If you don't have this knowledge, get it. It's your future that will be affected.

Mining, Security, and Government

Capricorn loves what is above and also under the ground. Mining stocks like United States Gypsum are a good investment for the long haul. The U.S. has vast resources of coal, and investment in coal may be a good long-term investment On the bright side, all those businesses associated with protection, like fences, concrete, and rock, will all go up in value. Don't expect to shrink the government any time soon, for Pluto with Jupiter there this year infers he will be watching you closely.

2007 Winter Solstice: First Quarter

Be at war with your vices, at peace with your neighbors, and let every new year find you a better man.

—BEN FRANKLIN

What do the government and old Mother Hubbard have in common? The coffers of the government are bare. We have peaked out. Investors may want to position themselves defensively. There are always bright sectors, and given the current circumstances, look for the lawyers to reap the gains as litigation increases this season.

Consumer Reactions

A sense of worry that can be cut with a knife clings to consumers during the Christmas season. This may be the second lukewarm holiday season in a row for retailers. The rich get richer and the poor get poorer. Lower-end retailers, like Walmart, feel the squeeze as the holiday shopping season gets off to a lackluster start. Meanwhile, Tiffany's and Coach do well in times like these. This is an odd boom, because the middle class is getting squeezed. We don't feel as invincible as we once did, and the real-estate slump has put a damper on consumer spending.

Equities

One sector's loss is another's gain. In the past year, equities have gained great momentum in the face of the real-estate sector's demise, and may have already peaked. If you have not done so, this

may be a good time to do some serious reallocation. When there are too many stirring the pot, good money can turn bad rather swiftly, so follow the Girl Scouts' lead—be prepared.

Military

Armies do not run on good intentions alone, and there could be some tough times ahead for our men and women in uniform. Our military is burnt out. They are caught between a rock and a hard place, and it is becoming harder to recruit troops and raise the money to pay for them. This ugly war can be a boon to the number-one maker of prosthetic devices: Stryker Corporation.

Spring 2008: Second Quarter

Any society that would give up a little liberty to gain a little security will deserve neither and lose both.

—BEN FRANKLIN

The Spring Ingress chart is the most important chart of the business cycle. Most astrologers pay much closer attention to this ingress than all the other seasons combined.

With jolly Jupiter perched on the money sector of the Ingress chart, traders are feeling pretty good about themselves, but markets can stay sweet for only so long. The moment when everybody is happy is exactly when we should worry about the markets.

Transportation

Mars is waiting in the wings, poised to pounce, and when he does, volatility will follow. Markets may overheat toward the end of April. Transportation stocks again feel the heat as global tensions push energy prices upward by the end of May. Worries about inflation may force the Federal Reserve to raise interest rates, resulting in volatility to the downside. Transportation stocks again feel the heat, when global tensions push energy prices upwards. The consumer stays home.

Military

The U.S. may see challenges to its military superiority over the next six months as more countries vie to go nuclear. In this atmosphere, it is not unusual to see some major swings in the global markets. Each time the market goes up, another international incident threatens to slap it back in its place. Risk does have its rewards, but only for those who have the stomach for it. The window of opportunity has narrowed considerably. Seventy percent of stocks go with the trend, and the trend may be downward from here on out.

Summer 2008: Third Quarter

If you would know the value of money, go try to borrow some; for he that goes a-borrowing goes a-sorrowing.

—BEN FRANKLIN

There seems to be less faith in government than ever before. In a climate like this, the Democrats need only to run against Bush. Our leaders seem to be afraid to make the necessary changes in the economy to compete in the modern world. George W. Bush is far more than just another lame-duck president. Expect to hear numerous reruns of the president's failures, not only regarding the war in Iraq but also about his fiscal mismanagement, from candidates on the campaign trail. Will the Democrats come up with some tangible ideas about how they are going to win the White House? We need more than nebulous ideas, but any ideas are better than none at this point.

Volatile Prices

If you are not ready for a rough ride, you may want to stay on the sidelines. This market is not for the weak! We may see relaxed gas prices just in time for the conventions. Lower gas prices bring more profits to well-run transportations stocks like Fed Ex. Look for a bump up in tech. Even lowered gas prices cannot bring the party back to a market that sees the handwriting on the wall. There is a lot of uncertainty out there, which may translate into sideways markets.

Fall 2008: Fourth Quarter

Beware of little expenses. A small leak will sink a great ship.
—BEN FRANKLIN

Autumn may be a season of great swings. Look for technology to take a "perhaps" with a vengeance come October. Even as computers and communication stocks give good numbers, there is just too much uncertainty in this market. It may be wise to stay on the sidelines, until the election dust settles, before making purchases in this market climate.

2008 Election

Who will be the next president? What will he or she be like? At this writing, neither party has chosen its candidate, but Americans have never felt more restless with the country's leadership. They want real change, not rhetoric. Celestial forces favor women in the political arena this year.

Interest Rates

Americans have a lot of questions, but no clear-cut answers. With so much of the future up in the air, we may feel a bit queasy. Higher interest rates could radically dry up what little was left in the ebbing real-estate market. Precarious housing lending practices could come to light and put the final nails in its coffin.

Market Week 2007

Money never made a man happy yet, nor will it. The more a man has, the more he wants. Instead of filling a vacuum, it makes one.

—BEN FRANKLIN

November

There could be repercussions from the trillion dollar curse. When China coughs, the whole world feels it. Disruptions abroad could mean buying opportunities at home. Markets are frothy and may even go up on bad news. Hedge your bets and get ready for a ride. The wise seize opportunities when they can, but always remember, nothing lasts forever.

December

Lock in profits around December 3. The market may lose that lovin' feeling as the month progresses, when potential trouble on the high seas, geopolitical intrigues, and a sluggish consumer combine to make for a jittery start to the shopping season. Negotiations head off trouble the third week. Look for adjustments in the pharmaceuticals sector as generics take control. Foreign demand brings a boom to the mining sector.

Market Week 2008

January

New year starts out on a positive note. Retailers smile, flush from a good holiday season. Look for upward trends to continue. Meanwhile, all that glitters is not gold. Read the fine print and make certain to have all documents signed, sealed, and delivered by the end of the month, when Mercury turns retrograde and wreaks havoc on agreements.

February

What a difference a month can make. The market may be getting a bit overheated. With possible inflationary forces looming on the horizon, accompanied by fears of interest rate hikes from the Federal Reserve, a pall falls over the market. Hold off making commitments or major purchases until after February 21, when Mercury turns direct.

March

Not even sweet spots last forever. Prices are near peak levels and people are getting restless. Expect global tensions and tightened energy supplies to bring higher prices at the pump by midmonth. Combined factors may put a damper on equities by midmonth. The balance of power may be shifting sooner than most expect. Prepare accordingly.

April

Tensions ease and the market bounces back. We may make some real breakthroughs in medicine, and biotech firms reap the benefits. The consumer is clearly driving this market to further peaks; however, nothing—not even bull markets—can last forever. The transportation industry, airlines in particular, may have problems at this time as heightened terrorism alerts abound, raising concerns for trouble in the air.

May

The threat of terrorism and the global game of oil are not necessarily over. The market is priced for perfection. The run on emerging overseas markets may be peaking now. In view of this, we may want to reallocate for safety as growth may falter from here. The threat of terrorism rears its head again. Get all your ducks in a row by May 25, because more forces than just Mercury going backwards will collude. Be prepared.

June

Franklin Delano Roosevelt said the only thing we have to fear is fear itself. This is a good thing to remember as markets turn frosty. Gas prices rise, making the consumer jittery. World tensions and inflation worries combine forces, turning buoyant optimism to nervousness almost overnight. Tension eases midmonth, but the damage is done. Investors are glum as oil prices rise. Hold off on important decisions and signing documents until after June 19, when Mercury turns direct. At all times, read the fine print.

July

The party's over. A combination of global tensions, interest rate increases, and a nation bent on driving will push oil and energy prices back up. At first, the market adjusts, but it is temporary. Rising unemployment and threats from abroad may wreak havoc on the market. Potential troubles may be brewing in both the military and the health care industry as well, despite the demographics.

August

As global tensions recede, so do oil prices, which cheers the market positive. By the last week of August, though, prices could creep back up. Everybody knows good times can last only so long. The market is priced to perfection, which forces wise investors to the sidelines. We might want to take some profits if you're holding certain gaming stocks.

September

Make certain your investments are solid now. Diversity is paramount, because rapid growth in stocks lead to bubbles. Get ready to put shorts in place. In other words, fasten your seatbelt and seek shelter for a rough ride ahead. Seriously consider selling unproductive issues or overpriced stocks into any highs this month. Adjustments may be painful, but less so if you prepare yourself accordingly. Depressing news from abroad puts a damper on market performance.

October

Reality rears its ugly head. We may see some volatile times this month. Earnings are mixed. What has gone up could come down now, and you should know when to say when. As leaves turn gold, the market may turn blue. There may be some real market adjustments midmonth, as confluent factors knock the wind out of the market. The only thing that markets hate is uncertainty, and there is plenty of that now.

November

Some stability returns to the markets in the first week. This is one of those times we might be see leadership topple. November 8 marks a pivotal change in the markets. Hopefully, you have prepared your portfolio for the long haul. The negative wind still permeates the air, even as markets adjust. The consumer can no longer buy his way out of everything, especially on credit.

December

There seems to be a collective sigh of relief. The rich are getting richer, but even this market might be too rich for most. There are a lot of assets chasing less and less in potential profits. At times like this, it may be time to take some profits and place our investments in safe issues. This may not be the jolliest of holiday seasons, especially for retailers. With so many uncertainties, shoppers play it close to the cuff.

About the Author

Dorothy J. Kovach is a traditional astrologer and timing expert from Northern California who specializes in helping people and businesses alike with their problems. You can reach her at Dorothy@worldastrology.net or through her Web site at www.worldastrology.net.

A Plan for Living by the Moon

By Sally Cragin

When Sharon, my editor, mentioned the topic of living consciously with lunar cycles, my first thought was—oh, that's easy, I'm doing that all the time! But then I remember how I'm usually astonished by the crescendo of activity that invariably happens between the first quarter and Full Moon. And also how often I have to remind myself not to start projects just before the New Moon.

I make a living writing a column called "Moon Signs" for the *Boston Phoenix* newspaper, so if I'm surprised by lunar phases and signs and other celestial movements, I can only imagine that the interested layperson or astrological aficionado would appreciate advance notice of when the Moon is telling us all, "Hey, look up! Pay attention to what I'm doing!"

The Easy Part Is Looking Up

When I've taught classes focusing on astrological or lunar topics I invariably say this: "If you remember nothing else from our time together, remember this: when the Moon is light on the right, it's waxing. When it's dark on the left, it's waning."

Sounds simple, but it's easy to get confused because the Moon is tipped on its axis and the New Moon to crescent phase looks more like that Cheshire cat smile than something directly across from us. The waxing lunar phases having to do with the increasing of the Moon are these: New Moon, waxing crescent, first quarter, gibbous Moon, and Full Moon. The waning lunar phases having to do with decreasing phases are these: Full Moon, last quarter, Balsamic, waning crescent, dark of the Moon, and New Moon.

What's the Difference?

Waxing Moon phases are about beginning, building, growing, increasing, adding. Waning Moon phases are about taking apart, declining, decreasing, subtracting, completing. Relationships that end on or around the New Moon are more likely to stay broken-up. Projects that reach a climax around the Full Moon are in tune with the phase. Beginning a project on or just after the New Moon gives you a twenty-eight-day cycle to explore your options.

Living Consciously During the New Moon

I'm going to write about the time just before and just after the New Moon, since it's wiser not to do too much separating of phases. The New Moon is an ending and beginning time all at once. It's a quietly freighted time just before the New Moon. This is an excellent time for meditation. During this phase, the Sun, Moon, and Earth are getting into alignment, although the Moon is behind the Earth, which is why we only see a sliver and then no Moon at all. However, this interlude can be emotionally draining, and a time when feelings are magnified. Beware of inappropriate pessimism or overreacting to adversity.

The waning crescent to New Moon period is a time when everything "shakes down," and sometimes relationships, projects, endeavors, and activities just need to come at an end. When things end during this period, you have an opportunity to contemplate the appropriateness of an ending. Sometimes it's easier to come to terms with a conclusion you may not have expected.

Living Consciously During the Waxing Moon Phase

This phase lasts until three or four days before the Full Moon. Optimism comes easily during this phase. When I've had clients born on or around that first quarter Moon, they're generally cautiously optimistic (as opposed to folks born on or around the Full Moon, who sometimes need lots of stimulation!). During this phase it's easy to get into a rhythm, so "consciousness" is sometimes compromised. The first quarter phase is a turning point for projects or relationships. Look back to days near the time when the Moon was new to see what started in your life. Where is it now, at the first quarter Moon? Sometimes the very day of the first quarter isn't the best time to take action, no matter how tempting.

Living Consciously as the Moon Races Toward Full

The gibbous Moon phase occurs between the first quarter and Full Moon, when the Moon really looks like a lopsided peach. This is when life gets very intense, and it's usually the day or two before the Full Moon that you hear people saying, "everything's so crazy—it must be a Full Moon!" However, this can be an excellent time to put the pedal to the metal in a number of areas in your life. Some people thrive on this energy, which can be the opposite of "living consciously." They hurtle pell-mell through their days in cars littered with empty coffee cups. Throw in a Full Moon and you've got manic Monday seven days a week!

Use the time during a Full Moon to work late hours, expand an operation, or extend the reach of a project. Even having a party means you're in the right zone with this phase. We all know that how we live our lives is very different from the way our parents did. Heck, even the lives we led ten years ago were different. It's been just about a decade since E-mail and cell phones have become commonplace items. As useful as up-to-the-minute information can be, sometimes we don't allow enough time for things to unfold in their own good time. And during a Full Moon, moving more slowly has got to be a conscious decision—circumstances are all about acceleration!

Living Consciously Between the Full Moon and Last Quarter/Balsamic Phase

It may take a few days to feel like your life is slowing down, because the days before and after a Full Moon have their momentum. But deceleration is in the stars. During the Full Moon, the spotlight is on. Well, on! Because the Sun and Moon are aligned with the Earth, when there is a high tide, it's the largest high tide of the month. This is also true of New Moons. Because the Sun, Moon, and Earth are still in a line, these tides are called "spring tides" and account for the highest high tide and lowest low tide. Now, say what you will about the scale of tides versus the scale of liquids in our cerebellum (not to mention distinctions with local geography, e.g., the spectacular high tide at the Bay of Fundy, Nova Scotia), but my experience is that whatever's sloshing in our heads gets some stimulation from lunar phases.

If you have pets, particularly nocturnal animals like cats or rodents, notice their activity during the Full Moon phase. They don't have to live consciously because they're in tune with natural processes. I have arboreal tree crabs for pets, and they invariably choose to change shells when the Moon is either new or full. There's much more clattering in the aquarium during these two phases as well.

Scheduling a party or an important social occasion between first and last quarters can help with the turnout—people are in a festive mood, willing to be among others, and eager for more stimulation.

Living Consciously During the Last Quarter Phase

This phase can signal getting results. Are you cashing in on a project that began around the New Moon, or changed radically during the Full Moon? The last quarter to new phase is about finishing projects. Lingering over problems may not be as expedient as cutting the cord, so to speak. If something in your life is going to fall apart, this is the natural phase for that to happen. If one is of a brooding state of mind, this is the period where it feels like life is slowing down.

And it becomes infinitely easier to regret words said or unsaid, deeds accomplished or left undone. This is the natural time for cleaning out the clutter. Unless you're sentimental or acquisitive by nature, you should be able to discard unwanted items. If you're trying to phase out a relationship, you can put on the brakes now, or make yourself less available by phone or E-mail. But this is also a good time to look for bargains and to get goods for less than what they're worth. If you're in the mood to acquire, that is!

Back to the Beginning

I wanted to write about the "dark of the Moon," which is that day before the New Moon (sometimes it's two days before the New Moon, depending on the actual time of the New Moon). This is an accident-prone time, but it's also an extremely useful time for figuring out what you want. Your subconscious wants to be heard during this phase, and if you do not make time for yourself, the universe (the Greeks called this "the Fates") will find a way to slow you down. Could be the stubbed toe, could be moving too quickly in a slow zone, could be speaking too brashly or insensitively.

If the dark of the Moon falls on a Thursday or Friday, and there is pressure on you to complete a project, do your best but don't be surprised if you put the finishing touches on over the weekend or on Monday. Here's an image—you may feel that things are moving more quickly in the way that water seems to move more quickly when it's draining the last drops out of the tub. In fact, the water is moving at the same speed from the moment you pull the plug. It's just your perspective that's different. And whatever preoccupies people (even you!) during this phase will be of limited interest once the Moon has turned new again.

New Moons, Birthdays, and Strategy

Here's an easy way to remember what sign the Moon is in when it's new: it's always the same sign as the Sun. So when the Moon is in your Sun sign during your birthday month, it's always the New Moon. And since New Moons are all about fresh starts, give yourself the birthday present of a new project or different perspective—at least for that lunar phase.

Full Moons—Do We Have a Choice?

Depending on how we react, my response is—not really! As conscious as one can be during the waxing Moon phase, something happens, and happens at mach-5, and we're lucky to be hanging onto the steering wheel.

Remember that the Full Moon is in the sign opposite the sign the Sun is in. That means that if you're having a birthday, that month's Full Moon is as far from your natal Sun as it can get. And this can bring a tidal wave of emotions that one is not entirely prepared for. And, when the Full Moon is in a particular sign, it can bring out that sign's attributes in darn near anyone. So a Full Moon in Aries can make people seem more impetuous than they mean to be, or a Full Moon in Virgo can make people seem pickier than they think they are, and a Full Moon in Aquarius is a time of wandering attention span for normally sharp-witted and grounded people. Are you reading this article during a Full Moon? Probably not—taking in information is easier when there's less illumination in the sky. That said, here are some comments on how to live consciously during a New or Full Moon.

2008 New and Full Moons

Full Moon in Cancer • December 23, 2007 and January 10, 2009

Domesticity rules. Pamper yourself. This is a great time for a massage or taking up pottery. (This is not a reach—Cancer rules bakers, and bakers knead. I've had more Cancer clients say, "That's a great idea," when I suggest bread-baking, pottery, or massage classes as a hobby.) Note: There is no Full Moon in Cancer during 2008.

New Moon in Capricorn • January 8 and December 27

Work-work-work. Hey, sometimes it's fun! This is another good interlude for planning long-range financial plans. It's easier to see the structure of something, and you're less likely to be swayed by appearances. Conversely, this is a blunt sign and so diplomacy goes right out the window. But who's noticing? This is not the easiest period for Libra and Aries.

Full Moon in Leo • January 22

Parties. Everywhere. Go to a party, put yourself near people in power, and don't hesitate to be forthright about what you want and don't want. If you're usually a very hesitant, diplomatic person, be blunt.

New Moon in Aquarius • February 6

It's midwinter, and we need a lift. This New Moon is all about having fantastical, unlikely ideas and making them happen. Remember that air-sign Moons (like fire signs) are good for the quick social encounter or communicating. A taste for fantasy could be awakened during this phase. This is a tricky time for Taurus and Scorpio.

Full Moon in Virgo • February 20

Clean like crazy! Organize, declutter, throw out expired vitamins and other medications, take charge of your health, and consider another variety of exercise or self-healing.

New Moon in Pisces • March 7

The zodiacal year comes to a close and since Pisces is the last sign of the zodiac, it must accommodate all the other feelings and events that didn't fit at other times. This could be a hypersensitive time (particularly for Gemini and Sagittarius), but for the rest of us, it's a period in which getting to causes, conditions, and roots of a situation emerge with gentle pushing rather than energetic shoving.

Full Moon in Libra • March 21

The ability to agree prevails and the more quality one-on-one interactions you have, the happier you'll be. Some signs find it difficult to make decisions, but usually, for Libra, this is one of those times when they know exactly what they want.

New Moon in Aries • April 5

Fire Moons mean ignition, and reaching out. Since Aries is the "baby" of the zodiac, see whether childish folks or the willfully innocent wander into your life. Other themes include barbeque, rams, climbing, and easterly aspects (Aries is on the eastern cusp—remember, we read horoscopes with our compass rose upside down). Things begun during this phase could easily fizzle, however. Make sure your interest is maintained through Moon in Taurus. Cancer and Capricorn aren't always thinking clearly.

Full Moon in Scorpio • April 20 and May 19

Secrets are so interesting. Are you drawn into some kind of drama or intrigue? Are you attracted to some kind of cultural movement or activity that would be considered edgy? (Of course, with all and sundry getting various flesh tags pierced and inked, what is *outre* these days?) Note: The May Full Moon is also in Scorpio.

New Moon in Taurus • May 5

Earth-sign Taurus has to do with practicality, security, and money (as in "show me the money"). This New Moon is an excellent time to think about long-term investments or projects that will not come to fruition immediately. Luxury goods could be a temptation, or starting a project that's going to be "elegant-swelegant." Leo and Aquarius won't be at their best.

New Moon in Gemini • June 3

This is a chatty Moon that is excellent for making and pursuing new contacts. Casual conversations could turn into more significant communications. It's another changeable Moon, so if you're not fully committed, you could still seem like you are. It's a good time to begin projects that have opportunities for collaboration. Virgo and Pisces could be off-kilter.

Full Moon in Sagittarius • June 18

Anything goes when the Moon is in Sagittarius, an unpredictable sign that can confer everyone with a "what the heck, let's fly to

Vegas for the weekend" mentality. That urge to escape is strong, but if you have to stay where you are, do try something exotic that would make a good story.

New Moon in New Moon in Cancer • July 2

This is domestic "ground zero." Feelings are at an all-time high since Cancer is highly sensitive to nuance. If you're someone who's a little bit oblivious to those in your immediate surroundings, you may find the social blunder comes easily. However, this is an excellent phase for rethinking your home and home-comforts. This can be an awkward time for Libra and Aries.

Full Moon in Capricorn • July 18

Read Sagittarius (June 18) and think of everything mentioned there in reverse. This is actually an excellent time for getting very serious about the stuff we're all supposed to have in hand (insurance, wills, and important paperwork). This is also a time when you can see how things work, inside and out.

New Moon in Leo • August 1

Since this Moon comes in the dog-days of August (often), this period could include a planned party that doesn't quite come off, or an impromptu gathering that is actually quite enjoyable. Remember, fire-sign Moons are about taking chances and being assertive, and even though the New Moon can be a hesitant time, you could be conflicted about taking action. Wait until the Moon is in Virgo to get a more critical perspective. Scorpio and Taurus could be feisty.

Full Moon in Aquarius • August 16

La-dee-dah. Here's another "anything can happen" Full Moon. This is a great one for having faraway friends return, or meeting exotic oddballs, or having a taste for what is referred to in other cultures as a hejira, odyssey, or dreamquest, but on a short-term scale.

New Moon in Virgo • August 30

Since this is the "back-to-school" month, this New Moon comes at just the right time to settle down to serious business and get organized. Planning the contents of a schoolbag (pencils vs. mechanical pencils, binders vs. spiral-bound notebooks) could stand in for planning a larger project. This Moon heightens critical faculties and also is excellent for cleaning. Gemini and Sagittarius may be too critical.

Full Moon in Pisces • September 15

This one comes around the Autumn Equinox, and if you feel sad about summer fun ending and back-to-the-grind routine starting, this phase can bring out your maudlin side. But it is a very useful time for making art or finding creative ways to spice up something routine.

New Moon in Libra • September 29

Like to juggle? This is the time. This could be a phase in which justice-seeking Libra impulses stray into a gray area. I mean, what happens when two events are scheduled at the same time, or choices must be made? Some signs (air and fire) try to fit extra activities in, but in my experience it's Capricorn and Cancer who have a hard time prioritizing.

Full Moon in Aries • October 14

Be spontaneous and make yourself available for the impromptu gathering. Leave yourself open for the unexpected explosion also. If you've been irked, it could come out right now.

New Moon in Scorpio • October 28

Fall is well-underway, and water sign New Moons are always emotionally intense. Since Scorpio is usually the least forthcoming sign in the zodiac (though they always think they're as frank as can be!), this New Moon is a time in which hidden agendas get even more deeply buried. But if you're looking for erotic activity/possibility/drama, you've waited for the right time. Leo and Aquarius would give this a miss.

Full Moon in Taurus • November 13

Be acquisitive. Is there some object or garment in your life that you really love but that has gotten shabby? Replace it. Grudge-holding is never attractive but it's a behavior that's extremely easy to slip into. Be aware of others being peeved and try not to wallow with them.

New Moon in Sagittarius • November 27

Starting a long journey, even if that's a figurative turn of phrase, is a smart activity. Getting interested in exotic cultures, cuisine, fields of study could also be of interest. Sagittarius Moons usually lighten everyone up, and this New Moon is lovely for nurturing friendships or relationships with quirky personalities. Virgo and Pisces aren't always comfortable however.

Full Moon in Gemini • December 12

Be in touch with a lot of other people. Make connections among disparate social groups. Be willing to consider unusual ideas. Don't try to dwell on any one person or project. Being scattered is natural.

New Moon in Capricorn • December 27

Another good interlude for planning long-range financial plans. It's easier to see the structure of something and you're less likely to be swayed by appearances. Conversely, this is a blunt sign and so diplomacy goes right out the window. But who's noticing? Not the easiest period for Libra and Aries.

About the Author

Sally Cragin writes "Moon Signs," an astrology column for the Boston Phoenix newspaper in New England. She also writes about theater- and arts-related topics for the Boston Globe.

The Magic of Porches

By April Elliott Kent

I grew up in the country, in a small farmhouse built by my grandfather. It was a fine house, but it's not what I remember most; to a kid, a house is just a house. All of the really interesting, really magical spaces were outside: the barn, the wheat fields, the playhouse—and the front porch.

I spent hours on our porch when I was small. It was just "outdoors" enough to let me feel independent, yet still connected to the house so I felt safe. For my sister and me, the front porch was a place to exercise our imaginations by acting out complicated plays of our own invention, and to exercise our bodies by taking turns shoving each other off the porch railing. It served, too, as a stage for celebrating the changing of the seasons. Whether it was carving pumpkins for Halloween, standing on tiptoe to knock down icicles from the eaves, or posing for our annual Easter photograph, many of our most cherished memories seem to have been posed against the backdrop of that porch.

We moved to the suburbs when I was ten, first to a house without much of a porch and then to one with no porch at all. It wasn't until I was a newlywed in my early thirties that I lived in another house with a real front porch, a rented 1920s Craftsman bungalow in San Diego. Its broad porch, half sheltered in colorful bougainvillea, replicated that happy mixture of public and private space that I remembered from childhood. My new husband and I promptly installed a comfortable bench and a little table and spent many long, happy hours lounging on the porch. We ate our breakfasts there and decorated it for every holiday, and on one memorably hot summer evening we actually hauled the dining table out onto the porch and hosted a dinner party there.

When we moved on, I missed that old porch. Our next few rentals hadn't much more than a front stoop, though one did at least have enough space for a couple of chairs. It was in the heart of a lively, interesting neighborhood, which almost made up for the lack of a proper porch. Almost, but not quite.

A Porch of One's Own

Finally, in 1997 we bought our first house, a 1927 Craftsman bungalow not far from our first home together. Almost everything about our new place was a mess, including the horrid, shoddily enclosed front porch, complete with an offensive tin awning over an ugly front door and two nasty, uneven steps. It was so ugly that I nearly cried every time we drove up to the curb.

Even so, sitting inside that ugly little porch was magical. Despite its cracked floor, crooked windows, and horrible door, we loved having breakfast there. Looking out over the two large pine trees in the front yard was like sitting in a tree house. We could watch, unobserved, as neighbors came and went, picked up their newspapers, and walked their dogs. On Sunday mornings we dawdled on the porch for hours, drinking endless cups of coffee and littering the floor an inch deep with newspaper.

It was ugly, though, and truthfully it had become a safety hazard as well. So in 2002 we refurbished our porch as part of a whole-house renovation project. Removing those crooked windows and that terrible door and awning was our opening salvo in the renovation battle. What emerged was stunning: the bones of a beautiful Craftsman-style porch, complete with graceful, tapered columns, that showed off the house's original front door and picture window.

Your House's Smile

Opening up the porch of our house changed its look as radically as a smile opens up a face; and like a smile, it made the house—and by extension, its inhabitants—seem much friendlier. Today, we know almost all our neighbors by name and consider most of them friends. Just the other evening, enjoying a drink on our porch swing, we caught a glimpse of a neighbor we hadn't seen for a while and called him over for a glass of wine. Soon another neighbor drifted over to join us. In no time at all, we were having a relaxed, informal party!

That kind of spontaneous gathering never happened on our old, closed-in porch. It certainly never happened when we lived in houses with no porch at all! People in the city tend to respect one another's privacy, and without a front porch there is no clear signal that we're home and, in the parlance of a more formal era, "receiving." And so what begins with the good intention of giving our neighbors "space" often contributes to a sense of isolation from one another.

The Architecture of an Era

Not long ago I was visiting my sister when she excitedly pulled me over to her computer. "I have a picture of our old house! It's really been fixed up. Let me show you." She pulled up the picture, and I felt a rush of delighted recognition. It wasn't just the

nostalgia of seeing my childhood home. Painted in three earthy colors that accentuated its decorative features, that little farm-house looked just like the Craftsman bungalows I've lived in for most of my adult life! In all my years of gravitating toward simi-lar houses, I never noticed that I was simply trying to recreate what had felt comfortable when I was small.

And it's not just me. For Americans who grew up during a particular era—say, after World War I and before architecture all but abandoned the front porch in favor of the three-car garage, sometime in the 1970s—a gracious front porch is a symbol of many warm memories. It was on porches like these where our grandmothers rocked us to sleep for our afternoon naps, where we gathered with neighbors on hot summer afternoons to share gossip and glasses of iced tea, and where Jack-o'-lanterns greet-ed us on our annual Halloween trick-or-treat expeditions. The front porch sheltered us from rain and sun and gave us a place to relax, imagine, and dream; they offered a sense of community and coziness, all in one. Was there ever a more comforting sensa-tion than pulling up in front of your house after a long, difficult day and seeing a porch light blazing to welcome you home?

Welcoming the Four Seasons with your Porch

Not only does it seem that fewer houses are being built with a full front porch, but even in neighborhoods like mine, which abounds with old-fashioned porches, few of us seem to have much leisure time to spend on them. From a magical point of view, this is a real loss. In a very real sense, the porch is the threshold of your home, a liminal space that marks the transition from public to private domains. Spending time there is a way to give energy to both sides of your life and remind you of the need for balance.

In the practice of feng shui, the porch and front door assume great importance as the primary portal through which energy enters your home. It's considered important to keep your porch clean, uncluttered, and in good repair. The entrance should never be blocked, not even with plants or decorations, and certainly not with discarded items. You should always be able to open your front door wide!

To that sage advice, I would add that porches help us keep rhythm with the cycles of the seasons. Part of the Arts and Crafts movement that inspired bungalows like mine was the notion of blending indoor and outdoor spaces and incorporating motifs from nature in a home's design. The porch is a space where indoor and outdoor elements combine seamlessly, a place where we are always reminded of the time of day and the season of the year.

Whether you are the proud owner of a full porch, a small landing, or a simple stoop, why not use all of the charms of magic, nature, and hospitality to transform your entryway into a space that's both inviting and protective? Welcome each season with the decorative and practical elements that suit the work of that season. Here are some ideas for enlivening your porch with the energy of the seasons, using the natural calendar of the zodiac.

The Spring Porch

Where I live, spring announces itself in the softest of whispers. There is no dramatic thaw of ice and snow, no tender buds dotting deciduous tree branches, just gradually longer days and perhaps a little rain and wind. Our porch can always benefit from a good spring cleaning in late March, though it doesn't always get one. The cobwebs that gather along the crown molding need to be swept away. The porch swing could use a coat of oil. The wicker chairs and the concrete floor cry out for a good scrubbing.

These are energetic tasks well suited to the Sun in Aries season, which begins at the vernal equinox in late March. Aries likes to stay active and happily takes on projects that seem overwhelming to other signs. After your labors are done, decorate your porch in hearty blooms such as carnations and geraniums in white and red, the colors of Aries. Haul out a wicker trunk to use as a table, and stash a light blanket inside to ward off spring's occasional chill. Aries is a fire sign, so invite that element onto your porch with lanterns and candles.

As the Sun moves into Taurus in late April, comfort and luxury are the order of the day. Lie in cushions—lots of cushions! Taurus is an earth sign and loves aromatic plants, so arrange a lush bouquet of cut flowers from your garden to fill the porch with fragrance. Ensconce afternoon guests in comfy chairs, and serve lemonade in crystal tumblers along with a big slab of cake or a giant cookie.

By late May when the Sun enters Gemini, the pace of life picks up speed. Everyone's busier now and flying off in all directions. Weekends are full of graduations and weddings, kids fresh out of school are whizzing around on their bikes, families prepare to leave on vacation. There is little time for languid relaxation but plenty for socializing, so use your porch to extend your entertaining space. Streamline your collection of planters and add additional seating for parties that spill over from inside the house. Make it easier for guests to see your street address from the curb, either by hanging up a plaque with larger numbers or focusing a spotlight over your existing numbers. And since Gemini is an air sign, catch more of the soft, late-spring breezes by hanging up windchimes and sticking pinwheels into the base of your planters.

The Summer Porch

Summer is when the porch comes into its own, since it's the ideal season for enjoying a porch's ample charms. The porch is a cooling oasis for meals, afternoon drinks, or even naps on a hot summer afternoon. Long days and sunshine lure neighbors outside to work in their yards and wash their cars, and porches become impromptu gathering places for catching up after long months spent mostly indoors.

The Sun enters Cancer at the Summer Solstice in late June, when the days are hot and lazy. The Cancer season is ideal for dining outdoors, so you'll need good serving facilities—a serving cart or tray, a table, maybe an ice bucket. Cancer is a water sign, so even if you don't live near water, invite an aquatic motif onto your porch with a small fountain or a garland of seashells.

From late July through late August, the Sun is in dramatic, party-loving Leo. Drape your porch in strands of sparkling lights, torches, or colorful paper lanterns and candles. Incorporate tropical plants and rich fabrics in gold, orange, and red—the colors of the Sun, ruler of Leo. Keep a portable CD player on hand and stocked with batteries so you can enjoy your favorite background music on the porch.

As the Sun enters Virgo in late August, the air and the mood turn brisk. Vacationers return to work and kids go back to school. After a busy summer, it's time to give your porch some practical attention in preparation for crisper days ahead. Clean the windows and porch floor. Caulk windows. If necessary, install storm windows. If you're lucky enough to have fruit trees on your property, keep a big wicker basket handy on the porch for gathering autumn's bounty.

The Fall Porch

After the last dazzling Indian Summer days of early October, the days turn cool and you'll need a sweater to enjoy much time on the porch. But fall is a seductive time of year, and the crisp air and dazzling sky beckon us outdoors for a while longer before winter sets in.

The Sun enters Libra, the sign of beauty, harmony, and socializing, at the autumnal equinox in late September. Festoon your porch with garlands of autumn leaves and long strands of ribbon covered in shiny beads or small mirrors, to catch the autumn breezes that delight Libra's air sign nature. Keep a beautiful, artistic bowl on a table, filled with inviting fruit in season.

Various festivals commemorating the cycles of life and death converge in late October and early November, as the Sun enters Scorpio. Acknowledge the spirit of the season with seasonal pumpkins, gourds, and pomegranates. Flickering lanterns and a tall vase filled with long, bare tree branches are appropriately sober tributes to the beauty of all life's transitions. This is also an appropriate time for replacing rotted wood in eaves or floorboards.

As the Sun enters joyful Sagittarius right around Thanksgiving time, our spirits lift as we look ahead to the celebrations of the winter holidays. By now, the days are growing shorter and

colder. Bring in plants that need protection from late autumn's chill, and liven up your porch with hearty swags of evergreen and bright, plum-colored accents. A cozy lamp pays homage to the ebullient fire sign nature of Sagittarius.

The Winter Porch

Unless you have an enclosed porch or live in a very temperate climate, you're not apt to spend much time on your porch in winter. Instead, it often becomes an important staging area for practical winter gear such as a handy shovel. Provide a special space to stow the muddy boots and umbrellas that tend to accumulate like snowdrifts.

The Sun moves into Capricorn on the Winter Solstice, the shortest day of the year. Festivals of light abound during the Capricorn season, so hang lights, and plenty of them. Capricorn is an earth sign, so acknowledge the bounty of the Earth with a wreath of pine or holly branches and dangle a sprig of mistletoe over your door. Most porches are nearly unused for socializing at this time of year, but don't let this important space fall into neglect. Capricorn is the sign of career and earthly stature, and the porch symbolizes the entry point of this energy into your life, so make a conscious effort to infuse your porch with light, fragrance, and color as often as possible.

At the end of January, the Sun moves into Aquarius, a sign of ice and snow and barren landscapes. Introduce shimmering, reflective touches of electric blue and silver into your porch's décor. Aquarius is also an air sign, with an affinity for creatures that fly, so reach out to your avian friends with a winter birdfeeder or a wreath made of birdseed.

As the Sun in Pisces season begins in late February, hang musical wind chimes to evoke Pisces' artistic nature. Like his fellow water signs Cancer and Scorpio, Pisces enjoys a bit of water or least aquatic colors. Throw pillows embroidered with fish, a tabletop painted aqua, or crystals hanging from chains (in feng shui, crystals represent the water element) will celebrate the whimsical spirit and imagination of Pisces.

The Magical Threshold

Your front porch is a vital symbol of the interplay between your home and the rest of the world, offering visitors their first glimpse of your home and the people who live in it. It also provides for the kind of no-pressure social opportunities that are in short supply in these days of solitary freeway commutes and hours spent indoor, in front of flickering screens.

Far from a mere decorative element, the front porch is a magical portal where the practical world meets imagination and play—a threshold both safe and sociable. It is a stage on which to enact the great annual play that is the changing of the seasons, so pull out your favorite props and wardrobe pieces, and play your part. Sweep your porch, sit a little while, and wave to the neighbors; and when dusk falls and you go inside, be sure to leave the porch light on to welcome weary travelers back home.

About the Author

April Elliott Kent, a professional astrologer since 1990, is a member of NCGR and ISAR and graduated from San Diego State University with a degree in Communication. April's book Star Guide to Weddings *will be available in February 2008. Her astrological writing has appeared in* The Mountain Astrologer *(USA) and* Wholistic Astrologer *(Australia) magazines, the online magazines* MoonCircles *and* Beliefnet, *and Llewellyn's* Moon Sign Book *(2005, 2006, 2007). April lives in San Diego with her husband and two cats, in a house with a great front porch. Her Web site is: http://www.bigskyastrology.com.*

Your Home's Curb Appeal

By Alice DeVille

Homeowners take pride in the interior of their homes, spending time and money to personalize living quarters for a desired standard of comfort. As a realtor in the Commonwealth of Virginia, however, my first glimpse of a property is usually from the outside, looking toward the main entrance. I park my car away from the home and stand across the street to take in a visual picture of the premises. Whether I'm about to list the property for sale or show it to prospective buyers, I want to capture the most attractive exterior features with my eyes as well as my camera. I'll scan the house and any portion of it visible from the outside, including the porch, stoop, garage, siding, roof, gutters, doors, windows, and window treatments.

With a critical eye (and my expertise in feng shui), I look at the sidewalks around the house, the walkways leading to it, the yard, and last but not least the landscaping. Why? Because good landscaping has been known to hasten the sale of a home by weeks and sometimes months compared to other homes in the neighborhood.

I recommend that buyers visit property not only during the day but also at night, to see if light from neighbors' homes shines directly into key living spaces, or whether the surrounding trees provide adequate screening for privacy and a restful night's sleep. If I am working with a home seller whose lawn is full of weeds and overgrown shrubs, I provide pictures of similar properties with appealing landscaping so they have an idea of how to modify their façade to compete with the other listings. Most realtors have firsthand knowledge of where to find exciting gardens with a variety of plants, shrubs, and stately trees.

Today's buyers are Internet savvy and locate homes of interest through online searches. Maybe you're one of them. What you see can entice you to make an appointment, or you judge the house unfit based on the lack of attractive outer attributes. Perhaps you just bought your home, and now your job is to maintain the lush appearance of the lawn and keep the landscape, flowers, and trees trimmed and healthy. Whether you are a prospective buyer or already a homeowner, and no matter how large or small your yard, you'll find tips in this article for planning and planting the perfect green space.

Seasons of Beauty

Landscaping is all about bringing life to outdoor spaces—color, variety, density, form, and grace. Landscaping is also about cycles, and understanding climate and weather patterns in your locale so you can highlight each season with plantings that please your eye and your psyche. If you acknowledge these cycles starting with spring, you are following the astrological wheel, which begins with Aries. Each sign and season has its own beauty for you to enjoy, and its own tasks to be done. With thoughtful planning and planting, your outdoor environment will add color to the skyline and contribute to the quality and character of your neighborhood.

Curb Appeal Begins with a Plan

You have all seen the popular HGTV shows that address a home's worth by looking at the exterior façade and landscaping—or lack of it—and then coming up with a plan for making the property the most appealing home on the block. The idea is to correct existing landscaping, get rid of eyesores (dead plants, shrubs, weeds, unruly limbs, and dirt patches), and give the grounds a makeover.

First, Assess What You Have

While you may not be selling or buying a home, you can make sure your home has the curb appeal it deserves. Start by crossing the street and assessing your property as though you are viewing it for the first time. Would you want to ring the bell? Consider the landscape of your home in terms of what it can do for you. Mature plantings add value by framing your home and providing cooling properties in the summer months. The sunny spots on your lot make perfect places for installing a patio or for growing sun-loving flowers, herbs, vegetables, and grass. Do you have room for recreation and relaxation? What scenic vistas exist? When you sit on your deck or look out your front door, do you see any visual barriers such as tool sheds, structures accessed by utility companies, or water storage tanks? Clever landscaping with shrubs or sculpted hedges hides these eyesores. Improving your outdoor living space can increase your personal satisfaction and your enjoyment of living in your home.

Check Drainage

Look at the way the water flows away from your home. Notice the slope of the land. Is it steep or flat? The answer determines what you plant and why. Certain elements are more difficult to change. You may have to regrade the slope to ward off erosion or puddling that simply drown plants in the soggy soil. Depending upon where you live, the soil is unlikely to be in prime condition to support a variety of plantings. For example, in northern Virginia, where I reside, the native soil is red clay and requires a clay cutter additive and other soil amendments before it can sustain a serious landscaping project. You may have to work the soil for several years, and then keep it fertile with a maintenance program that balances alkalinity and acids.

If you are in doubt about the quality of your soil, you can have it tested by a county soil scientist in your community to learn what composition of additives will make it rich enough for your gardening projects. Address any drainage problems your lot has or you will constantly be replacing plants and shrubs that drown from too much water runoff. Swales and contours that send rain

flowing into the wrong location could lead to a flooded basement. Homes that sit at the bottom of a hill are often the coldest because cold air flows downward and frost pockets form in the low areas. Add extensions to downspouts and bury the drains to carry water away from your home's foundation.

Be sure to note the lot boundaries on your plat map so you don't start digging on a neighbor's property. If you're not sure where your boundaries are, order a land survey and ask for the property to be staked or marked. You'll also find out if any neighbors have encroached on your lot with fences, sheds, or plantings.

Once you have assessed the terrain and topography of your lot, you are ready to take pictures and start making decisions about what you want to include in your green space. Take note of bare spots in the lawn, because these will need special attention unless they are under sprawling shade trees like oaks or elms. You can either plant on the bare spots or treat them to reseeding after your landscaping is in place.

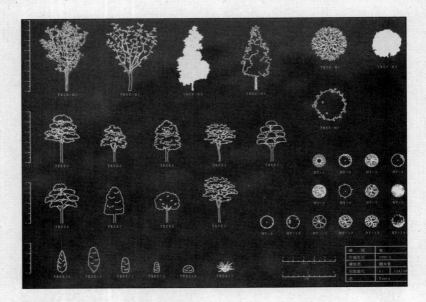

Now, It's Time to Design

To figure out what will work in your plot, you'll have to design it. You can either do this yourself or, if your budget permits, hire a professional landscaper. Do you have a balcony at your condo instead of a lot? Can you make room for hanging baskets, window boxes, or seasonal floor plants? In any case, sketch the area and include all the intended or existing planting areas—trees, decks, slopes, fences, walkways, patios, and decks—just about any area of your outdoor space that could use form and color. Make a very large drawing so you have plenty of room to write on it with specific information about your choices. Even if your sketch is crude, make sure you note your lot's dimensions so you don't overplant the available space.

First, plan your trees, because they provide focal points for your yard or garden. You may prefer shade trees that provide the most colorful foliage in the fall, or maybe smaller flowering trees that bloom in spring and summer. Trees can provide either a bold outline in your yard or an accent for a large grassy area of your lawn.

Next, consider plants that give year-round structure to your garden, such as ornamental plants that don't shed leaves, large bushes, and shrubs. At the same time, plan pathways, low walls, borders of brick or stone, raised beds, or placement of garden art—statues, bird baths, or arches. They will provide structure in the garden during barren months.

Now it's time to think about accents. Decorative flowering shrubs and grasses can be used to screen windowless garage walls, sheds, compost heaps, and utility structures, or as dividers between garden sections and attractive accents that frame the garden.

Finalize your sketch by including perennials, annuals, and bulbs. Bulbs provide early spring color, but normally have a short bloom life (think tulip, daffodil, or hyacinth). Annuals are relatively inexpensive and grow later in the spring and summer. A flat or two of these beauties adds an eye-pleasing swath of moving color to your landscape. Perennials take more time to develop and give your garden shape. They easily lend magic as border plants around your annuals, ornamental or vegetable gardens, and herbs. Since they return yearly, maintenance is relatively low.

Go on a Field Trip to a Garden Center

Plants and trees come in all colors, shapes, sizes, and textures, and you'll want plantings that accent the features of your home and surroundings. When you get this far, head to the local garden center and check with the landscape planner for advice. You'll learn about the suitability of your choices in terms of growing conditions. Plants and trees must be compatible with your zone, climate, orientation to the Sun, and soil. You can check catalogs, seed packets, and tree planting instructions for details, or you can log on to http://www.growit.com/ZONES to see what care your selections need to thrive. Once you have this information,

you're ready to purchase your nursery stock and start planting. Here's some insight into what you can expect.

Ten Years to Beauty

To become a work of art, gardens and landscaping need time to mature. You can plant a flower garden and expect excellent results in a year, but the "Big Picture"—complete with developed landscaping and all the trees—will take approximately ten years to mature. You will want to avoid planting any shade trees too close to your home. The roots could invade your home's foundation and sewage pipes, or the tree could fall onto your dwelling during a bad storm. Experts recommend a safe planting distance of at least twenty-five feet away.

Another reason to keep woody growths away from your home is to prevent excessive moisture that can rot the eaves. To discourage termites, keep plantings away from the foundation. Grass and flowers seldom grow under trees with spreading surface roots. If you have trees that prevent grass from growing, allow the lawn to decline instead of planting grass seed each season. If you have this condition, carve out a pattern around the tree and fill it in with decorative mulch or stones to minimize maintenance. An alternative presentation is to plant raised beds around these areas and incorporate shade-loving specimens such as bleeding heart, hosta (if you don't have a large deer population to contend with), day lily, ivy, pachysandra, and primrose. Shrubs that thrive in the shade or partial sun include azalea, japonica, ligustrum, rhododendron, and vinca species.

Trees with deep roots allow lawns and groundcovers to grow at their base. Apply mulch around the trees at least six inches away to hold moisture, but never apply it against the tree bark or base. A buildup of moist organic matter could cause root rot.

Perennials that grow to eighteen inches or less make suitable groundcovers, edging, or border plants. Besides bordering trees, use perennials in front of tall grasses, leggy plants, and larger shrubs to create a flowing contrast. Plants such as Lady's mantle, aster, blue plumbago, Dianthus (pinks), creeping baby's breath, and phlox have the additional quality of spreading by forming mats or trailing across the ground. They make useful bedding plants and look exquisite as bursts of color in formal gardens, around ponds or other water features, along pathways, and in tiered beds.

Flowering trees such as cherry, crape myrtle, dogwood, magnolia, eastern redbud, and tulip blossom in spring or summer and have the brightest foliage. You can plant these trees alone or surround them with attractive, low-growing shrubs and border plants or flowers. Small garden and patio trees include crab apple, Japanese maple (red and green varieties), plum, Japanese lilac, and evergreen pear.

Fast-growing ornamental trees like Leyland cypress, a needled evergreen, tolerate "wet feet" or roots. They are ideal to plant if you want to speed up the mature look of your landscaping. Use them as screening plants and allow generous space between them. They grow three to five feet per year, so they will close together quickly. Many new home owners plant this species along with slower growing deciduous trees (trees that shed leaves annually) and then remove some of the Leyland cypress when their more desirable plantings reach maturity. This species grows house high and beyond, but you can transplant them if you do so before the trunks and roots get too thick. Remove them altogether when they have lost their ornamental value. The deciduous green ash and red ash (native to Georgia and Mississippi) withstand wet soil and also survive in severe cold and drought. Flowering ash, grown in temperate zones, bears white to greenish-white clusters of fragrant flowers in late spring, and their shiny green leaves turn soft lavender or yellow in the fall.

Other fast-growing needled evergreens are Italian cypress (suitable for warmer climates), Arizona cypress, California redwood varieties (native to northern California and Oregon), and members of the Cedrus family, which are actually conifers (cone-bearing) and come in weeping, golden, blue, and columnar forms. If you plant these trees as a "live" fence, be sure to place them at least fifteen feet apart to allow for spreading and development in your ten-year plan.

Specimens that grow too fast include bamboo, willows, and privet hedges. The bamboo plant is so invasive it can take over your lot or your neighbor's, and is difficult to remove as the roots are very strong. And willows grow so high, planting them near utility wires, water pipes, or septic systems is banned. Privet, with its dense head and blue-black fruits, can get very messy if planted near streets and sidewalks, but they have a plus side. Privet hedges can be sheared and shaped, and they provide good wind blockers or privacy screens from eyesores or traffic.

More than likely you'll want a variety of trees and shrubs to accent your landscaping. Consider the beauty of adding one or more of the many species of holly in your yard. They range from dwarf shrubs to seventy-foot-high trees and grow in the temperate and tropical regions of both the northern and southern hemispheres. You need both male and female plants to produce berries, which may be black, red, yellow, or orange depending upon the species. Hollies need acid soil to thrive; they won't survive in a downhill frost pocket. Some are tree-shaped and grow up to fifty feet high and twenty feet wide. Leaves of English holly varieties are often spiny, glossy, and dark green. They also come in golden variegated forms and with smoother leaves. American holly, native to the eastern U.S., has been known to grow successfully in more northerly regions with selective site requirements such as good drainage and wind protection. Red is the most common berry color, and the species survives in moist or wet sites in the southeast.

Care and Feeding

If you begin by preparing good soil for planting, your maintenance will be reduced. Supplement soil and plantings with a slow-release fertilizer, or organic amendments such as peat moss or compost according to the species' recommended schedule. Develop a watering routine for new plants and trees and put established plantings on a maintenance schedule. Water deeply at least once a week, more often if the summer season has been particularly dry. Heat will quickly evaporate the moisture if you water too shallowly. Early morning or late afternoon are preferred times to water. Bark chips, mulch, and organic compost feed the soil, help to retain moisture, reduce erosion, protect roots, and slow weed growth.

To stay feng shui savvy, remove all broken, diseased, dead, or awkward limbs by cutting them back to the nearest branch or shoot. Deadhead flowers to encourage new blooms and get rid of unsightly dried-out blossoms. Prune trees to strengthen branch structure and promote graceful form.

Don't worry if some of your plantings don't survive. Keep good records and discover what works best in your soil. Learn as you "sow" from the body of knowledge available to you in books and publications, and from experts in the field of landscaping. Celebrate the seasons with living color. Then watch your home's value grow and blossom with curb appeal.

About the Author

Alice DeVille is an internationally known astrologer, writer, and metaphysical consultant. She grew her first vegetable patch at age eight and has been interested in gardening ever since. In her busy northern Virginia practice, Alice specializes in relationships, health, healing, real estate, government affairs, career and change management, and spiritual development. Some of her expertise in trees and shrubs comes from her past employment in the Department of Agriculture, Forest Service, which has stewardship of over 193,000,000 acres of forest land. She has developed and presented over 150 workshops and seminars related to astrological, feng shui, metaphysical, motivational, real estate and business themes. Alice is a licensed Realtor® in the Commonwealth of Virginia. She served on The President's Commission on Consumer Affairs for two years. Numerous publications and Web sites, including www.StarIQ.com/ feature her articles. Quotes from her work on relationships appear in books, publications, training materials, calendars, planners, audio tapes, and Oprah's Web site. Alice is available to write books and articles for publishers, newspapers, or magazines, to conduct workshops, and for radio or TV interviews. Contact Alice at DeVilleAA@aol.com.

The Many Faces of Green Living

By Morris Goodwin III & Stephanie F. Meyer

This we know: the earth does not belong to man, man belongs to the earth. All things connected like the blood that unites us all. Man did not weave the web of life, he is merely a strand in it. Whatever he does to the web, he does to himself.

—CHIEF SEATTLE, 1854

Some may believe that green design and conservation measures are relatively new practices, forced into existence by the limitation of natural resources we have come to depend on. Interestingly enough, our existence on Earth began with complete dependency on nature. This is still true today.

Throughout history, individuals have worked together to form communities that nurture their daily needs. The most basic needs—food, shelter, and water—were directly connected to people's existence on the land. As individuals grew to recognize this relationship with the Earth, cultures developed common practices and rituals that sustained life. Whether in the ancient civilizations of Greece and Rome or in a present day village in the Himalayan Mountains, self-sufficient "green" communities preserve nature to enhance the quality of life.

Water, Soil, Wind, and Light Are an Influence

Elements such as water, soil, temperature, wind, and sunlight often will influence the functionality of designs and inspire the aesthetics of architecture. The ancient ruins of Greece and Rome show that patterns of daily life were enhanced through careful city planning and site considerations. In Mesopotamia, a civilization not far from Greece (in present-day Iraq), the Hanging Gardens of Babylon, one of humanity's finest achievements, was designed around the limiting elements of nature. The city was built in the desert, yet it had the vegetation of a tropical rainforest. Babylon's center of life was the Euphrates River, which the people used to irrigate the lush gardens of the desert climate. The Hanging Gardens of Babylon could be considered the first green roof design to hold water, block the heat of the Sun, and provide ample fruits and vegetables for the people.

The architecture of the city consisted of vaulted terraces that raised one above the other and rested upon cubed-shaped pillars. These hollow pillars were filled with earth to allow for the planting of trees. What may appear to be artful design intentions also functioned as protection from the intensity of the Sun's rays, and as an irrigation system that allowed for water preservation.

Rome adopted these practices and continually improved them. Around the first century B.C.E., community-driven ideas such as markets, townsquares, civic centers, public pools, and gardens

were implemented. Villas surrounded by parks and buildings strongly influenced by the location of sunlight, water, and topography—the same key elements in sustainable design today—were built. Four main types of villas developed:

- Urban villa (urbana): based around public activities
- Country villa (suburbana): functional for family activities
- Agricultural villa (rustica): self-sustaining farms
- Villa with orchards and vineyards (fructuaria): in recognition of the art of horticulture

Villas addressed the individual needs of the community, while also enhancing the civic centers and social network of Greek and Roman culture. These villas are models for green design in both urban and suburban settings today.

When humans were given dominion over the land, water, fish, animals, and all of nature, the emphasis was on careful management and enhancement, not waste and degradation.

—JIMMY CARTER, OUR ENDANGERED VALUES

A period of recognizable change occurred during the Industrial Revolution and World Wars I and II. These periods in history

gave rise to dramatic socioeconomic change that influenced every facet of life.

The Industrial Revolution began in Britain during the middle of the eighteenth century and lasted through the late nineteenth century. With a large-scale trickle-down effect, the movement spread throughout Europe and into the Americas and Asian countries. The development of machines and the new factory style of work brought opportunity for greater economic achievements. The Revolution drove the standard of living for many to new heights, but it divided the nations: those who longed for stability and little change, the rural; and those who were captivated by the new standard of life, the urban.

The Industrial Revolution "created a specialized and interdependent economic life and made the urban worker more completely dependent on the will of the employer than the rural worker." The once rural, almost "organic" lifestyle, designed and based on localization and communal sharing within each town, village, and city, changed with the encroaching factories.

That lifestyle was replaced by high-density living in new urban settings and eventually it moved even into rural cities. With the influx of new people into the urban centers, apartment-like buildings grew quickly. Instead of single homes, dwellings became cramped. Buildings that contained twenty or more apartments were built along narrower streets. Centralized marketplaces, displaced by factories, moved toward the outskirts of cities. Across the globe, great cities were built upon the once-rural communities, and the green spaces vanished.

People like Karl Marx and John Stuart Mill saw all these new developments as a "dehumanizing" of man. Alexis de Tocqueville, a French political thinker said, "Technology and especially technical specialization of work, was more degrading to man's mind and spirit than even political tyranny."

This dehumanizing happened between the World Wars, by which time the steady progression to bigger and better machines and cities was an everyday occurrence.

The first skyscraper was erected in 1885, in Chicago, on the streets LaSalle and Adams. That nine-story building began a boom that would create a natural progression to build up instead of out. New York City became the metropolis of vertical monuments.

In America and parts of Europe, a great need to escape the cities for more open space came after World War II. The cities had grown too large, and the hustle and bustle of city life no longer appealed to soldiers returning from the war. They wanted a place to raise children and their own green space to tend. Thus, the first suburbs were born.

A Suburban Nation

It is an invention, conceived by architects, engineers, and planners, and promoted by developers in the great sweeping aside of the old that occurred after the Second World War. Unlike the traditional neighborhood model, which evolved organically as a response to human needs, suburban sprawl is an idealized artificial system.

—ANDRES DUANY, ET AL., SUBURBAN NATION

Presently, most people living in America are embedded into an "idealized artificial system," with faith that commerce and technology will continue to support this lifestyle. The model of city planning is based on this faith and involves five components: housing, shopping, business, civic institutions, and roadways.

Traditionally, these five components were designed to be reachable within a five minute walk. But suburban sprawl differs from traditional design, largely because it separates these components and makes them accessible only by driving or some other form of transportation.

Because the components of a suburb are disconnected it is difficult to sustain feasible transportation systems. From the Industrial Revolution onward, developments such as the automobile allowed for easier travel and opportunity. By the end of World War II, most families in America owned at least one vehicle. This willingness to embrace the automobile transformed the way we designed our cities. Thus, the pattern of sprawl began, and it continues to mold our relationship to nature and to each other.

Greener Cities

A world unlike the past, neither struggling against, nor exploiting nature, but a world where mankind and nature, thought and life, benefit each other. A world, in wisdom like the past, but conscious with new understanding.

—CHRISTOPHER DAY, SPIRIT AND PLACE

There are a number of communities that recognize the value in ancient cultures. For example, the Ladakhi Buddhist Community, located in the Himalayas of northern India, is completely dependent on nature's elements and its compounding effects on daily rituals. The designers used Ladakhi's culture as a foundation for renewing ancient practices in a modern construction project. In building the school, the site directly influenced the placement for maximal exposure to sunlight. Instead of an entirely stone structure, a timber

frame was used to allow for shifting in regional earthquakes. All the rooms open into the center courtyard that encourages community gatherings and events. Innovative preservation techniques, developed through the study of ancient customs, is far more prevalent in countries that have limited technological resources.

The continuous flux of change proves once again how design is influenced by community, history, technology, and human desire. The civilizations of Greece and Rome gave rise to landscape-influenced design, while the Industrial Revolution and the World Wars heralded an era of drastic movement toward the modern age. The elements most recognized in green communities are structures placed in relation to the Sun's movement for solar harvesting; in dry climates, conservation of water from rainfall and a return to material usage, indigenous to the regional geography.

Today we see conservation efforts being made in the hope of nurturing an environment that works with the Earth. This effort is leading to a new frontier in design that, as many hope, will become a standard across our global community. Green design is not a new idea. How we as humans live and develop throughout time has changed; so too has green design.

About the Authors

Morris Goodwin III has a love for the poetics of words and artistry. Morris spends most his time working on his first novel and going to graduate school in eco-architecture. He looks for inspiration both in nature and within the human psyche. He lives in Minnesota, but has a deep love for the East Coast, where he grew up as a child.

Stephanie F. Meyer is a designer and yoga instructor. Stephanie finds inspiration through travel, friends, and family. Captivated by the relationship society has with the Earth, much of her early adulthood has been spent exploring different cultures. Born and raised in Minnesota, Stephanie's love for nature is a fundamental force in her design objectives and artistic expression.

Works Cited

Carter, Jimmy *Our Endangered Values: America's Moral Crisis*. Simon & Schuster, 2003.

Campbell, Joseph. *The Power of Myth*. "Chief Seattle, 1852," page 42.

Duany, A. et al. *Suburban Nation: The Rise of Sprawl and the Decline of the American Dream*. North Point Press, New York, 2000.

Day, Christopher. *Spirit and Place*. Architectural Press, Oxford, 2002.

Architectural Record, 2003.

De Tocqueville, Alexis. *Democracy in America*. 1835.

References

"Industrial Revolution." Author unknown, *Columbia Encyclopedia,* Sixth Edition, 2006.

"World War II." Author unknown, *Columbia Encyclopedia,* Sixth Edition, 2006.

Architectural Record. August 2006 Vol. 194. McGraw-Hill Companies

Architecture. October 1999 Vol.88. BPI Communications, Inc.

"Eco Homes Get the Green Light." *The New York Times Magazine.* August 2006. New York: New York Times.

Voluntary Simplicity

By Maggie Anderson

The problem with the rat race is, even if you win, you're still a rat.

—LILY TOMLIN

Until the Bankruptcy Act was passed in 1800, individuals who could not pay their creditors were confined in debtors' prisons. Today's debtors find themselves limited in other ways, including a lack of work options. Many potential employers will not consider a job candidate who has a bad credit rating, especially if that employee will handle money or must be bonded. College graduates laden with heavy school loans must take positions offering the highest pay, even if the jobs are outside their majors and true vocations. With a softening economy, heads of families frequently opt to work overtime hours or take two, even three, jobs to pay down debt. Having debt puts severe strains on family life and creates stress on each family member.

For all of us who regularly run through mazes and never seem to find our way out, the key to inner peace and better health may be in learning how to simplify our day-to-day lives. Life has a way of issuing wake-up calls, and some recent four-alarm sirens have alerted Americans to the possible need for voluntary simplicity, which means living within the boundaries of our time, energy, and financial realities. Hundreds of self-help books have been written on how to reduce the stress of daily living in the modern world.

Voluntary Simplicity: Is It for You?

Our Puritan forefathers practiced simplicity in every aspect of their lives, including dress, speech, and religious rituals. Theirs was a spiritual reformist response to the opulent religious expressions and affluent lifestyles in their native England. Since Colonial times, voluntary simplicity has risen and fallen many times in popular culture—and it's making a comeback.

Today's voluntary simplicity movement is a reaction to the stress of modern lifestyles; environmental crises, including global warming; and the need to find spiritual development in an increasingly materialistic world. While these three broad issues often overlap, practitioners of voluntary simplicity are usually motivated by one of these issues initially. But they often embrace all three, eventually.

Changing Lifestyles

The goal of individuals who practice voluntary simplicity as a reaction to modern stress is to "have a life instead of a lifestyle." It holds appeal for many people who are caught in patterns of overconsumption and debt, who are overworked and lack leisure, who have disintegrating family lives and lack community involvement, and who have little time to pursue individual interests.

"Freedom" has been a keyword in simple-living literature from the beginning. Benjamin Franklin promoted frugality, hard work, and limited consumption in the *Poor Richard's Almanac* (published from 1732–1757). He warned readers of the perils of debt and that the desire for even small luxuries can lead to trouble:

> *What Madness must it be to Run into Debt for these Superfluities! Think what you do when you turn in Debt: you give to an end debt, the practice of voluntary simplicity helps individuals to distinguish between their "wants" and their "needs."*

Adopting simple living doesn't mean that individuals can't do it all or have it all—it just realistically points out that it's unlikely that they can have it all and do it all at the same time without creating enormous stress for themselves and everyone around them.

Simple living suggests that, at various stages of one's life, individuals choose what is most important and give it priority over other, equally attractive options. This puts us in the enviable position of being able to choose the way we use time rather than continually reacting to the agendas of our consumer society.

For example, practitioners may opt to have one parent stay at home with their children and live on one salary, or both parents might work part time and share child care. One couple of my acquaintance, both engineers, alternated full-time child care with full-time employment in three-year increments until their children finished high school.

Environmental Concerns and Sustainable Living

Nature provides a free lunch, but only if we control our appetites.

—WILLIAM RUCKELSHAUS, *BUSINESS WEEK*

Individuals who adopt voluntary simplicity out of their concern for the environment work toward maintaining an environmentally friendly and sustainable life. Their goals are to preserve the Earth so that our children and grandchildren may enjoy nature as it was intended, in its most pristine form. Since this often requires changes in public policy, the environmentally driven practitioners of voluntary simplicity also often lead politically active lives.

Henry David Thoreau (1817–1862) found peace, tranquility, and transcendence while living the simple life for two years on Walden Pond. He also is the original American proponent of living in harmony with the environment. However, much like modern practitioners of simple living, Thoreau did not abandon all modern amenities: he attempted to find a balanced approach to nature and civilization.

The majority of individuals who adopt voluntary simplicity for environmental reasons do not live without electricity or spend time plowing fields with mules. Many do use solar technology and other alternative fuels whenever possible, and make it their primary goal to live lightly on the earth.

This might include growing their own food, but they also can purchase food from many other organic sources, including food co-operatives, community subscription gardens, and farmers' markets. They practice widely accepted recycling processes in addition to adopting others that reduce the use of fossil fuels—such as walking, biking, and using public transportation instead of driving an auto if possible.

Amish, and some Mennonite, communities in the U.S. renounce modern technology as a way of keeping their lives simple. Although the majority of Americans would not embrace similar living patterns, it is commendable that these groups live in ways that have low environmental impact—and they are self-sufficient. These communities are not dependent on oil. When it's in short supply, they don't miss a beat.

Neither do these Amish and Mennonites groups become helpless when the lights go out. Their food supplies are not subject to disruptions because they grow and store their own. We can all learn a lot from their simple ways, even though they are more adaptable to rural living than urban life.

Thoreau's book *Walden* (1854) experienced a revival in the 1960s and 1970s, not only because of environmental issues, but also for his political views. In our consumer-driven society, voluntary simplicity is countercultural and can include a political component. Those who promote a continually expanding economy sometimes find the voluntary simplicity movement threatening. Their fear that if enough individuals live within their means, the economy will experience a slow-down or grow at a slower rate.

While individuals in the voluntary simplicity movement appreciate the wonders of modern technology, they also recognize that there can be too much of a good thing. Sustainable consumption of material goods can be compared to the consumption of food: our bodies need food for sustenance, we love good food and enjoy preparing and eating it—but we also recognize that the overconsumption of food can damage our health.

Voluntary Simplicity as a Spiritual Discipline

Manifest plainness, embrace simplicity, reduce selfishness, have few desires.

—Lao Tzu (604 to 531 B.C.)

All of the major world religions associate simplicity with freedom from desire, envy, and unhappiness. The goal of simple living in these traditions is twofold: to detach from material possessions as a form of spiritual discipline, and to make do with less so that others may have more.

The public often confuses voluntary simplicity with voluntary poverty. Those who were educated in parochial schools may have memories of clergy who belonged to orders that embraced poverty as part of their spiritual disciplines. Certain religious orders of monks, nuns, and priests do take vows of poverty, but, with rare exception, those who practice voluntary simplicity do not.

Voluntary simplicity may, in fact, be one of the best ways for individuals to avoid poverty. The goal is to always live within one's means, whatever that may be. Those who wish to adopt a simple lifestyle may do so, but deciding where to spend the extra disposable income is always optional.

Early in their marriage, one couple in my county agreed to live on half of their joint incomes. They were typical middle income earners, but for over fifty years they've donated 50 percent of their earnings to meet the special needs in this community. Their gifts have touched thousands of lives. Their own spiritual rewards are evident: both have remained youthful, glowing, healthy, and joyful well into their advanced years.

If you are currently a member of a faith community, inquire about the resources it provides for individuals who wish to explore voluntary simplicity as a spiritual discipline. You may be surprised at the rich history of this movement in your own denomination of church, mosque, synagogue, or temple.

How to Begin

Voluntary simplicity requires a change of heart and mind, followed by action. It's a philosophy that nudges people toward making significant change, but is not pushy. Individuals who are new to the movement usually begin by making small changes and work up to the big ones. For instance, some might begin by limiting their family's television time in favor of family time spent biking. Others may attempt to eat a more healthy diet from sources that are Earth and animal friendly, and give up fast food. Individuals who are new to recycling might take a few months to make that a habit. .

If there is one necessary starting place, however, it is coming to a reasonable understanding of the difference between wants and needs. The public is bombarded with advertising on a daily basis. What used to be a luxury—for instance, having two cars in one family—now seems like a necessity. New products like cell phones spring up virtually overnight and make their way into the necessity category in a flash. Initially, this is not easy to sort out but, after a bit of practice, it becomes more obvious and easy.

If one chooses to begin living a life of voluntary simplicity, the second step is to get out of debt as soon as possible. Being debt-free increases all options and gives us greater choices around our work lives. The film *Affluenza* helps parents understand and deal with their family's overconsumption and the negative influence that it has on young people.

What It Is and What It Isn't

Although the kind of voluntary simplicity that is associated with religion does include identifying with the poor by living in a similar kind of poverty, it is not part of the movement for individuals who live in the secular world. Few of us could duplicate the life of Mother Teresa, or lead the life of other monks and nuns. What we can do is lower our desire for material possessions, following the lead of spiritual leaders from all religious traditions.

When embracing voluntary simplicity, one does not promote poverty for oneself or for others. Rather, the movement advocates living within one's means, avoiding debt, and, if possible, using some disposable income to enhance the lives of others. The key-word is always "sustainable," and individuals are encouraged to live within their means, no matter how affluent or meager.

Many Resources Available, but Beware of Imitations

Sensing a growing movement, some enterprising commercial interests have co-opted the language and appeal of voluntary simplicity in recent years. For instance, recognizing that over-consumption leads to clutter, entire retail stores and mail order catalogs are now devoted to helping the U.S. homemaker "get organized." The new occupation of "professional organizer" has sprung up, with some professional organizers exhibiting their skills on reality TV shows.

Voluntary simplicity only includes purchasing expensive, built-in closet organizers if you don't have to acquire them by increasing your debt load. The same is true for items that appeal to the environmentally conscientious. Although the movement recognizes quality over quantity, the purchase of 100 percent cotton organic sheets for four hundred dollars is not necessary. A rule of thumb? If items appear in a slick, glossy magazine, seem overpriced, and you'll go into debt to buy them, you're veering off the voluntary simplicity trail if you bring them home.

The voluntary simplicity movement is more about shedding "stuff" than adding more. It is tough to resist a bargain and all the advertising that surrounds us. Adopting a more simple lifestyle is also easier if you gain the cooperation of partners and your children if you have them. It does help to have a support group, and you will find them in many religious settings and nature centers.

You could even start your own! Some of the sites listed below will show you how to do this.

You can find excellent resources for voluntary simplicity and simple living online, as well as in the self-help section of local public libraries, religious, and secular book stores, and on environmental Web sites.

About the Author

Maggie Anderson lives in Mount Vernon, Iowa, and she practices voluntary simplicity in her everyday life.

Resources

"Affluenza." Retrieved from http://www.pbs.org/kcts/affluenza/
"Take Back Your Time." Retrieved from http://www.timeday.org/
"Alternatives for Simple Living." Retrieved from http://www.simpleliving.org/
"Seeds of Simplicity." Retrieved from http://www.seedsofsimplicity.org/

Composting: An Alchemical Recipe for "Black Gold"

By Pam Ciampi

My interest in composting was born out of sheer desperation. Many years ago in Vermont, as I was making an attempt to seed a lawn and grow a garden on five shady acres of acid soil littered with rocks, I was desperate to find a way to enrich and amend the thin coating of topsoil I had to work with. I had heard of composting and decided to give it a try. My first attempts were blissfully ignorant, free of form, and not restricted by a container or a technique. My compost piles consisted of loosely built haystacks set at irregular intervals around the yard.

I would add leaves in fall (plenty of those in Vermont), kitchen scraps daily, lime when I had it, and manure once a year, whenever the farm down the road would agree to deliver. I watered the piles when they started to smoke and turned them when they got too clumpy. After a year went by, to my amazement the garbage and leaves magically began to morph into the most wonderful, porous black dirt. When one pile got too tall, I would start another haystack and eventually there were seven stacks working in different stages of development. I loved those compost piles almost more than my gardens. They were amazing, alchemical experiments right in my own backyard, working day and night to turn waste into "black gold."

One day, when working the compost, it occurred to me that composting could be a metaphor for that part of the natural life cycle that causes breakdowns and death. As an astrologer, this sounded like a perfect description of the higher manifestation of Scorpio. In ancient mythology, the higher side of Scorpio is representeented by the Phoenix. The story of this remarkable bird, which was said to resemble an eagle, was that after living for 500 years it met its death in a blazing fire. After it had died, the Phoenix was magically resurrected and rose up from the ashes to live forever in the heavens. If we take the resurrection concept into the personal realm, the compost then becomes a template for how to recycle and reuse our emotional "waste materials." In this way, by creating an emotional compost pile, it might be possible to turn negative emotions like hate, regrets, and envy into a kind of psychological "gold."

What's Good for the Garden Is Good for the Soul

If you are new to composting, it might be helpful to look at the process as a new recipe for a special dish you want to try out. The first step any good cook takes is to find out what ingredients the recipe calls for, and the next thing is to see if they are at hand. In our compost recipe there are only four basic ingredients that,

interestingly, correspond to the four natural elements of fire, air, earth, and water. The first two ingredients are the yang and the yin of composting, and correspond to the elements of fire (dry and hot), and earth (wet and moist). These ingredients will be referred to as "browns" and "greens."

Browns provide a carbon-rich base that is one of the key elements in the successful compost pile. The browns are yang in nature, and include dry materials such as dried lawn clippings and weeds, and kitchen scraps that have little or no moisture. The best example of browns are the dead leaves that fall off deciduous trees in autumn, when the moisture has withdrawn into the tree roots in preparation for winter. Dead weeds, dry grass clippings, straw, and wood chips are other examples of browns.

Greens are waste materials that are yin in nature (wet and moist). Greens include any fresh garden waste, such as fresh grass clippings and garden weeds, and kitchen scraps that still hold plenty of water, such as coffee grounds and vegetable leavings. (Tip: Never put fish, meat, or oils in the compost because they attract animals.) Well-cured farmyard manure also comes under this category. All greens provide a nitrogen-rich atmosphere that creates the heat that the compost pile needs to support the microorganisms that facilitate the process of decomposition.

Balance Matters

How much of the browns and greens do you put in? The lazy woman's composting rule (highly recommended by the author) is to always try to keep it full. This rule is followed by dumping all wastes into the compost bin, while trying to maintain a standard ratio of two-thirds brown to one-third green. This is easy to do by simply layering generous portions of browns on top of generous portions of greens according to your whim and their availability. Remember that the more greens you have, the hotter the compost will get and the faster it will decompose.

For example, a pile made up of 25 to 50 percent greens will heat up in the shortest time. But you must also consider that more is not always better. If you see smoke coming out of your compost, you might be creating a dangerous fire hazard and making the pile too hot for the microorganisms to live. Using too much of the browns will cause the opposite affect. The pile will dry out. Try experimenting with different brown-to-green ratios until you find the balance that works best for you.

Turning It On

The last two ingredients of the compost pile are available in the natural elements of air and water. A healthy compost pile needs frequent aeration and the right amount of moisture. A pitchfork or long rod (a piece of rebar) is a handy tool that will help you to turn the compost pile. Turning the pile frequently helps to blend the materials as well as to increase the oxygen flow. This will allow the microorganisms, earthworms, and insects to work more efficiently. If space is not a consideration, another method of aeration is to knock down the whole pile with a shovel, mix it up, and then build it up again. Composters, like cooks, have their own special methods and part of the art of composting is in finding out what works best for you.

Last but not least, a happy compost pile is a moist compost pile. The moisture content of your compost will depend on your weather zone. If you live in a hot, dry climate, your compost will need frequent sprinklings. On the other hand. if you live where the rainfall or snowfall is heavy, you may need to cover the compost pile to protect it from becoming too wet. But whatever your weather pattern, the goal is the same. You want to maintain a moisture level that is not too dry and not too wet. The aim is to create a friendly climate for those tiny but beneficial organisms that will work diligently to decompose the waste in your compost pile and transform "garbage" into "black gold" that you will use to enrich the soil in your lawn or garden. By adding nutrients and balancing the acid to alkaline ratios, you can make sandy soil hold water and clay soil less dense.

Composting by the Moon

The most favorable times for composting activities can be determined by observing the natural rhythms of the Moon. Each month the Moon signals the best times for various composting activities as it makes its journey through its phases and the different signs of the zodiac.

Best Days to Start a Compost Pile

According to natural rhythms, there are good times in each month of 2008 to start a compost pile. These times occur at the time of the New Moon. It is recommended that you use the tables on page 300 in conjunction with your local weather conditions.

In 2008 the dates of the New Moons that are favorable for starting a new compost pile are listed in the "Start a Compost Pile" table on the next page. The best New Moons for starting a new compost pile are the Pisces New Moon, the Cancer New Moon, and the Scorpio New Moon. These occur in March, July, and October.

Start a Compost Pile

January 8	May 5	September 2
February 7	June 3	October 28
March 7	July 3	November 27
April 6	August 1 and 30	December 27

Best Days to Turn a Compost Pile

The best days to turn the compost pile are in the two weeks after the Full Moon, when the Moon is waning. The dates are listed in the table below.

Turn a Compost Pile

January 1–7, 23–30	July 1–2, 19–29
February 1–6, 22–25	August 17–29
March 1–6, 22–31	September 16–28
April 1–5, 21–30	October 15–27
May 1–4, 21–31	November 14–26
June 1–2, 19–30	December 13–26

Best Days to Aerate a Compost Pile

The best days to aerate a compost pile occur when the Moon is waning and in an air sign (Gemini, Libra, Aquarius). These days are listed in the table below.

Aerate a Compost Pile

January 1, 27–28	July 1, 19–20,28–29
February 6, 23–25	August 24–25
March 4–5, 22–23	September 20–21, 29–30
April 1–2, 28–29	October 17–18, 26–27
May 26–27	November 14–15, 22–24
June 22–23	December 20–21, 30–31

Best Days to Add Waste and to Water a Compost Pile

Adding wastes and watering the compost may be carried out on any day, as needed.

What Kind of Bin to Use

Compost bins, like gardeners, come in all shapes and sizes. There are many different types to choose from, including trash-can bins, block bins, wire bins, wood bins, plastic bins, and rotating bins. Contact your local recycling or garden center to find the one that is right for your needs. When I first started composting, I didn't use any kind of bin. Although these days, my needs are better served by a plastic shelf bin, those early compost piles produced a better quality of soil amendment than anything I've tried since.

Conclusion

Composting is satisfying, useful, and productive on many levels. It is my hope that this article has encouraged you to get in touch with your garbage and to participate in the simple process of turning that garbage into gold. Composting has many benefits, but the greatest in the eyes of this author is that it helps to explain why decomposition (the Scorpio process) is integral to, and a necessary part of, the life cycle.

About the Author

Pam Ciampi is a certified professional astrologer with over thirty-two years of experience. She loves gardening and has authored three almanacs titled Gardening by the Light of the Moon, using gardening practices that are based on zodiac signs and Moon phases. Pam was president of the San Diego Astrological Society from 1998–2005, and is currently serving as the president of the San Diego chapter of National Council for Geocosmic Research (NCGR). Besides her busy private practice, Pam also teaches intermediate astrology classes in the San Diego area. Pam can be reached at pciampi@sbcglobal.net. Her Web site is: www.pciampi-astrology.com.

The Moon's Many Faces

By Lesley Francis

There's something ancient and truly familiar about the Moon. She watches over us—from a distance. Her light is reflected but that doesn't dim her beauty. She shines into the darkness as she grows, showing us how the cycle of life works. She reminds us that everything begins in darkness, in what appears to be nothingness, and then evolves into something meaningful and useful. It's probably the most significant reason the Moon's cycles have always been used to plot the best time for planting a garden, cutting your hair, hiring a servant, etc. The folklore around this is based on observable results. It's just not made-up hocus pocus.

However, we often neglect to make use of the knowledge the Moon reveals in the area of feeling. She is the key to what we sense, how we feel, how we respond, what we cherish. And it is the Moon that calls upon us to feel life, feel ourselves, feel what is possible. Then, she invites us to take the leap.

Leap into the Unknown

Each of us has our own emotional blueprint that guides us and supports us. The cycles of the Moon remind us to take note of that blueprint, to find ways to manifest it that are not just meaningful but effective. If we are blocked in our feeling world, it can make the rest of our lives distorted.

But we live in a time when the feeling world is considered to be inconvenient at best. So this complicates the need to connect to your inner feeling world. It's okay to focus on the practical side of the Moon's energies—the running of daily life and the nurturing of others. But we're advised to avoid all that emotional stuff. Get over it and get on with life. After all, feelings don't last. Right?

All I have to say to that is @#H&*! I remember being seventeen, not the happiest year of my life. I didn't want to go to school. I didn't want to talk to anybody. I was depressed. I felt alone and disconnected. Finally, I just couldn't stand it anymore. I summoned all my courage and told my parents how I felt. Their reaction? You shouldn't feel that way. I was stunned, hurt. I withdrew, bottled up my feelings, and carried on. And I bear that imprint to this day. It wasn't until I was in my late thirties that I started to open up to my own feelings, and even then, it took a divorce, a custody battle, and the loss of my mother to get that "feeling" process kick-started. All because no one taught me about the feeling side of life: about its value, about its importance, about it being necessary to live a balanced, healthy life.

There are so many reasons why being emotionally plugged in needs to be a top priority. It helps us to be physically healthier, to be more aware of what works for us, to know who to trust, to feeling secure within ourselves, to handle whatever comes our way, and to avoid other people's garbage. In short, you can know yourself and have a deeper connection to your own life, instead of feeling like you are watching it from a distance.

The list goes on. I know there's something you could add to this list if you just listened to yourself. Try it and see what you come up with.

I teach a workshop called "Buried Treasure." Its purpose is to help people become emotionally present in their lives in order to further their spiritual growth. I am an Aquarius with an inordinate number of planets in air signs (the signs that view talking and thinking as recreational sports). That in itself makes it ironic that I would be teaching such a workshop. But, the real irony is that the first time I taught this workshop, all the participants were water signs: Cancers, Scorpios, and Pisces. The people who are supposed to know about emotions. Well, just because your primary response to the world is emotional does not mean you know how to connect to those feelings, trust them, and use them to guide you.

We're all stuck in the same boat. We have forgotten how to use our feelings as a barometer for what our next step should be, no matter how big or how small. Understanding the Moon's cycles offers us an opportunity to regain that balance so we can become familiar with the deeper aspects of ourselves and honor our feelings at the same time.

There's no doubt that we must take care of the practical matters of life, but we seem to have lost sight of the fact that perhaps knowing ourselves (and I think the Moon is key to that) might make our lives work better.

It then makes sense that we can use the cycles of the Moon to cultivate the most precious thing we have. Ourselves. We, like our gardens and our homes, are a work in progress. That may be difficult for the perfectionists on the planet, but the Moon clearly demonstrates to us in the unfolding of our daily lives and daily routines that things change. Why? Because perceptions change depending on how we feel, what we sense. Not everything is linear. Nor is it meant to be.

The cycle of the Moon shows that everything begins within, moves outward, and then comes full circle as we experience the results of our efforts—not unlike the fisherman who waits to cast his net until the time is right, and then gathers in the fruits of his labors.

To me, using the cycles of the Moon to connect to myself means taking the time to know how I feel and acting in accordance with the deeper feeling nature, which I call our Internal Guidance System. It's there in all of us. And it really does run the show. So, being unaware of the program that's running on that channel makes it difficult to recognize what's really going on. We fail to see the following truth: life is a mirror of what is within.

This is something our ancestors understood. So, they made time for the Moon. They revered her and honored her and lived in ways that reflected their awareness of her role. She was part of nature, something bigger than they perceived themselves to be.

They sought a partnership with nature, out of equal parts necessity and intuition.

Today we believe that nature exists to serve us. We don't revere the natural world except in a picture-postcard way. We are disconnected. That makes the cycles of the Moon even more important. She is our constant companion, our pathway back to a sense of ourselves and to our home. No matter where you live, embracing the cycles of the Moon and the opportunities represent will bring you a greater passion for life, a more peaceful heart, and a deeper sense of who you are and why you are here.

The Moon's Phases

There are eight phases to the Moon's cycle—new, crescent, first quarter, gibbous, full, disseminating, last quarter, and balsamic. Each phase lasts about three and a half days.

Because the Moon represents daily functioning, it's important to find an activity, a ritual that symbolizes each phase of the Moon and nurtures you at the same time. You need to get out of your head and into your heart. Choose something personally meaningful. Otherwise you'll feel stilted, like what you're doing is a requirement instead of a pleasure.

I will suggest an activity with each phase as a guideline, but I do invite you to create your own. Don't stick with them religiously, either, because you'll find that as you get more connected to your emotional self and come to know yourself at a deeper level, what works for you will change.

New Moon

We are quite literally in the dark. The new Moon asks us to take time to listen to the whisperings of our inner selves. We are cleansed and purified following the end of the previous cycle. And now we begin anew. Our energy is wide open and there's anticipation in the air. How would we like to grow during this lunar cycle? The sign the Moon is in during this phase may often offer a clue. A New Moon in Aries might give us opportunities to test our self-reliance, a New Moon in Cancer a challenge to handle hurt feelings from the past.

Try standing outside and wishing on the Moon. After all, this is the wishing phase, the time to set your intent. What we often forget is that the Moon does not require that these wishes be momentous to anyone but ourselves. The Moon connects us to all those things that give our lives meaning. Take time to feel. Notice any physical sensations that occur. Sometimes we're so busy that we don't notice our own responses because there's too much going on. So review your feelings during this period. Honor them. Respect them. Listen to them. But don't act. It's too soon.

Crescent Phase

Okay, so now your intent has taken root. This is the weighing and balancing time. Security issues arise. Fears, worries, and concerns can crowd out all those glorious desires. Just know that resistance is as important as acceptance (something I learned from William David, a spiritual teacher who pioneered work on color and sound). Examine the negative or challenging feelings that crop up. All those ingrained habits, behind the endless you-can't-do-that chatter in your head that will keep you stuck if you don't air them. Where did they come from? Why do they have such a hold on you? Acknowledge them and recognize that they have served a purpose—to protect you—that may no longer be valid. Doing all this will focus your vision and remove any unnecessary blockages before you take action—or at the very least, neutralize them. It's like pulling all the weeds out of your garden so the plants will grow strong and tall. Part of what this phase is about is building inner strength and confidence.

One activity that can really help is writing. Don't worry about grammar and all that structural stuff. Just write your feelings. In single words if necessary. Take a time out and then go back and read them again. See what else comes up.

First Quarter

Do you remember Kevin Costner's character in the movie *Field of Dreams*? He really exemplifies the whole process of the lunar cycle. He listens to his heart's desire and decides—despite opposition—to build a baseball diamond in his corn field. Well, the first quarter is the "build it and they will come" phase. Decisions are made, plans begin to jell, and the first steps toward making things happen are taken. You're going to feel, you just have to get the job done. You might be a little pushy and irritable at the same time, especially if those around you just don't get what the big deal is. Yet you feel you've just made the next big discovery that will change the world and you want to hold a press conference. You're literally bursting at the seams and taking charge; taking action seems to be the only thing that will satisfy you. You definitely don't want to deal with any limitations. Underneath all this is just a little bit of uncertainty. And that's not a bad thing. It's there to keep you from rushing headlong into things without the proper planning. Physical activity can really help—walking, dancing, anything that allows you to blow off some of the excess energy before you throw caution to the wind. This is a period when you need to feel grounded.

Gibbous

The key word for this phase is "adjustment." The dream is taking shape, but things aren't unfolding the way you envisioned them. You push harder for perfection. The predominant feeling here is usually frustration. You really wonder what you were thinking when you started this whole thing anyway. For example, you may have decided at the New Moon to transform your relationship with your mother. Take a different approach. You got all your ducks lined up and yet she's still talking to you like you're five years old. What went wrong? Well, nothing really. Every plan needs tinkering, or sticking with it, or both. So, stop and analyze what's going on. What's working and what's not. Back to Mom. Just because you had your heart set on creating a different relationship with her doesn't mean she's ready to change. You might have to stick to your plan for a while longer. Right now you have to process, then integrate the unanticipated roadblocks that cropped up while you were working to put your plan into action.

Any kind of physical bodywork right now is good to help release the tension you're building up. Or try working on some project that lightens your mood and helps you put things in perspective because you can get pretty compulsive in this phase and overwork the program.

Full Moon

This is the "nowhere-to-run, nowhere-to-hide phase." Things come to fruition and now it's time to put things into perspective. This is the gift of the Full Moon. The lights are on and you can see everything—the good, the bad, and the ugly. Resist the urge to push aside what doesn't fit the original wish. The Moon's message is often similar to the Rolling Stones' lyric: "You can't always get what you want, but if you try sometimes you find what you need." Trade your subjectivity for objectivity. That, after all, is the road to awareness and growth. Avoid being your own judge and jury; it will inhibit any chance of finding the hidden treasures in your experience and using them to know yourself better. And isn't that the real purpose of anything we undertake—to come to a deeper and more profound awareness. I am not talking about navel gazing here. I am talking about gathering food—emotional, practical, intellectual, and spiritual—from the events of our lives so that we feel fulfilled. That can't happen if we polarize ourselves into good, bad, right, wrong, success, failure. Reward yourself in whatever way is special to you. It's a way of celebrating yourself, which is something we all need to do more of.

Disseminating

Now that you know what you know it's time to stretch yourself. Move forward with wisdom and understanding, not just a set of facts or bare bones information that describes what you've just been through. Here's your chance to shine by sharing what you've learned. That is the true harvest, which gives meaning and purpose to your life experiences when you wear them proudly. Live your expanded awareness. Be an example. True leadership comes from those who not only followed through on their commitment but had the courage to talk about it without pulling any punches. This is the phase we all have the greatest difficulty putting into practice. We're too busy trying to be the model of perfection. So, whatever we learn lies dormant inside us or is pushed aside because telling our truth might tarnish the whole idea that we are always in control, that we always have all the right answers. Nowhere is this more obvious than in parenting. Rather than using our life experiences to enrich our children's lives and prepare them for a life of ever-expanding possibilities, we present them with a Cliff Notes version: "Just the facts, ma'am." Nothing else. But life isn't in the facts; it's in the experience itself.

Your ritual at this phase? Try creating a chart with your goals written on it. Leave a space to observe what you gained from the experience and then give yourself a gold star for a job well done.

Last Quarter

This is a time for rest and reflection. Take stock of what has transpired from the beginning of the cycle. What impact has this had on you? How has it changed you? What did you accomplish? What do you need to get rid of, what no longer serves you? In the middle of this accounting, there is a slight feeling of restlessness. This phase is symbolized by the fall ritual of digging up the garden. The satisfaction of what was created by all that hard work lingers, but it's not enough to sustain you. Yet it's not quite time to turn your attention to what comes next. You're not quite ready for the future. You feel the glimmer of something promising, but it's still an unknown. You're still busy re-evaluating and re-evaluating

and re-evaluating. The experiences you've had may have so profoundly impacted your life that a wholesale change is required in order to facilitate the future that tingles just out of your reach.

Meditation can really help sort out the jumble of thoughts that keep on trucking through your brain. Sometimes it's hard for us to realize that assimilation takes place on many levels, and that we must make knowledge of the head into knowledge of the heart.

Balsamic Moon

It's time to let go, clear the decks, and prepare for a new wish—mentally, emotionally, physically, and spiritually—because a new phase beckons. But it cannot take root if you're still holding on to the past. The challenge of this phase is to blend the past and the future. Take the essence of what you've experienced forward without hanging onto it. You might feel that what transpired during this lunar cycle is so profound that you can't let yourself forget it. Trust is the key. Trust that what was meaningful to you will move forward with you because it is now a part of you. And trust that you can safely release the experience itself. Holding tight to things doesn't actually contribute to long-term growth. It crystallizes them and destroys their original value. Plus, the new seed waiting for development will not grow in an already-crowded psychic Earth, because all your energy is focused on maintaining the status quo not on creating new opportunities for yourself.

What you need to do in this phase is to remain open to the world of all possibilities. Allow feelings and thoughts to flow in and out. Acknowledge them but do not pursue them or develop them. Only then can the wish that our heart desires to fulfill in the next lunar cycle make itself heard over the din of everyday life.

So, welcome the Moon and her phases into your life. You'll find it nurturing and enlightening. In this time of rapid advancement, we need something that can keep us connected and grounded. And it's comforting to know that the lunar cycle tells us that the opportunity for growth keeps on knocking on the door of our consciousness.

About the Author

Lesley Francis is a professional astrologer, writer, journalist, and teacher whose five planets in Aquarius have led her on a fascinating journey through life. Her study of astrology began thirty-three years ago after interviewing her future astrology mentor for a story in the local daily newspaper. It proved to be a passion and an avocation until ten years ago when her journalistic career gave way to her new life as a professional astrologer, psychic, and teacher. Lesley has lectured across Canada and recently spoke at the 2007 NORWAC conference. She can be contacted by E-mail at lesley_francis@hotmail.com or by going to www.andnow.ca.

Natural Cycles of Living

By Deborah Ooten

At times, our lives take on a momentum of their very own and we live life at top speed. It is vital that we begin to slow down, take stock of how we spend our time and energy, and look at what life has to offer us. Three areas of life—work, play, and self-care—must remain in balance for us to be in optimal health.

We typically spend eight to ten hours at work each day working to make a living for our families and provide the necessities of life. Work can be a job, career, or vocation. The highest form of work is an energizing vocation that helps us wake up saying, "Yes, I get to do what I love and get paid for it!" Unfortunately, most of us do not work in our true vocation; most of us have jobs or careers that can take energy from us, depleting us at the end of the work cycle. Therefore, it is essential to keep work in perspective and balance it with play and self-care. Although

money is important, it can be of little use if we are out of balance, unhealthy or sick.

Notice the Change of Seasons

Like nature, people cycle through distinct seasons. Autumn is the season of "harvest"—it is a time when we turn our attention inward to reflect on what the year has brought us so far. It is also the time to take stock of what we need to carry us through the winter. Often we lose sight of the changes that the natural cycles of life bring. We may find ourselves fighting an uphill battle to connect with family, friends, and even ourselves, as we maneuver in a fast-paced world. I suggest that we take time to view the change of seasons as a way to move gracefully into the fall. We can start by taking an inventory of the blessings and the challenges that are currently present in our lives.

It is important to begin our inventory with the positive accomplishments or blessings that exist in our lives. So begin by making a list of the ten most important positive events in your life this last year, remembering to give yourself credit for all that you have learned and for those things from which you have benefited. Be sure to focus on the positive aspects of your life regarding family, friends, work, play, and self-care. Try to notice the things in life that have given you pleasure, or those events that have brought joy into your life. Are you aware of how you feel and think. Ask yourself if you are living in sync with the natural rhythms of the time. You may notice that you are slowing down, taking stock, and preparing to make the necessary changes to your house, your wardrobe, and your life that will enable you to embrace the coming winter. As you make these changes, try to access that part of yourself that finds joy in the changing seasons.

Next, look at the challenges that this past year has presented to you or your family. Make a list of the "tools" that you used to survive the difficulties. Remember that "tools" come in many forms. Tools can be your family, friends, religious affiliations, social groups, financial resources, and life lessons that you have accumulated. I find it very helpful to look at the challenges in life as opportunities to learn new skills or acquire new tools, and as opportunities to renew your faith and to reconnect with your friends and family. Challenges are never fun at the moment, but they can tell us that we need to change something in our lives. They can be invitations to look at the ways we are holding on to those old patterns, relationships, or behaviors that are not supporting the changes that we need to make in order for us to grow. Challenges also offer us a way to be more aware of what needs to be cleared out of our lives. Fall is all about change and release, letting go. Be sure to remember the lessons or learning that you have reflected on and hold on to the blessings that come from change.

Our lives are full of opportunities to learn, and it is vital to take stock of where we have been in order to know where we are going. Remember to keep a balance in the three centers: body, mind, and heart. The Buddha said, "The path to enlightenment (awareness) is not difficult if we have no preference." So, just as the seasons change, bringing times of reflection, darkness, birth, and rebirth, so must we change. The fall gives us the opportunity to take stock of our lives and to hold on to what works, releasing all that no longer nourishes us.

Taking time to appreciate the natural beauty of each season can be a way to experience the balance of body, mind, and heart. Making time for a walk in a wooded, serene place can provide an experience of rest and meditative reflection. Fall, for example, with its beautiful colors that presage the darkness and barrenness of winter, can give us an opportunity to experience melancholy, to acknowledge the grief that we may feel about losses over the past year, and to reflect on our own mortality and the gift of life.

Remaining in touch with the changes of the seasons allows our bodies to be healthier, our minds more focused and less chaotic, and our hearts open and compassionate. Enjoy the seasons, then let go and embrace the next one that comes.

Life Isn't Just About Work

Play, games, and pastimes were a part of life for all ancient peoples. In some excavation sites in Egypt, Babylonia, China, and in the Western hemisphere, we have found toys, games, drawings, sculptures, and evidence of early theater. Play is an essential ingredient to balance our lives for optimal health. The ancient Egyptians and Greeks prescribed recreation/play as a means of treating the sick. Often the recommended treatment for recovering from an illness included walks, reading, theater performances, and traveling.

Include play of some sort in each and every day, or at least a few times a week. And let what you do for play and recreation shift along with the seasons. Play ball and picnic during the summer, take yourself to the theatre or visit art museums in the fall, and see a Broadway musical of the symphony in the winter.

Self-care is the act of attending to or being present to ourselves. Self-care involves being present to body, mind, and heart
in the present moment.

Remember to take care of your body by exercising, consum-
ing the amount of calories your body needs to maintain a healthy
weight, getting plenty of water each day, finding time for massage or other bodywork. Most importantly, don't forget that we
all need a heavy dose of physical affection and hugs each day.
The body will reward us by remaining healthy if we attend to its
needs in a conscious way.

The mind needs stimulation in order to remain healthy, and we
can do that by reading, researching on the internet, doing cross-
word puzzles, taking continuing education classes, challenging
ourselves to learn new things, and staying in open conversations
with family and friends. Meditation, or simply quieting or clearing our minds for twenty to thirty minutes each day, can help us
to hear our true inner voice. When we are quiet, we often can
find the true answer to any question that is at hand. Our minds

love diversion, so engaging in activities that involve the arts is also a wonderful stimulation.

We keep the heart healthy by being aware of our feelings, sharing our feelings with others, being compassionate with ourselves and others as we make our way through life, and by remaining kind in all of our interactions. The heart is nourished by worship, by attending plays and musical events that touch us in some deep way, and by maintaining healthy, open, caring relationships.

The key to living better is to balance all aspects of work, play and self-care, and remaining happy, healthy, and vibrant is possible by attending to the mind, body, and heart centers. Be compassionate and kind to yourself and others as you work, play, and take care of yourself.

This article originally appeared on the author's Web site and was reprinted with permission.

About the Author

Deborah A. Ooten, Ph.D., is the founder/director of the Conscious Living Center. She has her doctorate in clinical psychology, and is an occupational therapist, a trained craniosacral therapist, and a certified enneagram teacher in the narrative tradition. Deborah believes that lives can be transformed by attending to how our personality separates us from ourselves, others, and the divine. Deborah is a powerful presenter, a compassionate listener, and a dynamic change agent. Her Web site can be found at http://www.goconscious.com/

Root for Root Vegetables

By Maggie Anderson

If you're one of the softies who always roots for the underdog, you're probably very fond of root vegetables. Their very names are sometimes blighted by being used as insults, like "couch potato" or "turnip head." Potatoes come loaded with politically incorrect carbs; turnips are reputed to be peasant food that taste all turnipy; and parsnips are so not in demand that, if you try to buy one at a supermarket, your purchase will be held up for half an hour while you try to explain to the eighteen-year-old checkout girl who has never seen or eaten one before that it is not an overgrown radish.

One reason that root vegetables are so disparaged is because they've been associated with poverty since the early Middle Ages. Rather than have their wheat fields burned to the ground by marauding armies,

317

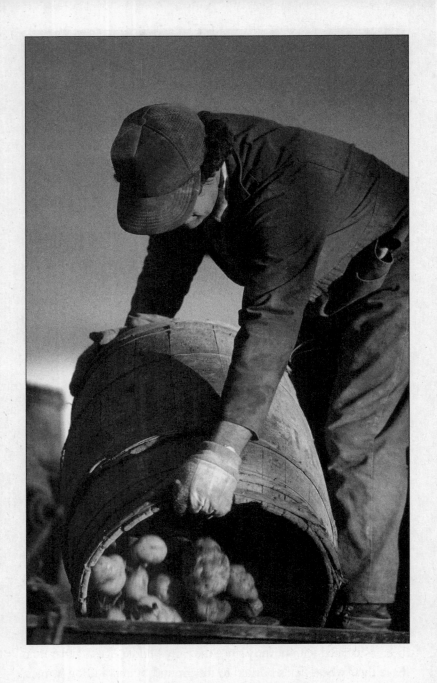

European peasants wisely made root vegetables the staple of their diets so that their crops could be grown and stored safely under-ground, well hidden from the Huns. From then on, this lowly sub-terranean fare became known as the diet of the poor. Rich people, of course, ate further up the food chain. One author and poet, Sadi (1184–1291), suggested that if one were hungry enough, a turnip might taste every bit as good as chicken:

> *While, in the sight of helpless poverty, Boiled turnip will a roasted pullet be.*

During the Great Depression, root vegetables again became as-sociated with the eating habits of the poor, and Huns were not to blame. With unemployment at 25 percent and other incomes meager, many Americans became survival gardeners, growing root crops in their backyards. Turnips were as popular as pota-toes because they reached maturity quickly, set lots of seed, and stored well. However, after the economy improved, many who survived those lean years vowed never to eat another turnip—as long as there were real pullets in their pots like the government had promised.

The Infamous Potato

Of all the root vegetables, potatoes are the most newsworthy and have status in the popular culture too. Regular potatoes, AKA "spuds," "taters," or just plain "fries," are the subject of myth and legend. Used raw, they are said to cure warts when one chants the proper incantation: "Rub a half potato on your wart and wrap it in a damp cloth. Close your eyes and whirl three times and throw. Then bury rag and spud exactly where they fall."

Potatoes are the only vegetable to have a major economic di-saster named after them. Their sudden disappearance gave rise to the Irish Potato Famine, leading to the resettlement of thousands of Irish people and the annual St. Patrick's Day Parade in New York City. Evidently monocultures are prone to disasters that

include being wiped out overnight by blight. This proves that biodiversity is a very good thing and that, if you grow potatoes, make sure that, when you plant their "eyes," they are not all the same color.

Having made an about-face in the potato famine-feast cycle, potatoes played a supporting role in the documentary film *Super-Size Me* (2003). The problem with potatoes today is not too few but too many, especially when in the form of French fries. Food purveyors are trying hard to break the potato's association with the underground. Supermarkets now feature entire sections devoted to them. Frozen and boxed potatoes are morphed into odd shapes, not only fries but also wedges, pancakes, and something called "tots." The one thing that all sliced, diced, chipped, minced, and mashed potatoes have in common is their lack of potato-ness. Unfortunately, despite their new disguises, potatoes are still extremely high in carbs.

Potatoes have also played a prominent role in international politics. There was a short period in recent U.S. history when patriotic restaurant owners and several Congressmen called for renaming potatoes boiled in oil "freedom fries." That was when the U.S. was mad at France for not doing its part to spread democracy in the Middle East. Surprisingly, the French, who know better than to gorge themselves on fries, can stay thin, shapely, and fashionable, did not change their foreign policy because of the potato incident. This should be a lesson to people who make their living writing menus: never name a popular vegetable dish after a foreign country that your next elected officials may not get along with. This reminds me: there is also a favorite American children's game titled "Mr. Potato Head."

Orange-colored Potatoes

Your words are wise, the women said. It is foolish to sit here and hunger, when near at hand yams are thick in the ground, and many fruits wait but the plucking.

GOOLOO THE MAGPIE AND THE WAROUGAH
IN AUSTRALIAN LEGENDARY TALES

Yams and sweet potatoes are as popular in some cultures as American (French) fries and in some exotic tropical lands were once used as currency. In the U.S., their peak consumption comes in November, and they are mostly forgotten for the rest of the year. This may be because the public is perpetually confused about the difference between yams and sweet potatoes and doesn't know where to look for them in recipe books. One is a tuberous root while the other is a real tuber, but only people who were born below the Mason-Dixon Line can tell the difference.

However, the cable Food Channel does feature scrumptious yam and sweet potato dishes, like sweet potato pie and candied yams, during the winter holidays. While traditionalists insist that yams and sweet potatoes be served at Thanksgiving and Christmas, it seems that only guests over sixty actually eat them. Children regularly shun them, and most every other root veggie in every form, because they are "different."

What's on the Salad Bar?

Many people in the modern, fast-food addicted West eat more vegetables from salad bars than at home. Because three root vegetables are regularly featured there, a common belief is that this category includes only carrots, radishes, and beets. Carrots can be shredded, diced, or sliced but, piled on top of a mix of arugula, radicchio, and mesclun, they come closer to being adult fare than the dried-out sticks that are put into first graders' lunchboxes with peanut butter sandwiches. Carrots are touted as being good for dieters, and sucking on one is said to be helpful to individuals who are trying to quit smoking. There is no downside at all to carrots unless you mistakenly try to inhale one.

Sadly, there are more rose-shaped radishes left over at the end of each day on the salad bars of America than any other root vegetable. The upside of radishes is that they are easy and quick to grow and the first crops gardeners can show off to their neighbors in the spring. However, a quick glance at the index of your cookbooks will tell you that there are no recipes for radishes. You can brag about the big ones and dare people to eat the hot ones but, after that, they are only good for slicing, dipping into a bowl of sour cream, or cutting into fancy shapes with devices available on late-night infomercials.

Beets on salad bars are usually modified by pickling or total immersion in a hot sweet vinegar sauce invented at Harvard University. Raw beets are not particularly edible, but cooked they make a superior dye for neckties, napkins, and children's tongues. Russians make their beets into a majestic soup called borscht—a tasty value-added root food—the added parts being other roots and tubers like carrots, turnips, potatoes, and onions.

Recipe for Borscht

3 tablespoons butter
1 small cabbage, finely chopped
1 cup potatoes, diced

½ cup carrots, sliced or diced
1 celery stalk, minced
1 onion, coarsely chopped
2 quarts beef stock
2 cups canned tomato juice
½ cup juice from beets
1 cup cooked or canned sliced beets
1 tablespoon cider vinegar
sour cream
chopped dill or parsley (for garnish)

In a large, heavy pan, melt butter and lightly sauté cabbage, potatoes, carrots, celery, and onion for approximately 5 minutes. Add beef stock. Add tomato juice and beet juice to stock. Cover and simmer over low heat until vegetables are firmly tender but not soft.

Add the chopped beets and vinegar. Season well with salt and pepper and remove from heat before the beets begin to lose their color.

Garnish with a dollop of sour cream and a sprinkling of dill or parsley over each bowl. Serve. This recipe freezes well.

The Other Round Root

Onions, and other members of the allium family that grow beneath the ground, like garlic, appeal to only one gender: they are widely consumed by real men and real men wannabes. Guys like them greasy and fried on burgers and Philly steak sandwiches and, when they are showing off, raw. Adventuresome women might order an "onion blossom" in a restaurant occasionally, but otherwise avoid them in fear of having bad breath when they kiss onion-eating males. If they find onion bits in their spaghetti sauce, preteen girls like to spit them out between the braces on their teeth, while rolling their eyes and saying something that sounds a lot like "pfaaphitt-eh!!!"

Rooted Oddities

Jerusalem artichokes are not from Jerusalem, nor are they artichokes. They are bumpy tubers that try to disguise themselves as sunflowers by setting tall stems with cheery yellow flowers. They originated in abandoned backyards of neighbors who insisted that you share the joy of growing them. When you plant Jerusalem artichokes on your property, they will be a consistent food supply for you, your family, and the rest of the neighborhood for the next fifty years. You can dig them up each fall, but you'll never, ever find all of them and every one you miss will live to multiply another year.

The Chinese eat day lily bulbs and consider them a delicacy. They are plentiful in the gardens and country ditches of America, just waiting for hesitant cooks to dig them up and put them in a pot. Evidently, day lily bulbs are good pickled and boiled, and recipes for them can be found in many "survive in the wilderness" books. It is probably only the warnings about potential kidney failure from eating day lilies that hinder their popularity.

Increasing the Consumption of Root Vegetables

There is no improving on nature, so root vegetables are perfect foods just as they are, bumps, lumps, and all. We all should eat them and do more to promote them too. Food vendors could help the reputations of these neglected veggies by hiring product placement firms that will get root veggies into show business.

If the public saw films of Johnny Depp munching on a raw turnip or Angelina chowing down on mashed rutabagas, it could change the diets of American overnight. When Hollywood celebrities start naming their firstborns "Sweet Potato Pete" or "Radish Rose," we'll know the campaign was a success.

About the Author

Maggie Anderson makes her home in Mount Vernon, Iowa, in the Heartland of the U.S., where she maintains an astrological practice and teachers astrology. Maggie specializes in "affairs of the heart," which allows her to use her experience as a family therapist. In her spare time, she is a gardener and author.

Wine by the Sign

By Robin Ivy

Wine is one of life's great pleasures. When we gather for holidays, special events, and even some religious rituals, wine is served, and its presence indicates the importance of coming together to mark the occasion. The Thanksgiving Day table would not be complete without a crisp white or fruity red, and New Year's Eve and champagne have become synonymous! Wine is a prerequisite for celebrations of love, from anniversaries to weddings. A special selection is chosen for the toast, and we raise our glasses to the guests of honor. Couples entwine arms as they take their first sip, marking their married life or a renewal of their commitment.

Today, collectors seek prized wines from Web sites and wineries, and people plan vacations in the vineyards. But our fascination with the juice of the vine dates far before modern times. Stories of wine go back to the biblical anecdote in which water was miraculously changed to wine to accommodate thirsty wedding guests; and even further back in the Old Testament where, in the book of Genesis, Noah planted the vines and became drunk from the wine the grapes produced.

Classic literature is dotted with wine references as well. Shakespeare, for example, refers to wine in many of his works, including *Julius Caesar*. In Act IV, Scene III, Brutus demands, "Give me a bowl of wine. In this I bury all unkindness, Cassius." In the Bard of Avon's play *Othello*, Iago proclaims, ". . . good wine is a good familiar creature if it is well used." The virtues of wine were recognized not only in Shakespearean times, but even further back. In early Persian and Egyptian mythologies, wine was associated with fertility, love, and health. Wine was the drink of the gods, and often associated with femininity. In Persian lore, a woman was said to have discovered wine as she consumed fermented grapes, which cured her chronic head pain. The Greek goddess of the harvest, Demeter, was linked to wine, and the Greeks would break bread and toast in her name, and in the name of Dionysus, the god of indulgence and celebration. Ancient Egyptians produced wine as well, and often had shrines to Renentet near their wine presses. Osirus, an Egyptian god, was considered the first to plant the vineyards, and Egyptians held a holiday in his honor. Hathor was regarded as the goddess of wine and intoxication. The fact that these societies linked wine to their deities and commonly used it as an offering shows that it was highly regarded as a precious commodity.

Like our ancestors who immortalized wine through literature, spiritual practice, and celebration, we mark our own milestones and raise glasses to friendship, love, and success. However, choosing the perfect wine for an occasion usually requires some deliberation. One consideration is seasonal, and the connection between the two is often simplified. We tend to serve rich reds in the cooler months and switch to lighter whites in summer time. However, some of us are loyal to a certain chardonnay or cabernet regardless of the weather outside. Our tastes and personalities often influence our choice of wine as much as they do our attire, our car, or the neighborhood we live in. Could it be that our preference for wine has to do with our zodiac sign? And if your favorite wine were a sign, what would it be? Just as our close friends and family members have their distinguishing traits, so do the many varieties of wines. Let's explore the characteristics of wine by the sign and expand our notion of which wine is right for which occasion, taking Moon signs, seasons, and our own inherent tastes into consideration. Bon appétit!

Red Wines

Red wines can range from heavy and rich to more light and refreshing, depending on the variety or blend of grapes used in the

making. Traditionally, red wine was served with red meat, lamb, and stews, and thought of as a warmer during cooler weather, but now red wine is popular year round partially due to the health benefits its antioxidants provide. Wines in the red family vary quite a bit in their characteristics. Cabernet Sauvignon is strong and mature, while at the other end of the spectrum is the smooth, light Pinot Noir. Enhance the mood of your next dinner party or occasion by considering the qualities of each variety of red wine and aligning it with the sign of the Moon, the Sun, or the feeling you hope to create among your guests.

Cabernet Sauvignon

The true Cabernet Sauvignon is a full-bodied wine named for the grapes associated with the Bordeaux region of France, though today Cabernets are produced in California, Chile, Italy, and other regions of the world. In fact, the cabernet is now the most widely planted grape of all. Cabernet Sauvignon is often described as a noble wine. It can be aged for longer periods than some other varieties. The result is a dark red wine with complex character and depth. In a good Cab, you may find rich fruit flavors such as currant or black cherry, spice, chocolate or cassis, and a long satisfying finish.

Who does this description remind you of? Do your Scorpio and Cancer friends come to mind as you share the deep, mysterious nature of the Cabernet Sauvignon? These two intense water signs, known for their emotional complexity and connection to maturity, ancestry, and old age, fit the descriptor of a great Cabernet. This makes it an excellent choice for a milestone anniversary celebration or retirement party. Offer a Cabernet to provoke meaningful conversation at a dinner party as well, particularly under a Cancer or Scorpio Moon, or when the Sun visits Scorpio in late fall.

Merlot

Merlot is another red wine originating in the Bordeaux region. The merlot grape differs from a small, thick-skinned cabernet in that it is a soft, plump fruit instead. The wine it produces is lush and fruity, and as a result, Merlot is a friendly, approachable wine, palatable to many tastes. Generally, Merlot is early ripening and doesn't require much time to age in the bottle. Cherry and black currant flavors characterize this wine, which can also have the tobacco and spice tones of a Cabernet Sauvignon. While the two varieties are often blended for balance, the Merlot is not as intense and is therefore a very popular choice, a wine of the people. Merlot has become the Chardonnay of red wines.

If this wine were a sign, who would it be? The softer red wine is reminiscent of Venus' signs, Taurus and Libra. The social graces of these two signs make them easy to befriend, and both make charming hosts. Aquarius, the sign of friendship and popularity, also shares traits with Merlot. Serve a Merlot when you expect a wide range of personalities at your party, and chances are it will be a crowd pleaser.

Pinot Noir

A lighter alternative to Merlot and Cabernet is Pinot Noir, a native to the eastern Burgundy area of France. Pinot Noir is now produced widely in California, Oregon, and New Zealand, too. Pinot Noir fills the senses with raspberry, plum, and strawberry sweetness, making it an excellent choice as a summer red. A youthful wine that generally evolves in a short period of time, Pinot Noir can be floral or spicy, like sandalwood, but is always smooth and berry sweet. Pinot Noir is rumored to appeal to the heart!

Considering the qualities of youth and heart, it seems that Pinot Noir was born to be a Leo. The Lion is ruled by the heart and known to retain the appearance and spirit of youth into old age. The plum shade of many Pinots even reflects purple, one of Leo's colors. Another popular, easy red wine choice, Pinot Noir has the versatility of being a summer or winter wine and can be served with a variety of foods. Choose a Pinot Noir when the Moon or Sun shines in Leo, but also when a romantic, elegant atmosphere is what you hope to create. Remember that Pinot Noir is the wine of the heart.

Zinfandel

Red Zinfandel, with its origins in Europe, has migrated throughout the world and is known as an exotic grape. The zinfandel grape has a distinctive black color and produces a robust red wine, closer to purple in color. Another friendly, approachable red, Zinfandel shares the berry tones of a Pinot Noir or a Merlot, with more hints of pepper and spice. While popularly planted now in the California hillsides, the origins of Zinfandel are sketchy. But Italy and eastern European roots have been traced, and Zinfandel came to North America via Austria during the nineteenth century.

The robust character of this wine makes it a nice fire sign selection. Zinfandel is sometimes described as prickly, as it has a peppery zing we might equate with the sign Aries. And like gypsy Sagittarius, this grape has traveled the world. The purple-red color blends the colors most associated with these two signs, Sagittarius purple and Aries red. Described often as having character and flair, Zinfandel is a great choice when your guests are worldly and cultured. Discussing your travels, collections, and photographs over a few glasses of Zin would make an interesting evening. An art opening also lends itself to Red Zinfandel's qualities. Look for Aries and Sagittarius Sun and Moon times as other occasions to open a special bottle.

White Wines

Traditionally associated with summer months, warmer weather, and lighter meals, white wines are actually very diverse, even in color, which ranges from clear white to golden yellow. Consider too the wide variety of influences in whites, from oak and vanilla to more tropical or floral flavors. It is impossible to make a general statement about white wine. While whites often complement fish, poultry, and salads, some are also excellent choices for holiday gatherings during the winter months. Exploring the distinctive qualities of some popular white wines can expand both your perspective and your options next time you're asked to choose the wine to go with dinner.

Chardonnay

The king of white wines, Chardonnay is pressed in the majority of wine-producing nations. Arguably the wine with the most massive appeal, Chardonnay is complex and rich. Some Chardonnays fill

the palate with pear, apple, melon, or other fruit flavors, while others are distinguished more by toasty, oak, or honey traits. How a Chardonnay is aged has quite a bit to do with the flavor of the final product, and a buttery, smoky, or particularly savory version may be due to oak aging.

The qualities of Chardonnay are reminiscent of earth in many ways. The floral, oak, and fruit essences all connect to the earth, linking Chardonnays with the signs Taurus, Virgo, and Capricorn. A hearty, full-bodied Chardonnay mimics the qualities of Taurus, the bull. A well-aged variety with character has the maturity and character of Capricorn, while a "Virgo" Chardonnay would have the warm, oak, aromatic quality of later summer and the change of season. Chardonnay also relates to the physical, material traits of the earth signs, since its widespread appeal makes it a favorite and prosperous grape for winemakers internationally. You can almost never go wrong if you serve a Chardonnay. It is strong enough to complement a holiday meal with all the trimmings, and also stands up on its own at a cocktail-style gathering. Serve it when the Moon or Sun cruise through earth signs Taurus, Virgo, and Capricorn, or any time you want a fine wine with down-to-earth flavor.

Pinot Grigio

Pinot Grigio, or Pinot Gris, dates back to the fourteenth century, where monks discovered the grapes in France. France and Italy are home to this variety, though it is now often produced in California as well. This is a light, vibrant, summer-like wine with pear, apricot, pineapple, or citrus flavors. Some Pinots also have nutty or smoky scents and tastes.

Like the air signs Gemini, Libra, and Aquarius, Pinot Grigio is lively and fresh! The crispness of most Pinot Grigios lend versatility and makes them easy to pair with foods. The flexibility and summer flavors reflect the sign Gemini. Some Pinot Grigio blends are a bit more complex, and with a bit of Sauvignon or Chardonnay to enhance it, a Libran balance is achieved. When Libra, Gemini, or Aquarius is the sign of the day, or when you hope for light, but intelligent, conversation, choose a Pinot Gris and let the party begin!

Reisling

Reisling is originally a German wine, although today Australia, New Zealand, and the Alsace region of France are known to produce varieties of this dry, crisp white. This wine ages well, and at its best has a perfect balance of sweetness and acidity. An older Reisling will take on a toasty quality and can rival the best of Chardonnays. Since individual Reislings are strongly expressive of the land they are produced on, they range from delicate to complex.

Since the finest of Reislings embody ideal balance, Libra, Gemini, and Pisces, the signs of dual imagery, represent this wine well. The sweet, fruity variety may lean toward the rich, imaginative quality of Pisces, while a drier, crisper Reisling has the air sign feel of a Libra or Gemini. All three signs strive to reconcile their dualities and find the yin-yang harmony between intellect and emotion, while the choice Reisling achieves a similar balance, neither overly sweet nor acidic. Serve a Reisling with appetizers, cheeses, and lighter meals, or to cool and mellow a spicy dish. Under a Pisces, Gemini, or Libra Moon, Reisling is a refreshing choice to complement the mood.

Sauvignon Blanc

Sauvignon Blanc is another youthful wine that requires little aging in the bottle. The grapes are native to France's Loire Valley although they are now notably grown in New Zealand and also in California. Sauvignon has the grassiest flavor of all the wines considered here. It is also described as herbaceous, tropical, or flinty. Generally speaking, Sauvignon Blanc is a light, refined, and naturally crisp variety.

Sauvignon's qualities can range from simple and fruity, with hints of gooseberry, passion fruit, and nectarine, to moderately complex with nuances of minerals, foliage, and herbs. The earth-sign qualities of Sauvignon Blanc are reminiscent of Virgo, pure and refined. Virgo attunes to the details, and this wine is recognizable for its' specific flavors and aromas of earth. Sauvignon Blanc makes a good choice for Virgo-type occasions such as a business dinner or garden party. Uncork a bottle at the end of summer, Virgo's time, and savor the extended daylight before longer, colder weather sets in.

Quick Reference by Sign

Aries: Robust and peppery selections such as Red Zinfandel

Taurus: Earthy, full-bodied varieties such as an oaky Chardonnay or soft Merlot

Gemini: Light, fruity, lively choices such as Pinot Grigio

Cancer: Rich, hearty, romantic selections such as Cabernet Sauvignon or Sangiovese

Leo: Festive, elegant choices like Pinot Noir and champagnes

Virgo: Fresh, earthy selections such as a refined Sauvignon Blanc or aromatic Chardonnay

Libra: Lively choices like Pinot Grigio and blended varieties such as a Cabernet/Merlot

Scorpio: Deep, rich Cabernet Sauvignons and strong, buttery Chardonnays

Sagittarius: Exotic, worldly choices like Rioja and Red Zinfandel

Capricorn: Mature wines with varietal character such as Cabernet Sauvignon and Chardonnay

Aquarius: Fresh, lively varieties such as Pinot Grigio or Pinot Noir

Pisces: Rich, deep, berry-like varieties like Pinot Noir and blends like Semillion/Chardonnay or balanced Reisling

About the Author

Robin Ivy is a radio personality, educator, and astrologer in Portland, Maine. She fuses her passion for music and the metaphysical in Robin's Zodiac Zone, a feature on her morning show on 94 WCYY, Portland's new rock alternative. Visit Robin's Web site at www.robinszodiac.com.

Light, Plants, and Rhythms

By Bruce Scofield

Plants are more sensitive to light than most other kinds of life on our planet. Light is what they seek, use, and live by. Plants know what direction light is coming from and will move themselves out of shade. At the tip of a plant shoot are chemicals called auxins that influence cell division—with more light comes more cell division and consequently more growth and extension. In this way, plants will always bend toward the light, something that is obvious to any indoor gardener. This response to light is called

phototropism. While plant shoots are positively phototrophic, the roots are negatively phototrophic and grow away from light.

Light is essential to plants, and further more, plants are essential to us. We are what are called heterotrophs, organisms that must get their energy from somewhere else. So are all other animals and all fungi. But plants are autotrophs, or self-feeders, that make their own energy from light and water. The secret of plants is in photosynthesis, the process that occurs in the chloroplasts of the plant cell. In these tiny organelles, photons of light are used to split water and make carbohydrates that the plant uses to live. And of course we owe our lives to plants, directly as in a salad, or indirectly as in a cow that ate grass. Interestingly, the tiny chloroplasts found in all green plants are the remnants of formerly free-living bacteria, cyanobacteria to be exact. Cyanobacteria (sometimes incorrectly called blue-green algae for marketing purposes) have been on the Earth for at least three billion years, and they are what initially made our oxygen-rich environment.

These bacteria invented photosynthesis, and plants merely carry on their tradition. The bottom line here is that we are living off cyanobacteria in one form or another—and ultimately, the Sun!

All plants have a daily cycle of photosynthesis that changes as the Sun moves through our sky. Plants know exactly when to turn this cycle on and off each day, and this is in response to the alternation of day and night that is caused by the rotation of the Earth. This cycle is an example of what are called *circadian rhythms*, a type of biological clock. There are many kinds of circadian rhythms in the cells of plants, and some plants have daily leaf motion rhythms, as well, that serve to limit water loss by evaporation. Circadian rhythms allow plants to know when to close their flowers at night to keep the pollen dry, and they use them to give off special odors to attract insect pollinators.

The study of biological rhythms in modern times actually began with plants. The French astronomer Jean Jacques d'Ortous de Mairan observed in 1729 that the sleep movements of a species of heliotrope varied in a consistent way throughout the day. He thought that the plant was following the alternation of night and day, but to test this he placed the plant in continual darkness. Amazingly, its leaf movements persisted, suggesting there was an internal clock in the plant itself. A century later, Charles Darwin wrote a book on this topic called *The Power of Movement in Plants,* and throughout the twentieth century many researchers continued to probe the basis of these rhythms.

Another important adaptive rhythm found in plants is related to the cycle of the year. Many plants live at latitudes that have a yearly cycle of day-length change. In the northern hemisphere, days are longer in summer and shorter in winter, and this becomes more extreme as one moves north. The reverse is true in the southern hemisphere. Tracking this seasonal rhythm is central to the reproductive cycle of plants and in order to do so, plants must measure changing differences in day and night length. The first report of

an organism measuring the length of day was published in 1920. Researchers writing for the U.S. Department of Agriculture, concerned with efficient tobacco propagation, discovered that the flowering of the tobacco plant at specific times in the year was influenced by the day-to-night ratio within the cycle of the year. They named this property *photoperiodism*.

During the course of the year, the days vary in length. In spring (in the northern hemisphere) the days lengthen until they reach a maximum at Midsummer's Day (June 21), the Summer Solstice. Then the days begin to shorten and by the Winter Solstice (December 21), they are as short as they will get. The length of the days and nights varies according to latitude. If you compare the longest and shortest days of the year near the equator, and the difference will be in minutes. At temperate latitudes, which covers most the United States, the longest day could be fifteen hours and the shortest nine hours. At very high latitudes in the Arctic, days could last for a season or more. These are the facts of life for plants, and since they need the sunlight to live, they must adapt to these changes and make the most of them.

The most dramatic evidence of photoperiodism in many species of seed-bearing plants is shown in the timing of flowering. Plants flower at the most opportune times of the year in response to the changing light-dark ratios caused by the yearly cycle. There are very good reasons why plants need to time their flowering periods perfectly. Many flowering plants have coevolved with insects that are needed to move pollen from one plant to another so that reproduction can occur. Plants have done this by making their flowers attractive to the insects, but also by having their flowers open at the same time of day that the insects are active. There are many examples of this, the most dramatic being the night-blooming cereus plant, which blooms for only one night and is pollinated by one type of moth.

Plants that have photoperiodic rhythms are of two basic types. Short-day plants time their flowering by registering long dark periods—that is, long nights. Long-day plants register long day lengths, which then induces them to flower. Of course, the length of day and night during the year is related to latitude, and plants of the same species that have a large north-to-south range will compensate for this. Plants will also measure the range of temperatures during the year, and this can be another factor in the timing of flowering. There is also a third category of plants that are said to be day-neutral and utilize several signals in the environment to induce flowering.

The actual mechanism in the plant that allows it to read day-length is located in the circadian clock. Here's a simplified explanation of how it works. The circadian clock itself is located in special cells where certain proteins are made at a fixed rate. As these proteins reach a certain level, protein making shuts down. When there is not enough of this protein, the process starts again. It's a bit like a thermostat that keeps a house within a certain

temperature range. The genes that drive the cycle are affected by light, and they become entrained to the light-dark cycle of the day. When light hits them earlier or later, depending on the species, the cycle adjusts itself. This continues throughout the year and results in a good adaptation to the natural cycles of Earth and Sun. When a critical day or night length is reached, the plant knows that it is time to flower.

Because different plants flower at different times of the year, gardeners place plants such that there are continuous blooms in the garden. And since different plants flower at different times of the day, gardeners place plants to provide continuous blooms during a single day. With careful arrangement, a gardener can place different types of plants in a circle to create a flower clock. The flower clock has been credited to Carl von Linné or Carl Linnaeus (1701–1778) of Sweden, one of the great figures in biology.

Linnaeus was a passionate collector and organizer of nature. He is the person who created the modern system of classification for plants and animals in which each organism has a genus name and a species name, like *Homo sapiens*—us human beings. He walked through Europe studying nature, naming and describing over twelve thousand species of plants and animals. While it is not known to be a fact, it is thought that Linnaeus made a floral clock that allowed one to tell the time of day. From his careful observations he came to know at what hour a particular plant would flower, and he placed that plant in a clock-like circle at its appropriate time. For his clock, Linnaeus selected local flowers that would bloom even on cloudy days. Linnaeus also noticed that some flowers would open and close according to the weather. He noticed others that opened and closed according to the length of the day—plants that were responding to photoperiodism. A third type changed, opening and closing times according to the time of day—and these are the ones he used in his flower clock. Some of these are listed below with their approximate flowering time. As you can see, not all hours are covered and for the most exact reading of this clock, the timing of the closing of certain species must be used.

Before Noon

5:00 Morning glories, wild roses
6:00 Spotted cat's ear, catmint
7:00 African marigold, orange hawkweed, dandelions
8:00 Mouse-ear hawkweed, African daisies
9:00 Field marigold, gentians
10:00 Helichrysum, California poppy
11:00 Star of Bethlehem

Afternoon

12:00 Passion flower, goatsbeard
4:00 Four o'clock plant opens
6:00 Evening primrose, moonflower
8:00 Flowering tobacco
10:00 Night blooming cereus

Some common plants that can be used to make a functional, though not precise, flower clock include morning glories and wild roses that open just after dawn. These are followed by dandelions, gentians, and California poppies, which open near noon. In the afternoon the morning glories close and then later the four o'clocks open, followed by evening primroses and moonflowers. In making a garden flower clock, you should know when each type of flower closes, as that can also be a way of telling time.

Serious gardeners will grow plants that bloom at a wide range of times during the growing season. The flowering of daffodils in spring, day-flowers in summer, and chrysanthemums in fall are all set by the plants' responses to changes in the length of day. Even varieties of plants within the same species have been developed that will flower at different times of the year as well. A goal of a good gardener and landscaper is to have a constant series of blooms throughout the growing season, a constant stream of color from plants—a kind of seasonal clock. And all of this is possible due to the complex biological clocks in plants that allow them to read the sky and bloom when the time is right. Plants have evolved to be closely in tune with the natural astronomical cycles that are such a fundamental part of our environment—and we couldn't exist without them.

About the Author

Bruce Scofield is a professional astrologer with a full-time practice in Maine.

Pumpkinfest

By Dallas Jennifer Cobb

On the rise of a hill in my home town of Wellington, in Ontario, Canada, is a giant orb—luminous and bright. It's not the Moon, it is a giant pumpkin. Giant pumpkins are growing everywhere, overtaking gardens with their Sun-seeking vines, tendrils grasping onto fences. Townsfolk care for their pumpkins like babies, guarding them from frost and pests.

Remember Peter Peter Pumpkin Eater, whose wife lived inside a giant pumpkin shell? Well, the pumpkins of Wellington are growing to those proportions. While they may sound spooky, the giant pumpkins are not a threat to the town, but a blessing, bringing local economic development to the area. Growing giant pumpkins has stimulated agricultural innovation, economic renewal, and tourism.

In a predominantly agricultural area, many of the family farms struggle to survive. The global economy has meant they must compete against the low prices of foreign-grown produce, easily imported from across the world. In order to survive, many long-time agriculturalists have become innovators, creating novel new ways to make money from farming. In rural areas the face of agriculture is changing and adapting to survive. In Prince Edward County, Ontario, Canada, where I live, a festival called Pumpkinfest is an example of the many ways that small-scale family farmers have adapted their crops and sales techniques to survive and thrive.

A Small History of Giants

Canada has been producing giant pumpkins since the turn of the century, when William Warnock of Goderich, Ontario, Canada sent a 400-pound pumpkin to the 1900 Paris World's Fair. In 1903, Warnock produced a 403-pound pumpkin for the St. Louis World's Fair, a record which stood until 1976 when Bob Ford of Coatesville in Pennsylvania brought a 451-pound pumpkin to the U.S. Pumpkin Contest in Churchville, PA. In 1979, Canadian Howard Dill of Windsor, Nova Scotia, Canada won his first of four consecutive international pumpkinship titles at the Cornell Contest in Pennsylvania. He set a world record of 459 pounds in 1980, then beat it in 1981 with a 493.5-pound pumpkin.

Since 1980, the weight of world-record pumpkins has continued to increase. In 1984 it crept to 612 pounds, and in 1986 it reached 671 pounds. In 1989, three growers, including Gordon Thomson of Hemmingford, Quebec, Canada, who produced a 755-pound pumpkin, brought in pumpkins that broke the 700-pound barrier. In 1990, the record was set at 816.5 pounds; in 1992, it was 827 pounds; and in 1993, 836 pounds. So in 1996, when Bill Greer,

from Wellington, Ontario, Canada, broke the 1000 pound barrier, it was big news. Greer produced a giant pumpkin weighing 1006 pounds.

Giving Birth to Giants

Bill Greer, a retired farmer and food processor from the small town of Wellington, started growing giant pumpkins as a hobby in 1993. In the three years prior to producing a champion, Bill Greer's biggest pumpkin had been 378 pounds. Through his first few years of growing, Greer got to know other growers of giant pumpkins. They are a lively group that holds competitions world wide. He learned the secrets of growing giants and got seeds from champion pumpkins. He also kept abreast of the weigh-offs held commonly in Canada, the U.S., Australia, New Zealand, England, and Japan.

In 1996, he tried seed that he got from another pumpkin grower, Howard Dill of Windsor, Nova Scotia. Using that seed (680 Dill '94 (male) (792 Holland '93/500.5 Dill '89) and a 697 Ciliberto '94 (female) (502.5 Ciliberto '91/722 Holland '92), and Greer produced his 1006-pound beauty and won the Great

Pumpkin Commonwealth, or GPC. After winning the title, the pumpkin was purchased by the Nut Tree Theme Park in California for ten dollars per pound. In addition to the money, Greer and his wife enjoyed an all-expenses-paid trip for two to California. At the theme park, artists carved the giant pumpkin into a stylized face, calling it the world's biggest jack o' lantern.

Seeds from the champion pumpkin were divided between the Ottawa-St. Lawrence Growers Association (where they were made available to members and other giant pumpkin growers) and Bill Greer himself (he shared seeds with interested local growers and used them himself).

The following year, the 914-pound winner of the Great Pumpkin Commonwealth was a beauty grown in California, from one of Bill's prize 1006-pound pumpkin seeds. To date, Bill's pumpkin remains the GPC Champion and the Canadian Champion.

Pumpkinfest Lore

Thrilled with the renown that Bill Greer's pumpkin brought to the little village of Wellington, the Wellington District Business Association started to brainstorm ways to capitalize on it. A workshop was offered for anyone interested in growing giant pumpkins. Bill Greer gave participants free giant pumpkin seeds and shared his growing secrets with over forty interested growers. This group grew and eventually became the Prince Edward County Pumpkin Growers Association.

Meanwhile, the business association started planning an event for the following fall to recognize the successes of the growers. They decided to call it Prince Edward County Pumpkinfest. The third weekend of October was chosen because the Giant Pumpkin weigh-offs are traditionally held on the first Saturday of October, and the second weekend is Canadian Thanksgiving.

At the first Pumpkinfest, held on October 25, 1997, over fifty pumpkins were paraded down the main street of the village of Wellington. They were drawn in wagons behind tractors, lawnmowers,

and horses, and even pushed in wheelbarrows. After the parade, residents enjoyed contests and games like pumpkin bowling, pumpkin carving, and pumpkin pie eating. The public park featured food and entertainment, and Midtown Meats hosted the weigh-off of the giant pumpkins, their forklift shuttling the pumpkins to and from the weigh scale.

In that first year, Bill Greer placed first with a 727-pound giant, Eleanor Lindsay-MacDonald was second with a 519-pound giant, and third prize went to John Dempster and Robin Snooks from White Rose. Their pumpkin weighed 468 pounds. There were also prizes for giant squash, tallest sunflower, and smallest pumpkin. The Growers Prize Draw cash prize, drawn randomly from the names of all growers, was ironically awarded to the winner of the smallest pumpkin trophy, Dan Insley.

Pumpkinfest has continued as a successful local agricultural event, and a tourist attraction that brings thousands of people to the village on that weekend. At this two-pronged event, the Prince Edward County Pumpkin Growers organize the weigh-off, and the Pumpkinfest Committee organizes the parade and activities in town.

Founding president Bill Greer continued as president of the Growers Association until his death in 2003. Though ailing from Lou Gehrig's Disease (ALS), Bill Greer went out with a bang. In 2002 he produced an 1172-pound pumpkin—the biggest ever grown in Ontario, ranked fifth in the world that year, and tenth in the history of giant pumpkins. He died in the spring of 2003, leaving his wife, children, and grandchildren to carry on the tradition of growing giant pumpkins.

Growing Giant Pumpkins

Get some giant pumpkin seeds from a local giant grower, or through one of the growers associations. Please see the references following this article. These seeds can be sprouted indoors under grow lights, in small 4-inch peat pots, three weeks before the last frost and transferred outdoors when the danger of frost is past, or sewn directly into the ground after the danger of frost is past.

Giant pumpkins need between 110 and 140 frost-free growing days to come to maturity and put on weight. The time varies depending on the variety of pumpkin, the climate, and the number of daylight hours you get in the summer.

Bill Greer used Dill's Atlantic Giant seed, which requires 130 sunlight days to reach maturity and regularly reaches giant proportions, producing 400- to 500-pound fruit. Under ideal conditions, Dill's Atlantic Giant seed has produced pumpkins up to 1400 pounds. The shape of the Dill is also perfect for large jack-o'-lanterns, as it is an upright orb-like fruit. The color ranges from yellow to bright orange, and the skin is often slightly rough to the touch.

Lunar Growing

Many farmers swear that lunar growing, or planting by the Moon's cycles, is a superior method of cultivation. Many farmers will tell you that the Moon's cycles affect seed sprouting, plant growth, and the stages of decline. Lunar gardening practices can be employed to help a seed sprout, a plant grow, and to effectively cull unwanted plants.

The Moon waxes (grows big) and wanes (decreases in size) over a period of roughly twenty-nine and a half days, a lunation cycle measured from New Moon to New Moon.

During the first quarter, the New Moon is not visible. It is like a seed sprouting under the Earth. The New Moon is the time to plant seeds to sprout in the garden or in peat pots, where the plant seeds will be urged along by the magnetic pull of the Moon.

The waxing Moon is called the crescent Moon at the time it becomes visible to the eye, first as a thin sliver in the western sky in the late afternoon and early evening. The gibbous Moon rises before sunset. As the Moon is waxing, seedlings and plants grow stronger and bigger. The Moon's effect is to increase energy and promote new growth. Generally, more babies are born in this waxing cycle, and it is the time to plant annuals that produce their fruit above the ground. This includes pumpkins, as well as squash, tomatoes, beans, eggplant, and peppers.

Incidentally, if you can use a lunar almanac to identify days when the waxing Moon is in the sign of Cancer, Scorpio, Pisces, or Libra, these are the ideal signs under which to plant pumpkin seeds.

The Full Moon marks the midpoint in the lunation cycle. The Full Moon rises as the Sun is setting, spreading luminous moonlight across the fields. On the night of the Full Moon the maximum effect of the Moon is felt, not just by us, but by plants and animals. For culling unwanted plants or weeds, the waning Moon cycle is considered beneficial to your efforts

What Pumpkins Like

Pumpkins like a spot with full sun exposure that is sheltered from the wind. At a very minimum, the plants must get at least six hours of direct sunlight daily. Build a large mound for the seedlings, about four feet in diameter, with a moat surrounding it. The moat should be about four inches wide and four inches deep to help direct water toward the roots of the plants. Build the hills up by mixing lots of organic compost into the soil to provide lots of nutrients to the babies. Compost not only feeds the pumpkins, but with a high humus factor, it helps to conserve moisture around the roots.

Plant four to five seeds or seedlings per hill, spacing them six to eight inches apart. Space the hills about fifteen to twenty feet apart so the vines have lots of room. Pumpkin seeds grow up, regardless of how they are planted. Many farmers traditionally plant them on their side, with the narrow edge pointing up. You can soak seeds overnight to soften the shell, but it isn't necessary.

With sprouted seeds or seedlings in the ground, be sure to keep them well covered with a loose layer of moist soil, and protect them from birds who love such delicacies. Water sprouted seeds and seedlings with a light, sprinkling flow so you don't wash the soil away from the tender root hairs, or damage the young plant.

It takes seven to fourteen days for the seed to crack and sprout through the soil. The young seedling has two oval baby leaves, which look like a butterfly's wings unfolding.

Over the next two to three weeks, once the seedlings are established, take note of which vines are looking healthiest and most vital, and thin to two or three per hill. Thank the plants that you are removing, offer them to the compost pile, and leave the strongest plants to grow.

With well-spaced hills, your pumpkin vines have lots of room to grow, and many grow up to thirty feet long. The vines can be

pruned, trained, and redirected so they can be grown along with other plants. Because the vines seek out heat and light, they can climb fences, trees, stalks, and even up onto roofs.

When you want to direct your pumpkin plant somewhere, provide small stakes or nails for the tendrils to grab hold of, stabilizing the vine.

Feeding Your Hungry Pumpkin

When it comes to feeding plants, many farmers prefer to encourage the natural process with natural products, rather than push the process with manufactured products.

Compost and rotted manure are the best foods for pumpkins, and because they are considered heavy feeders, it is good to regularly add some to the root base. An easy method is to make compost tea by letting some compost sit, immersed, in a large bucket of water for three days, then use that water to soak the mound.

Some growers prefer nutrients like fish emulsion, which is a concentrate of fish by-products. It is nutrient rich, and smells quite strong. Mix it with water and saturate the pumpkin mound.

Water features prominently in the diet of a giant pumpkin because between 80 and 90 percent of the pumpkin is water. Pumpkins love a moist soil and use their broad leaves to shade the ground, conserve moisture, and inhibit weed growth.

Depending on the amount of rain, and the climate, water your pumpkins when the soil is dry on top, and stop watering them when puddles begin to appear in the pumpkin patch. Direct the water into the moat, and onto the growing mound, so that the water is directed to the roots of the plant.

Grow, Baby, Grow!

After the two baby leaves appear, the first true leaves, with jagged edges, grow from the center of the young sprout. It grows slowly until at least three true leaves are established, then it starts to grow wildly. During this eight-week cycle, the root base expands, and vines grow as much as six inches a day. The first flowers appear about ten weeks after planting, blooming for one day only. There are two kinds of flowers, male and female, on each plant. Males sit on long stems and are usually more numerous than females. Females sit close to the vine on fuzzy round bumps that resemble baby pumpkins.

Bees move pollen from the center of the male flower to the inside of the female flower, but you can do it too, pollinating the pumpkins manually. Just use a small paint brush to gather pollen from the males, and carefully brush it inside of the flower of a female. When you are done, use a small paper bag to cover the female. Some growers prefer to do this to control the seed line, and keep out all other potential pollinators.

Experienced growers suggest identifying the main and secondary vines on your plant, and then habitually trimming off the tertiary vines, or shoots, that develop off of these. Many growers also prune the fruit that the vine produces, selecting a few strong-looking ones and removing the rest. This actually helps the plant to concentrates its energy on fewer but larger pumpkins.

Secrets for Adding Weight to Your Pumpkin

- Keep your pumpkin patch well watered
- Keep the mounds well composted to feed the plant and retain soil moisture
- Add a layer of mulch to the mound to keep weeds down and retain moisture
- Use a balanced fertilizer, regularly
- Cover the vines with soil to promote secondary root growth, which helps to feed the pumpkin

Fruition

Are you wondering what to watch out for to keep your giant pumpkins safe? Because they are hardy and strong, the main danger to pumpkins are frost, strong wind, insects, and animals. Gophers and moles love the taste of pumpkin, and vine borers, beetles, and aphids seem to like them too. Finally, watch out for mildew.

Early detection of irregularities is the best way to prevent major problems. So keep a daily eye on your babies. Like with my own children, I prefer to treat my garden as naturally as possible. I like to keep conditions ideal, knowing that a healthy plant has the best chances of resisting disease, and recovering from it if it is affected.

Handle the fruit as little as possible, with the two following exceptions. To encourage a classic pumpkin shape, adjust the fruit so that its bottom sits squarely on the ground. Do this when the fruit is about a month old. To ensure a nice texture on the bottom, slip a thin shingle under the young pumpkin to raise it up off of the soil. This will prevent scarring, rotting, and bruising.

In late August the pumpkin plant begins to turn its energy inward, reducing the number of flowers produced, letting the leaves tatter, and allowing the fruit to change color, from green to darker yellow and orange.

Once they are fully orange, it is time to harvest them. Cut them from the vine, leaving several inches of stem. Leave them out in the sun for about ten days to cure, covering them at night if there's danger of frost. If you need to store them, pumpkins like a dry cool place.

About the Author

Dallas Jennifer Cobb lives in Wellington, in Ontario, Canada. She loves to garden and prepare fabulous food for her family. When she's not running on country roads for exercise, she can often be found walking on the beach. You can contact her at gaias.garden@sympatico.ca.

Xeriscaping

By Carole Schwalm

Observe the mountains and rivers to know the yin and yang,
Observe the streams and springs to know the source of the waters.

—SHIH-CHING, *BOOK OF POETRY*, (c. 600–800 B.C.)

The word xeriscape comes from combining "xeri," from the Greek for "dry," and "scape," or scene. Although that conjures up the image of camels trekking across the desert with barely a sorry-looking cactus in sight, it's more than that.

It is about you, living in and adapting to that desert instead of trying to plant maples and mighty oaks, sodding the sand with Kentucky bluegrass, and then using as little water as possible to maintain it.

And it isn't just about existing through a drought, or something unnecessary to think about, if you live in a rain-drenched environment. Water is precious. Many, many people who use gallons and gallons of water populate cities and towns. Water must be treasured, and remain able to continue to support life as we know it. It takes people like you and me, helping assist a stressed and tiring Mother Nature.

Trees and plants are necessary to keep nature in balance—and we love them. But multiply lush lawns, abundant trees, and blooming flowers, and yes, fertilizer spreaders, by millions of neighborhoods across the planet. Each requires a once-a-week thorough watering to a depth of four inches. Many people water incorrectly, like doing a quick misting in the noonday Sun. So lawns start to look scraggly and then require additional nourishment or chemicals, and even more water.

The Right Environment Is Key to Xeriscaping

Inappropriateness is water-loving Kentucky bluegrass in Phoenix, Arizona, or a palm tree in Nome, Alaska. The latter won't survive outside. The former takes high maintenance or it is stressful to the grass that is trying desperately to do its thing. Native horticulture grows best, because it needs less water and has a natural defense against disease and pests. It has learned to adapt to conditions.

The map of zones on seed packets and in plant books shouldn't be something you glance at, go "hmm," and then bypass. For one thing, it tells you the last killing frost dates, which can vary from April to June, and the killing autumn frost times, which occur as early as August in some regions.

For example, southern Florida is in Zone 10, where a magnolia tree can reside happily, as it can in Alabama and Georgia. South Dakota is in Zone 3. Nice for the catalpa, which wouldn't grow well in the above states. The honey locust thrives in all zones.

Many of us relocate and want to surround ourselves with favorite trees and flowers to feel "like home." Sometimes you can.

For example, the juniper-tree adoring New Yorker can move to New Mexico and enjoy them in abundance. He or she can live with a white birch in the northern part of New Mexico, but that tree won't be happy in the southern area. Some special flowers are sure to shrivel and die in the dry air and heat from the Sun. The good news is that these areas don't lack flora. There are beautiful blooms, shrubs, and trees that love the land they live on, and they are ready to welcome you.

You also need to look around and be aware of prevailing conditions and then use common sense. You do not cram a tree that thrives in an exposed place into a dense shady one. If you live in an arid zone, a plant that loves wet places will be miserable. There are flowers that endure heat and drought and others that need shade. Some, like marigolds, resonate with acidic soil. Others, like impatiens, prefer alkaline. You should also plant trees and flowers with "friends" with similar habits and needs. It stands to reason that you can't deeply water a plant living near one that prefers a dry, sandy soil.

A Dry Scene from Another Perspective

People tend to think that xeriscaping only encompasses rocks and sand. After all, isn't that the proverbial "dry scene"? They are used, but they can be combined with native growth, too. One example is a 500-year-old Zen rock garden in Kyoto, Japan, that has no plants, weeds, or flowers in its 98-foot-by-32-foot area. There are only white pebbles and fifteen rocks, symbolizing islands. The pebbles, which represent oceans, are raked in perfect circles each day. The whole thing is indescribably calming.

Rock Stars

In feng shui, there are "guardian rocks" and "spirit rocks," said to have the spirit of an animal or plant or the energy of the sky and earth contained in them. This is an interesting thought if you have the inclination and patience to sort through a ton of them.

If you don't, focus on discovering a few medium-sized or larger ones that resemble happy frogs, birds, or wolves. Avoid angry or sinister faces or destructive points aimed at the house.

Lastly, rocks and pebbles around the base of trees (or even tomato plants) keep water with vegetation where it does the most good. The stones, truly acting as guardians, absorb the dew, letting it drip back down into the ground during the day.

Ponds

Ponds are considered benevolent structures. A round one is best, and is symbolic of prosperity. Rocks can surround them, and native plants and grasses and bring life to the xeriscaped landscape. Fish in them are even better, but you take responsibility for the fish and need to see to their comfort and safety.

Where to Do Your Homework

You won't go wrong if you do the following: Visit regional botanical gardens and local nurseries, focusing on the sections called "native plants." You can also look online. Request information from your closest agricultural colleges or cooperative extension services. Check the County Government listing in your phone book. Ask about diseases, pests and local weather conditions that are dangerous for important horticultural strangers, but that natives weather well. Have your soil tested. If you haven't had it done in four years, do it again. Things change. All take time, but you learn and can save a plant stress and yourself money.

Finally, it is about learning to live in harmony with the environment we are supposed to be benevolent guardians and kind caretakers of. The tree, shrub, or flower you inherit and plant depends on you and deserves to live peacefully. In return you benefit from its beauty. You are rewarded a million times over, by treating it kindly.

About the Author

Carole Schwalm lives in Sante Fe and contributes astrological work for www. Astrocenter.com. Her interest in gardening comes from following after her grandfather, a life-long farmer, who never had a weed dare to grow in his perfect garden. The accent on every element but earth in her astrological chart made it mandatory for her to get her hands in the sod or risk floating away in the clouds of dust or drowning in tidal waves of emotion or spontaneously combusting.

References

Bush-Brown, James & Louise. *America's Garden Book*, Charles Scribner's Sons, New Revised Edition (1958).

Wong, Eva. *Feng-Shui: The Ancient Wisdom of Harmonious Living for Modern Times.* Shambala Publications, Inc., (1996)

Felice, Raymond. *Homeowner's Guide to Landscaping.* Ideals Publishing Corp; (1982)

Mayell, Helen. "Zen Rock Garden." National Geographic News (September 25, 2002).

Pruning Your Beloved Plants

By Carole Schwalm

Viewing bonsai should be a kind of rest, a green pause in the staccato pace of daily life, a brief contact with nature's great calm.

BONSAI: CULTURE AND CARE OF MINIATURE TREES

The "roots" of bonsai start in China and Japan over 1500 years ago. The bonsai is a dwarfed tree that should be ten feet tall, but is only ten inches tall. Yes, this is an article on pruning, not bonsai, but many theories associated with this ancient art can be translated into your outdoor or houseplants. Let's start with aesthetics, or visual elements, translated from this ancient art to your geranium or your maple tree.

First, You Observe

Before you pick up the pruning shears, walk around the tree and see it from all sides. Study your houseplant at all angles, not just the side that faces the living room. Look at the side toward the wall. You are looking for balance and proportion; pruning is nature and it is art. You want to not only preserve the original, but also to make it more beautiful and pleasing to the eye.

Now, focus on the tree trunk or your houseplant's main stem or supporting structure. There is always one trunk or stem that dominates—even though there may be secondary trunks or stems, one generally stands out. Unless you have severe damage, this "spinal column" must remain. This is because when this is cut, it takes years for another leader or torso to grow.

The height of the tree or indoor plant should be around six times the width of the trunk's base. As your eye moves up, the plant should taper gracefully. If you are topping your beloved plant, taper; don't lop it off straight across. Think of asymmetrical balance, like a triangle.

Scientifically, your plant's spinal column needs to receive sunshine. In other words, light has to get through the limbs and branches to it. You may want to visit the plant at various hours when the sun shines on it, to see if the trunk or stem is receiving life-giving light. Plants reach for the light and they need air to circulate. They need room for growth. Here, branches reach up, not out. Start styling the limbs and branches, keeping proportion in mind. Pay attention and be sensitive to its needs, not just your own.

Proportion

As you approach the plant like the piece of nature's art that it is, look to see if there is even distribution. Some plants have their own character; they are unique because they are mis-shaped. That is okay. You and the plant can live with that. They may need a little touch-up, but they are who they are. Others have prune-ability potential. And never prune a plant that isn't healthy. It has enough trouble.

One side of your plant shouldn't have lots of branches. If there is a heavy branch on one side, there should be something on the other to balance it. Don't butcher the tree. It will not only look sick, it will become so, temporarily. Never cut more than one-fourth of the tree per year, or one third its height. Prune to fit the house. A one-story dwelling doesn't need a giant redwood beside it. That's bonsai-ification.

For natural growth, prune from the top to encourage branching further down. When you thin overcrowded branches, you are also helping the tree or plant's future development. After pruning, plants stop producing roots and start focusing their attention on the leaves.

After looking at the trunk or torso, begin with the older and taller branches or stems—one at a time. Contemplate where the tree or plant is trying to grow. See if there are stray branches and stems that look like they don't belong. Prune under branches or those growing down. Branches shouldn't cross each other. Remove one of the pair.

Cut away root suckers, those little things we think are nice new trees coming up. They aren't named haphazardly. They suck the life out of your tree. The same is true for "water spouts," a tiny grouping of false branches.

Indoor plants aren't pruned; they are pinched back. However, the result is the same. The process allows sunlight in, encourages branching, and promotes development. You even have to pinch some of the new leaves. It's tough to do, but you are promoting fuller growth.

The Right Tools for the Job

The simplest tool for indoor plants are your fingers, perfectly designed for pinching back. If the plant is bigger, use a pair of sharp scissors. You need something more substantial if branches and stems are thick. For outside, use a good pair of hand pruning shears for smaller branches and twigs. Lopping shears are used for branches 1½ inches or more. A sharp pruning saw is necessary for large limbs. Make sure tools are sharp to limit damage and pain to the tree.

The Grateful Deadheaders

In another ancient art, feng shui, one is advised that it is bad chi to have a plant with dead leaves, flowers, etc. Conservative landscapers, nursery folks, and tree doctors may pooh-pooh the chi perspective, but for the tree or plant's health, it is important to remove damaged, diseased, or old wood. It retards growth. Dead branches steal from the plant. They should be cut approximately one inch below the part that is alive or green. Then, apply first-aid. Protect what you've cut with antiseptic tree-wound paint. Prune dead leaves, even in the summer.

Indoor plants get pot bound, and leaves begin to turn brown. When you repot, prune. Trim off exposed roots that are broken or damaged. There is a bonus in this job. You can recycle and propagate prunings. The fall is the best time for this task, as that is when many plants get straggly.

Flowering plants need deadheading. Pinch or snip dead blossoms so it can bloom again and again. Get in the habit of doing it and it becomes a worthwhile obsession.

When to Prune

I "googled" for information relevant to pruning by the Moon, but there are varying stories. Some say prune when the Moon waxing, while others recommend waning phases for the best results. The former slows limb and branch growth and increases yield if your plant is a producer. The latter is helpful if your plant is a "bleeder" during surgery. Some say prune the third week after the Full Moon. Others say, a little after the New Moon. Astrologically, prune when the Moon is in Aries, Leo, or Sagittarius. Horticulturally, prune deciduous, none-flowering trees and shrubs after the leaves are gone in the early fall. This allows you to see the bones of the tree. For the spring-flowering types, wait until the flowers have faded. Prune evergreens in May or June, after the new shoots have developed. Prune only the thickest branches.

References

Sunset Bonsai: Illustrated Guide to An Ancient Art. (1976).

Bush-Brown, James & Louise. *America's Garden Book.* New York: Charles Scribner's Sons. New Revised Edition (1958).

The Moon in the Workplace

By Lisa Finander

There you are, sitting at your desk at work. Yesterday everything was great, but today is horrendous. People are disagreeing with you, you are behind, your voice mail is full of angry clients demanding a call, and it takes everything you have not to walk out. Most days you brush it off as part of the job, but today you feel defeated.

Does this describe your most recent employment? Do you love it, hate it, or try not to think about it? Have you outgrown it? Does your anxiety about going to work on Monday morning consume most of your weekend? Think of all the people who show up at work tense, angry, and depressed versus the ones who are even-tempered, optimistic, and flexible. Whom would you rather work for? With? Whom would you rather be? If you feel emotionally overwhelmed by your work at the end of the day, maybe it is not the work that is the problem, but the environment in which you are doing it.

Because most of us spend a great deal of our waking life working, our employers and coworkers become another family. Our professional survival depends on how well we can adapt. Each of us brings emotional needs left over from childhood into our work environment. If we leave our feelings unexamined, we recreate the same emotive scenarios at our job that we thought we left safely behind at home. Inadvertently, the workplace becomes a crucible of fragmented childhood roles on public display.

It is not that difficult for us to revert into our early family roles, because in many cases the company configuration duplicates the family structure. Our bosses become surrogate parents, setting up the rules and holding the power, while our coworkers turn into our younger or older siblings, depending on where their job ranks in importance to ours. Now confronted with a myriad of family dynamics and dysfunctions that provoke us into the same battles, competitions, fears, fantasies, longings, and resentments that we harbored in childhood, we thrive or wither in these environments much as we did in our early life. You may not have chosen your family, but you can choose your work environment, and more importantly, with a little self-reflection you can make better decisions on what you need from your employment.

A positive work environment is one that supports who you are so you can do the work that is important to you. Not all jobs are careers, and not all careers are jobs. For some people, trying to combine the two is too much pressure. It might be that all you require from your employment is an income that allows you pursue the things you enjoy outside of work. Some people work to travel. Their job is just a means to an end. Others have different expectations from their employment. It could be status, money,

or doing something they believe is worthwhile. Each person gives and requires different things from their work environment based on their beliefs of what it represents. The type of workplace for a person who works for spending money, versus the person whose work is their identity, could be very different.

The Astrological Moon

Operating just below our awareness, the Moon is the feeling center of our astrological chart. Its input is purely subjective, but at the same time powerfully influences how satisfied we are with our lives and, in this case, our jobs. When we bring our unmet lunar needs and emotions to the workplace along with everyone else, work becomes difficult. Because the Moon moves so quickly through the sky, changing astrological signs every two and a half days, our moods and those of our coworkers change with it. How we feel on any given day influences how we view and treat our colleagues. We continually experience all kinds of emotions moving through the workplace in E-mails, phone messages, meetings, and personal interactions. Other's needs may trigger our own. Are we seeking love, power, or rightness as we respond to them? When we are feeling unsure and vulnerable at work, we instinctively seek out the people who we consider safe to gossip with and complain to. They find us, too. There is heaviness to that kind of emotional exchange that drains us. Day after day, as more people discharge feelings of anger and hopelessness into the workplace, the environment becomes more oppressive and it takes a conscious effort on our part to separate from it. Hopefully, people share their positive nature at work too, creating a sort of balance. Remember some of your most challenging times at work. How much of the stress resulted from other people's or your own immature behavior? You cannot change your coworkers, but you can decide how you will conduct yourself at work. Understanding your emotional patterns is the first step in creating a healthier workplace.

Observing the Moon's Cycles at Work

My first experience using astrology at work was over twenty years ago. All I knew at that time was that my Sun sign was Virgo. I purchased an annual astrology book for Virgo and faithfully read my daily forecast. After a few months of observing the Moon's placement, a pattern developed. When the Moon was in the sign of Pisces, I had a bad day. Everybody and everything hurt my feelings. I hated my job on those days, and believed I would continue to feel that way. In a couple of days, my mood altered and my job did not seem so horrible. I was unaffected by the same circumstances that felt intolerable previously. Later when I began studying astrology, I learned that when the Moon is in the opposite sign of your Sun sign (Pisces is opposite Virgo), a person experiences low energy or challenging days. My perception of the world challenged me and changed on those days, bringing me right back to my childhood. I reacted accordingly. Of course, I was not conscious of it at the time. I felt disrespected, personally attacked,

and vulnerable. My emotional responses to the behavior of others knocked me off balance. It took tremendous energy just to exist at work. As a result, I started to expect to have stressful days when the Moon was in Pisces, and did my best never to schedule meetings or audits during that time. I continued to track the Moon, and subtler patterns emerged as I journaled my experiences along with the Moon's cycles.

Although following the movement of the Moon and my moods made my work life easier and more predictable, I did not enjoy my jobs, and a lot of the time they were only bearable. I struggled to find the "right" career by trying out different occupations with some success, but when I decided to focus on what I needed, expected, and required from my employment based on my emotional temperament, my work life transformed.

I started by creating a resume that was an accurate description of who I was and what I wanted to do. Not an easy task, because so much of my work history included things I was good at but detested. I mediated this by looking at all aspects of each job, leaving out the duties I did not enjoy and including the ones I did. Writing your heart's desire and then printing it on expensive resume paper is very cathartic. Then I probed further because this is what I consciously wanted. Our lunar desires are subconscious and revealed to us through cycles, memories, and feelings.

There is a rhythm to my employment. I work for others for a while, and then I work for myself at home. It has always been that way, even when I was a teenager. The times I made the actual switch to leave my job or cut back on the hours, it did not depend on my marital status or income. Instead, it occurred when I reached a state of depletion. I did not have enough energy to continue doing my work. I had outgrown it like a relationship. It had come to the point where there was only decay. I was not good for the job, the job was not good for me, and therefore it was the wrong job.

I also discovered that, unconsciously, I continued to choose positions based on the role I played and conformed to in childhood: the caregiver, social worker, and referee. I became, at work, the selfless mother that my parents had rewarded me for being, thoughtlessly believing that was who I was. My Moon is in Leo, and Leo is anything but a selfless sign. What brings the Leo part of me joy is creating something, anything, and my heart longs to bring those creations into the world. None of my previous jobs allowed me to be creative, and if they did, only in a very limited way. I could only do the work for so long before I "needed" a change. There were many other things my Leo Moon wanted in a job, and I began to record them. Discovering what you need on a daily basis is the next step in creating a positive workplace.

These are some of the questions I asked myself. As you answer them for yourself, note how they compare to the places you have worked. Notice if you base your responses on what you think you should need. This is a feeling quiz, where your heart holds the right answers.

1. What kind of people do you want to work with?
2. What kind of service do you want to provide?

3. What kind of compensation do you require? Money? Education? Insurance? Free-time? Status?
4. What do you want to learn from your job?
5. How will you feel about yourself and your work at the end of the day?
6. What part of yourself do you want to bring into the workplace?
7. How do you want to grow?
8. How far are you willing to commute?
9. What does the place look like? Would you be sitting in a cubicle?
10. What do you want to avoid?
11. How hard are you willing to work for what you want?
12. Will you only apply for jobs where you can use your new "envisioned" resume?
13. Will you take a risk and try something new?
14. How will your personal life and work life support each other?
15. What type of work depletes you?
16. What do you need from your coworkers?
17. What is special about you?
18. In your life, what is most important to you?

Bringing It All Together

I have asked you to do a couple of things to enrich your work life. First, I suggested you pay attention to the sign the Moon is in along with your daily experiences to get a sense of your emotional rhythms. You may not undergo difficult days when the Moon is in the opposite sign from your Sun as I do. Every chart, like every person, is unique. It will not take long before you discover your own motifs.

Next, I asked you a lot of questions about what you want from your work and your feelings about it. At this point, you might believe what you really want and what you have seem far apart.

They are not, really. Once you consciously put into words what you need from your workplace, you can use that information to decide how you want to interact with others at work and what kinds of jobs you want to pursue.

This is how I apply these ideas to my work life. Each morning before work, I check in with myself emotionally. How am I feeling about going to the office today? If I feel apprehensive, I do not push through it. I stop and listen until I hear the answers. Sometimes it is because I have worked too hard and need to pull back. Other times it is because I am afraid that I will be unsuccessful at something at my job, or I might be dreading a meeting or a communication with someone. Once I am aware of this, I release my negative expectations about the outcome and allow myself to be open to other alternatives. Whenever I interact with others, I am aware of their mood and its effect on me. I continue to check in with myself throughout the day to monitor my reactions and notice if I am taking on the emotions of others. I pay attention to the signs and cycles of the Moon and anticipate my moods, remembering that I will feel differently in time. We are all striving for respect,

recognition, and appreciation at work, but we do not always get or give it. Therefore, I remind myself to acknowledge the support of my coworkers and others who I make contact with during the day. It makes all the difference. In addition, I recognize my bad days and allow myself to have them.

It is natural for our feelings about work to change and evolve over time. We were not the same person in our twenties that we are in our fifties. Employers and employment have changed. The majority of us will switch employers and careers many times. A job that once was exciting can slowly loose its wonder and become stagnating, letting you know it is time to move on.

Whether you have just started a job, been there for a while, or are looking for a new one, there are some simple things you can do to sustain your emotional health at work. Use your break, lunch, and commute times to support your dreams. Read books you enjoy or listen to tapes during your personal time to ensure that you take your needs seriously. Set a styrofoam cup filled with water in your workspace, which is consciously intended to collect pessimistic energy during the day from yourself and coworkers.

At the end of the day, pour the water out and throw the cup away, symbolically releasing and moving the negativity out of your environment. Journal, write letters, search for new jobs, or E-mail friends to give yourself a boost. Other ways to replenish yourself could be to prepare special meals, go out to lunch occasionally, write with nice pens or use special notebooks, carry something of meaning, or enter a word or a phrase that inspires you on your computer's screen saver. If connecting with nature revitalizes you, go for a walk, sit by a fountain, or find a quiet spot under a tree where you can quiet your mind and release the emotions of the day. Pause for a moment between tasks and breathe. Discover the things that energize you and make your life better, and question the behaviors and patterns that keep you stuck—bring as many of them into your work life as possible. Good jobs are not as scarce as are the people willing to believe that they exist. Affirm you can work somewhere you enjoy, and watch what happens!

About the Author

Lisa Finander is a writer, teacher, and consultant who works with symbolism, including the symbolism of astrology, tarot, and dreams. She receives much support and inspiration from her husband Brian.

Llewellyn's Complete Book of Astrology
The Easy Way to Learn Astrology
Kris Brandt Riske

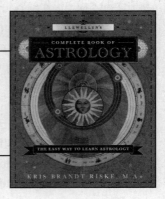

With *Llewellyn's Complete Book of Astrology*, you can learn to read and understand this amazing cosmic road map for yourself and others. Professional astrologer Kris Brandt Riske introduces the many parts that make up the horoscope, devoting special attention to relationships, career, and money. Friendly and easy to follow, this comprehensive book guides you to explore the zodiac signs, planets, houses, and aspects, and teaches how to synthesize this valuable information. Riske also explores the history of astrology going back to the ancient Babylonians, in addition to the different branches of contemporary astrology. Once you learn the language of astrology, you'll be able to read birth charts of yourself and others, determine compatibility between two people, track your earning potential, uncover areas of opportunity or challenge, and analyze your career path.

978-0-7387-1071-6
US $18.95 CAN $21.95
360 pp., 8 x 10

The Ex Files
A Zodiac Guide to His Former Flames
Rowan Davis

If your guy's ex is driving you crazy, check out this fun astrological guide to figuring her out. Blending the wisdom of the stars with tension-lifting humor, Rowan Davis takes an honest look at an unpleasant part of life—dealing with your man's ex. From vengeful Leos to secretive Scorpios, *The Ex Files* dishes the dirt on all twelve Sun signs and gives insight into what you can expect from each. There's also candid advice—based on your own Sun sign—for coping with a variety of exes. Learn how to ignore the scare tactics of the Aries, wise up to the Pisces' emotional games, and see through the Aquarius' ploy to win him back. And for those who want to take action, you can find out which signs are open to friendship, could use discouragement, or are best left alone.

978-0-7387-1044-0
US $12.95 CAN $14.50
216 pp., 5 x 6

Cosmic Karma
Understanding Your Contract with the Universe

Marguerite Manning

Marguerite Manning invites you on a spirited ride through the stars to see your soul's evolutionary journey. Based on astrology, *Cosmic Karma* can help you navigate the karmic crossroads and gain fresh insights into your soul's spiritual agenda. Where has your soul been and what are your karmic obligations in this lifetime? All the answers are in a celestial map of planetary energies—your birth chart. The Sun's house will help you figure out your "cosmic calling"—what you're meant to accomplish, while Saturn, the humorless taskmaster, reveals karmic lessons you need to learn. Lastly, peek inside the forbidding and intoxicating Twelfth House—where you can explore precious experiences, painful memories, and all your past deeds.

978-0-7387-1054-9
US $15.95 CAN $17.50
216 pp., 7 x 7

Star Guide to Guys
How to Live Happily With Him, or Without Him

Elizabeth Perkins

Is your hot yoga instructor a high-strung Virgo or a sensitive Pisces? Could the cutie in the coffee shop be the Leo of your dreams? Thanks to astrology, women can get the nitty-gritty on a crush before leaping into the murky depths of a relationship. The *Star Guide to Guys* dishes out the lowdown on men in all twelve Sun signs—covering their strengths, challenges, goals, desires, and other personality traits. Women can also depend on this entertaining, easy-to-use guide for insight into their own sign: what they're looking for in a mate, relationship needs, and dynamic compatibility with each sign. For ladies on a break from the dating scene, there's also astrological advice for living a fabulous single life and loving it.

978-0-7387-0954-3
US $12.95 CAN $14.50
240 pp., 6 x 9

Notes

Notes

Notes